THE
UNION
STATION
MASSACRE

THE
UNION
STATION
MASSACRE

The Original Sin of

J. Edgar Hoover's

FBI

Robert Unger

**Andrews McMeel
Publishing**

Kansas City

Photo of Otto Reed courtesy of Special Collections, Kansas City Public
Library, Kansas City, Mo.
Photo of Adam Richetti's grave courtesy of Marianne Unger.
All other photos courtesy of the *Kansas City Star*.

Library of Congress Cataloging-in-Publication Data
Unger, Robert.
    The Union Station massacre : the original sin of J. Edgar
  Hoover's FBI / Robert Unger.
        p.   cm.
    Includes bibilographical references.
    ISBN 0-8362-2773-5
    1. Murder—Missouri—Kansas City—Case studies. 2. Police
  murders—Missouri—Kansas City—Case studies. 3. Organized
  crime—Missouri—Kansas City—History. 4. Hoover, J. Edgar
  (John Edgar), 1895–1972. 5. United States. Federal Bureau of
  Investigation—History. 6. Kansas City (Mo.)—History. I. Title.
  HV6534.K2U54   1997
  364.15'23'09778411—dc21   97-18630
                                                  CIP

ATTENTION: SCHOOLS AND BUSINESSES

Andrews McMeel books are available at quantity discounts with
bulk purchase for educational, business, or sales promotional use.
For information, please write to:
Special Sales Department, Andrews McMeel Publishing,
4520 Main Street, Kansas City, Missouri 64111.

To Marianne,
who always shared the dream,

and to Bill and Caroline,
whose faith made the dream come true.

CONTENTS

CONTENTS

PREFACE

This book is fact

It is not fiction.

It is not "faction," that frustrating modern mix of truth and fantasy.

It is not creative nonfiction; it does not blend knowledge with speculation.

It is fact derived over a fourteen-year period from analysis of eighty-nine volumes of Federal Bureau of Investigation files. And, in the end, it is as close as I can come to the truth of what happened on the morning of June 17, 1933, in the parking lot at Kansas City's Union Station.

The book has limited annotation for the simple reason that 99.9 percent of it is rooted in that one massive primary source—FBI file number 62-28915. The twenty thousand pages of that file aren't even numbered, except by my own system, and those pages are chronological only in the broadest sense, apparently depending entirely on when the Bureau's clerks tossed a new stack of papers into the file drawer.

But it's all there.

So understanding the story of the Union Station Massacre must begin with some understanding of that incredible file and what it contains. Detailed information on the papers, their origin, and their journey toward daylight is offered in the afterword of this book. But a couple of points need to be understood from the very beginning.

PREFACE

First and foremost, the thousands of reports were written in a far, far different time and place. The agents, supervisors, and technicians—even J. Edgar Hoover himself—could not have conceived of anything like the Freedom of Information Act under which I obtained the file. So reports were written with none of the caution and awareness of prying eyes that shape reports filed by today's law enforcement bureaucracy.

No one contributing to the file, including the director, believed that anyone outside the FBI would see these reports: not defense lawyers, not historians, and certainly not a journalist. On the contrary, the agents were motivated by quite different impulses: their certain knowledge that "Mr. Hoover" wanted to know everything that went on in the field and would punish those who withheld information from him.

Beyond that, it was just a simpler time in a much smaller operation. Hoover counted his men in the low hundreds, not thousands, back then, and they were scattered in little groups all over the country. Most knew one another. Most were very young, usually in their twenties. And almost all, at least to some degree, brought pre-television skills of written narrative to their jobs. So when someone cried or sighed, they wrote about it. When a gangster glared or frowned or sweat, they put it in the report. When they saw something painful, they weren't afraid to convey the pain.

All this adds flavor to the story, though readers unfamiliar with the reports may mistake that flavor for literary license. Not so. If the book says someone smiled, that's because the file records a smile.

In the same vein, the two-volume transcript of Adam Richetti's trial, on file in the Missouri State Archives in Jefferson City, provided extensive information about the evidence and testimony presented in court. That transcript served as an invaluable comparison with the record long hidden away in 62-28915.

By design, this account seldom reaches beyond those two primary sources. When it does, mostly for historical context, additional sources are listed in the notes at the back of the book.

.   .   .

The FBI tracks its lineage back near the beginning of the century, but the name has not been around that long. The organization has always been within the attorney general's office, first as the Bureau of Investigation, then as the Division of Investigation, and finally, since 1935, as the Federal Bureau of Investigation.

Because all these name changes occurred during the period covered by this book, the name game has the potential to sow some confusion. I have attempted to avoid that by referring throughout to "the Bureau," even though that title is not always technically correct.

.   .   .

Finally, this book celebrates a city's wisdom. We Kansas Citians almost lost our proud old Union Station. Now it's officially to become a museum, as, in a sense, it always has been. There's already a monument of sorts gouged out of the polished granite facade, a hole no bigger than a man's thumb. For decades parents have lifted small children so they could run their fingers over that hole and feel its now-smoothed edges. And every time, Dad or Grandma or Uncle Fred would tell about the morning in 1933 when the machine gun bullets flew, leaving those ugly pockmarks on the stone. They'd speculate about what really happened that day, just as I have with my son. Now Union Station and all its history will be there for our grandchildren too.

Robert Unger
Kansas City, Missouri
May 7, 1997

ACKNOWLEDGMENTS

MY SPECIAL THANKS GO, as they have for so many years, to my beautiful wife, Marianne. Since those days in high school, she's never scoffed at a crazy idea, either mine or hers, and she's made my life a great adventure. We were friends first, and we'll be friends forever.

Thanks also to Pat and Kim McGuire for their encouragement when I was beginning to doubt and for sharing the kind of optimism that will not tolerate despair.

I am enormously grateful to Kim and Pat's lovely daughter Tracey and her brilliant husband, Frosty, for their patience, kindness, and computer expertise. One hot night in August they saved my manuscript and quite possibly my marriage after I accidentally erased a week's worth of revisions that Marianne had entered with great care onto a disk. The real trick was that they did it over the telephone with Frosty in Denver and Tracey in Kansas City—while three wonderful but determined Mohn children crawled all over her. She's a marvel. But then so are Justin, Joshua, and Bridgit Logan.

I thank JoAnn Ramsey for letting me litter her kitchen table with fingerprints, old photographs, and muddled ideas. And I owe a special debt to Floyd Ramsey for looking me in the eye one night near the beginning and making crystal clear why this book needed to be written. "It matters," he said, in the no-nonsense style of a good cop and an honest man, "because it's the truth."

Son Joe and his bride, Ann, never flagged in their interest and encouragement. It meant a lot, kids.

ACKNOWLEDGMENTS

I could not have sorted through the complicated ballistics and fingerprint evidence without the guidance of John Cayton, chief forensic examiner for the Kansas City Regional Crime Laboratory. He's an expert on firearms and tool marks who teaches and lectures all over the world. I'm glad he took time to teach me a little. Gary Howell, director of the crime lab, brought insight to many areas, especially in sorting out the conflicting currents in this enormous file. I owe both of them a lot. But if there are any mistakes or misjudgments on these pages they fall entirely on me. They would have to be in spite of, never because of, John Cayton and Gary Howell.

Several people were there when I needed them, and I'm not sure why. One day in Joplin, looking for tiny Sloan's Park and possessing no vauge notion where it might be, I walked to the door of a woman who once had lived there with her family, which still owns the place. She knew exactly where it was, and was well aware of Deafy Farmer and his gang. I was entirely on the wrong side of town, floundering without a clue, and yet hers was the first house I tried. What are the odds?

Another time a random conversation led me to the person who had heard federal judge William Becker's confirmation of what actually triggered the massacre. I promised you anonymity, but you know who you are. Thanks.

Matt Lombardi, my editor at Andrews McMeel Publishing, kept me working, and Laura Blake Peterson, my agent at Curtis Brown, Ltd., kept me hoping. Neither job was easy.

Finally, I am forever grateful to the people of New Lebanon, Indiana, who taught a little boy years ago that wrong is wrong and right is right. I can't list all of you, so I'll say it to one of your best. Thanks, Mom.

THE
UNION
STATION
MASSACRE

INTRODUCTION

On APRIL 24, 1997, Timothy McVeigh went on trial for his life in Denver, Colorado, accused of the terrorist murder of 168 fellow Americans in Oklahoma City.

But he was not alone in the dock.

The FBI's celebrated crime lab, at the epicenter of the Oklahoma City bombing investigation, had been the subject of ominous whispers for months. Then only days before the trial the Justice Department brought those dark rumors to sudden and startling light.

Crime lab experts, according to the inspector general, systematically had tilted evidence against defendants, consistently had given federal prosecutors the benefit of any scientific doubt, even had tailored laboratory test results to fit the government's theories.

The revered FBI crime lab, in short, was corrupt. Not all the time. Just sometimes. Usually on big, important cases.

"It makes us wonder," groaned a National Public Radio reporter the day after the rumors were confirmed, "just what the FBI crime lab was doing all those years when no one was watching."

I know, I shouted that morning. *And so does Adam Richetti!*

Pressure on the Bureau and the crime lab mounted as defense lawyer Stephen Jones hammered at the lab's skill level, professionalism, and, most of all, ethics and honesty. This paragon of twentieth-century forensic science, he contended, was in fact a scheming, manipulative house of fraud.

Not always, the Bureau and its apologists countered. *Not often*, *in fact. Consider the greater context. Look at our long, proud history. Judge the crime lab by its record. . . .*

Adam Richetti *is* that record, right there on the very first page. When Richetti went on trial for his life in 1935, J. Edgar Hoover's ambitious new criminal laboratory, soon to be the national focus of forensic science, was still an infant, only a year old at the time of the Union Station Massacre in 1933. Taking Richetti down would be one of the lab's first assignments and earliest claims to fame.

From the first days the incendiary Union Station Massacre case had locked young Mr. Hoover in the national spotlight. First it extorted the public dollars and personal dignity he believed he and his obscure Bureau deserved, then it threatened enormous penalties for any hint of failure to solve the crime he himself had promoted as America's disgrace.

So failure simply was never an option. Not after his pleas were heard and the purse was opened, not after a laundry list of new federal laws bestowed authority and jurisdiction he and his agents had only dreamed of.

In his hands lay the seeds of unprecedented power. Federal bank robbers suddenly were his responsibility. So were most kidnappers. And all interstate traffickers, whether in stolen goods, extortion threats, or crooks on the lam. Likewise, all who assaulted his or any other federal officers. His men at last could make arrests. And, best of all, carry guns like real cops. His boys would be laughed at no more.

Hoover nurtured those seeds into fruition unmatched in American history. His FBI, his crime lab, his persona, all grew to greatness. Without the Union Station Massacre, however, there would have been no such seeds. And without Adam Richetti, without the blood of public atonement, there could have been no fruition.

The stakes were too high; the massacre case was too big and too important to lose.

Hoover and his Bureau won every round, at least in the public eye. The spectacular identification of Richetti's fingerprint by the crime lab's new Single Fingerprint Section was ballyhooed as a giant leap for crime detection. The lab experts' seamless presentation of fingerprint testimony marked a historic milestone in criminal prosecution. Then the ballistics exhibits, blessed by agents' nodding approval, closed the show with a flourish.

But all that evidence was tainted, if not polluted beyond any genuine legal significance. And the Bureau's experts knew it.

Suspect evidence was presented with an air of deadly certainty. The dubious was allowed, even encouraged, without any hint of protest. And dead wrong, flat-out lies were covered by agent perjury.

Adam Richetti was condemned by that Bureau evidence. In the process, the young sidekick of Pretty Boy Floyd laid a symbolic cornerstone for the holy temple that would be built around both the FBI crime lab and the Bureau's ambitious director. Though Richetti was quickly forgotten, his twin nemeses grew into national icons.

Now it's Richetti's turn. The crime lab and the Bureau stand in the dock of public scrutiny, and Richetti can answer better than anyone the question still so vital to our national life: "How long has this been going on?"

Forever. From the very beginning.

Today, armed with the long-buried truth you are about to read, Adam Richetti almost certainly would win a new trial, perhaps even his freedom. But that won't happen. He's long dead, executed for the Union Station Massacre.

For the Bureau's crimes, if not his own.

CHAPTER ONE

THE LEGEND

UNION STATION already was alive and throbbing that Saturday morning.

Even at seven, the cavernous lobby heard and loudly repeated the rapid footsteps of cross-country travelers and the jabbering excitement of country folks just arrived for a long day of shopping in the city. Outside, porters worked their stations, lifting luggage to and from taxicabs almost as quickly as the people could climb in and out. Cabbies, wide awake and already a little edgy, crept forward in a long, curving line, then hesitated only seconds on the bubble before an impatient starter waved them on toward the wide doors of the massive station's southern face.

The Travelers Aid desk opened on time, precisely at 7 A.M., Mrs. Lottie West in charge. And Frank White pushed his broom and mop into a closet, his night's work done. Both knew, as did the rest of the station's family, that before the hands on the huge lobby clock could reach eight o'clock, a half-dozen trains would enter the maze of tracks below and behind the main floor, taking away most of those now hurrying about but depositing even more in their place.

A loose knot of men just outside the doors was interested in only one of those trains, the Missouri Pacific that had rolled all night along the Kansas-Missouri border, up from Oklahoma and, before that, Fort Smith, Arkansas. It was due to arrive at seven-fifteen, only fifteen minutes behind schedule, and it would carry, among many others, a chubby, bald bank robber named Frank Nash. He was an escapee from the federal penitentiary at Leavenworth, Kansas, and the men on the sidewalk were there to help him find his way back home.

Reed Vetterli was in charge, a twenty-nine-year-old Mormon who brought a strong sense of righteousness to his job as an agent for the United States Department of Justice's Bureau of Investigation. No one, according to those who knew him, wanted to get at and get rid of the bad guys more than Reed Vetterli.

With him stood a tall, broad-faced, smiling young man, his hair neatly trimmed and parted down the middle beneath his fedora. Ray Caffrey, recently arrived from the Omaha office along with his wife and young son, now worked for Vetterli. In fact, Caffrey's Chevrolet, at that moment in the parking lot, still carried Nebraska plates.

The two federal agents fit hardly at all with the other two men standing there on the sidewalk. Where the agents might look just a bit too slick, Bill Grooms and Frank Hermanson were more than a bit too seedy, both older, less proud, and worn in face and fabric in the way of city detectives. Vetterli's righteousness and Caffrey's zest struck no chord in the detectives' lives. After all, Hermanson and Grooms normally drove the Kansas City Police Department's muscle car, known as the Hot Shot, rigged with armor plating, stocked with a machine gun, and designed to seek out trouble and stomp it. Finesse was hardly the detectives' hallmark.

That car was close by, parked illegally, of course, at the curb in one of the busiest lanes, right in front of the station. But they'd just leave it there. This business shouldn't take long.

Nothing in particular caught the lawmen's attention, at least not enough to delay them in the bright morning sunshine. With a final glance around, they headed casually toward the wide set of doors to their right, called the east doors by everyone at the station because there was another set just like them toward the opposite end.

The four lawmen walked in a loose column, Vetterli leading the way through the milling crowd, past the restaurant, down the off-shooting lobby toward the trains, and finally downstairs to the platform. There they looked around again, slowly, watching for eyes to catch their own and hold the gaze even for a piece of a second, watching for others who might also be waiting and watching. But no one paid any attention. No one even seemed to notice.

The Missouri Pacific rolled slowly beside the platform, braking gently to a halt only half a second before an orchestration of porters stepped to the concrete and swung their small metal steps into place. Vetterli and Caffrey swept the train quickly with their eyes, scanning for the face they knew they would find. The detectives hung back and waited. It was not yet their time, and this wasn't their show.

A tall, thin, hawk-faced man stepped off the train almost before it stopped, his nervous eyes moving up and down the platform, looking for any sign of trouble. He had already seen Vetterli, who nodded and stepped forward, the others following closely.

Agent Joe Lackey had had little sleep during the previous forty-eight hours, and his demeanor showed it. He was clearly relieved to see his fellow agents striding confidently down the platform. And he welcomed Vetterli's quick assurances that everything was in hand, all arrangements made and executed, including the police escort car. Vetterli quickly introduced Lackey, who worked out of the Oklahoma City office, to the local officers, told him where Caffrey's and the detectives' cars were parked, and described the route they would take back upstairs. The plan was simple enough, as agreed by telephone overnight between Vetterli in Kansas City and R. H. Colvin, Lackey's supervisor in Oklahoma. They would load Nash into a car, get him out of town, and give him an unceremonious escort to his old jail cell in Leavenworth, thirty miles up the road.

Lackey reboarded the train, leaving the others on the platform, and walked quickly to Car 11's Drawing Room A. There he knocked softly on the door, careful to give his friends the signal that all was well. Frank Smith, an eighteen-year veteran of the Bureau, waited inside along with Otto Reed, the forty-nine-year-old police chief from McAlester, Oklahoma. Reed, who had known and chased Nash for years, had gone along with Lackey and Smith to Hot Springs, Arkansas, to make the bank robber's arrest official—and legal. Now he was eager to finish the job and go home.

In the farthest corner of the small drawing room sat the escaped federal prisoner, known as Jelly to his friends and by a string of aliases to lawmen throughout the nation's heartland. He hardly looked the part of the hardened criminal and certainly would have attracted less attention in a crowd than any of his captors. He wore a wig that didn't quite fit, had a hook nose much too big for his face, and was dressed far too casually for train travel in the 1930s. He looked more like a relaxed, forty-six-year-old vacationer who had been snatched off the streets on his way to the neighborhood bar—which, in fact, he was.

Nonetheless, the lawmen took no chances. Nash's hands were cuffed in front, and an agent gripped his belt from the rear. The federal men, at least, knew Nash had escaped from Leavenworth not by force or violence but by cunning and guile. He had first become a model prisoner, an avid reader with a special devotion to the prison's one-volume collection of the complete works of Shakespeare. Six years later in 1930 he was the deputy warden's chef and general handyman, a position that brought a lot of privileges, including running errands. One evening he was sent on an errand outside the prison, and he never came back. The next day the prison librarian discovered the Shakespeare collection was missing.

Once on the platform, the group hovered close to their prisoner. At no one's direction, they fell into a sort of fan-shaped formation, with Nash in the middle and the agents and detectives shoulder-to-shoulder out to the sides. In effect, they formed a flying wedge that by sheer intimidation virtually sliced through the dense crowd. And, intentionally or otherwise, they painted themselves indelibly into the memories of all who saw them pass. Their march across the wide, resonating lobby hardly could have been more dramatic, parting the flood of people like Moses at the Red Sea. Every head turned in their direction.

It was as if they knew they were marching into history.

The little formation quickly moved south across the lanes of traffic to Agent Caffrey's car in the first row of the Plaza lot, no one seeing anything that might raise the slightest alarm. The Chevrolet coach faced south, about one hundred feet from the east doors. A Plymouth sat to its right, a vacant space on the other side.

Caffrey unlocked the passenger door, and Nash started to climb into the rear seat, but Lackey quickly told him to sit up front where the lawmen could keep a better eye on him. Nash then slid across the front seat, all the way, so the passenger seatback could be pushed forward. Lackey, Smith, and Reed squeezed into the rear. Hermanson and Grooms stood together just beyond the open passenger door, talking with Vetterli. Caffrey, meanwhile, started around the car.

Suddenly, toward the right front, a man appeared. A raised machine gun blocked his face, but his words were clear enough. "Up! Up!" he shouted. Then, hardly a full breath later, another gunman yelled, "Let 'em have it!"

In Lackey's words, "The war was on."

Lead ripped into the car from three directions, cutting the lawmen to pieces before they could react. Outside, Grooms fell in the first volley, dead before he hit the ground. Vetterli dropped to the concrete, his left arm slightly wounded, and crawled toward the rear of the car. Unarmed and seeing that he could do nothing, he rose and sprinted toward the east doors, machine-gun bullets tracking but missing him—and leaving permanent scars on the station's granite face.

Near the driver's door Caffrey lay mortally wounded, a gaping hole in his head. He would soon be dead.

The prisoner, one of the first casualties, was already dead, his head literally blown apart by his would-be rescuers. In the rear seat, Chief Reed was dead, and Joe Lackey, with three bullets in his back, had collapsed forward over his knees. Hermanson now lay dead between the cars, his body under Grooms.

Still the shooting didn't stop as the gunmen circled the car, moving ever closer. Only Frank Smith was uninjured. But when he heard one of the gunmen coming toward the driver's side window, he threw himself forward across the collapsed seatback and lay perfectly still, not even breathing.

"They're dead," the killer shouted. "They're all dead in here."

At that moment, Mike Fanning, one of two Kansas City police officers routinely assigned to the station, ran out the east doors, drawn by the pandemonium and gunfire. Without hesitation, he fired toward Caffrey's car at the fleeing assassins.

Miraculously, the lawmen were not all dead. In fact, despite the shock and speed of the assault, surviving federal agents would be able to identify all three shooters: Verne Miller, a bank robber, killer, and friend of Frank Nash; Charles Arthur "Pretty Boy" Floyd, a notorious bank robber and killer; and Adam Richetti, Floyd's murderous sidekick.

There it is: the accepted version of what happened in those few minutes in Union Station Plaza. At least it's been the FBI's official version for over sixty years, taught to generations of Americans from old and new FBI press releases, sworn testimony by agents in open court, and congressional hearing testimony by the Bureau's leaders. It's been published in official Bureau histories and school textbooks; it's been repeated reverently as the Gospel According to J. Edgar Hoover by hundreds of loyal agents. The FBI's own for-public-consumption account of the massacre is enshrined in one fat paragraph, about four hundred words, near the end of the eighty-ninth and final volume of the Bureau's "Kansas City Massacre" file:

Frank Nash was escorted by the Head of the FBI's Kansas City Office, together with Special Agent Raymond J. Caffrey, two other representatives of the FBI, and Otto Reed, chief of police of the

McAlester, Oklahoma, Police Department. Police Officers W. J. Grooms and Frank Hermanson of the Kansas City, Missouri, Police Department, were also given important posts of assignment for this transfer. Frank Nash, upon being removed from the train, was immediately taken to the waiting automobile of Special Agent Caffrey, where he was placed in the left front seat in order that the officers might occupy the rear seat. At this instant two Special Agents took positions in the rear seat with Chief of Police Otto Reed. Police Officers Grooms and Hermanson, together with the Head of the FBI's Kansas City Office, were standing on the right side of Agent Caffrey's automobile during the time Special Agent Caffrey was walking around the car preparatory to entering the driver's seat. It was when Agent Caffrey approached the left door of this automobile that the three assassins surprised the officers from a point in front of and about fifteen to twenty feet to the west of the automobile. These men were observed carrying machine guns and other weapons and in approaching the automobile shouted, "Up, up." An instant later the voice of one of the gunmen was heard to say, "Let 'em have it." Immediately a fusillade of gunfire came from the weapons of the attackers. Shots were fired from the front and from all sides of Agent Caffrey's car. Police officers Grooms and Hermanson were instantly killed in the positions where they stood. Chief of Police Otto Reed was also instantly killed. One agent was severely wounded by bullets which entered his back, and he was confined to bed for several months. Special Agent Caffrey was instantly killed by a bullet which passed directly through his head as he stood beside the car. The prisoner, Frank Nash, was also killed by a misdirected gunshot that entered his skull, thereby defeating the very purpose of the conspiracy to gain his freedom. The other Special Agent escaped injury, while the Head of the FBI office received a wound in the arm. Apparently the assassins started at the front right-hand side of the car and at least two of them proceeded around the automobile, making a complete circle and firing recklessly as they went.

But it's not that simple. In fact, what really happened beyond the doors of Union Station that morning has been in dispute for well over half a century. Many saw the attack. Many more would claim to have seen it. And all of them described it, in conversation and print, in barrooms, brothels, and boardrooms. Often those eye-witness accounts featured the most elaborate—and thoroughly fictitious—detail. Scores of writers, most working with little more than curiosity and imagination, have explained those few minutes in dozens of ways over the decades.

Yet that FBI version has survived all challenges, first strengthened when Miller and Floyd turned up dead and then cemented when Adam Richetti was tried, convicted, and executed for the Union Station killing.

Unfortunately, it's just not true.

The FBI version is only marginally more accurate than the fancies of 1930s detective magazine writers. It is riddled with half-truths, deceptions, perjury, lies, cover-up, and what some would call official murder.

It's all in the file.

CHAPTER TWO

THE GREENHORNS

THE SMOKE has not yet cleared from the Union Station Massacre, in no small part because young John Edgar Hoover and the organization that he would build into the modern Federal Bureau of Investigation contributed enormously to the smoke. And it hasn't stopped yet.

Though some of the misinformation, disinformation, and outright lies should have been evident almost from the start, few Americans in the heat and panic of the moment in 1933 were very interested in labeling them as such. Other lies were slower to take hold in the public's consciousness, but they finally hardened to the point that periodic spurts of truth from a writer or a relative or a repentant lawman just rolled off, always leaving the legend intact, as it is to this day.

The essential elements of the legend are easily summarized; for years, any Kansas City schoolboy could recite them: Unarmed federal agents and lightly armed local lawmen were ruthlessly murdered in a blaze of bullets by machine-gun–wielding criminals, who cut them down without warning or mercy, giving the lawmen absolutely no chance to defend themselves.

Like all good legends, this one had its roots in truth. Take the guns, for instance. Hoover's federal agents were almost always unarmed in those days—at least, by federal law and department regulations, they were supposed to be. After all, agents of the Division of Investigation of the Justice Department were not really law enforcement officers. At best, they were investigators working for federal prosecutors, not at all lawmen in the spirit of the old U.S. Marshals or Texas Rangers, and not in any way organized as the national police force that the FBI is today.

"We were a bunch of greenhorns who had no idea what we were doing in those days," Kenneth McIntire, who worked the massacre case and went on to become a power in the Washington office, told the author in 1983. "I was the first one to buy a box of bullets for the Kansas City office. The only gun in the office was kept in a safe by the agent in charge."

Ray C. Suran, another agent who worked the massacre case, made the story even better. "We had one thirty-two caliber pistol in the Kansas City office. That was it. I was told one time to get the gun and some bullets and come to a particular office. When I got there, I found out the bullets wouldn't even fit the gun. They were the wrong caliber."

Great stories, even when told fifty years later by old men still fiercely loyal to the Bureau and J. Edgar Hoover. Such stories point up essential facts: that agents had few powers in those days, that they couldn't legally carry guns, and that they weren't even empowered to make arrests except in very limited circumstances.

Yet those great old stories are, for the most part, exaggerations told and retold to bolster the legend, and not just for the entertainment value of a good yarn. In 1933, the Union Station Massacre reached into America's heart; it saddened us and scared us when we were already sad and scared. The Great Depression was bad enough, but then came the gangs of killers and robbers terrifying the country's midlands, robbing small towns of their accumulated savings, and killing the guys next door.

Bonnie Parker and Clyde Barrow, Ma Barker and her boys, Harvey Bailey, the Underhill brothers, Baby Face Nelson, John Dillinger, Charles Arthur "Pretty Boy" Floyd, George "Machine Gun" Kelly,

Alvin "Creepy" Karpis: They were killers, every one, and Hollywood had not yet made them otherwise. Now came the slaughter of lawmen in the heart of a major city—and no one to fight back.

The legend changed that. Within a year, almost on the anniversary of the massacre, nine major anticrime bills were signed into law by President Franklin D. Roosevelt. It became a federal offense to transport stolen property over a state line, to use interstate communications in extortion attempts, to flee across state lines to avoid prosecution, to assault or kill a federal officer, to rob a national bank, or to take hostages or kidnap victims across state lines. Agents were given full police powers anywhere in the country. And they were empowered to carry weapons at all times.

The national law enforcement system took on the basic shape it maintains to this day, because, in very large part, of the legend. And because of the legendary man who shaped it.

■   ■   ■

Some say that the histories of the FBI and J. Edgar Hoover are the same, but that's a bit of an oversimplification. In fact, the Bureau's history predates Hoover's government service, though not by much.

John Edgar Hoover, who never lived anywhere but Washington, D.C., went to work for the government partly because it ran in the family, his father being a supervisor in the U.S. Coast and Geodetic Survey, and partly because a filing clerk's job at the Library of Congress would qualify for an accelerated night-school program at George Washington University. He'd been offered a scholarship at the University of Virginia, but he didn't want to leave his hometown Seward Square neighborhood and, more specifically, his mother. So he worked, studied hard, and joined the Kappa Alpha fraternity, where Annie Hoover became the unofficial housemother.

An avowed patriot and a former leader in his high school cadet corps, Hoover missed World War I, forced to stay home when Dickerson Naylor Hoover suffered a nervous breakdown and left his job with no pension benefits and little money to support his family. So the younger Hoover, then twenty-two, took his brand-new law degree to the United States Justice Department. He started work three months after the war began, thus rooting his lifelong claim to biographers that he couldn't serve in the military because his job was essential to the war effort.

With many of the department's bright young stars gone to France, Hoover did very well. In no time he was in charge of the department's Enemy Alien Registration Section, a specialty he extended during the war years to cover other enemies of the government, such as radicals and, eventually, Communists.

Hoover's first big break came in 1919 when the home of A. Mitchell Palmer, the new U.S. attorney general and Hoover's boss, was blown up, and everyone quickly concluded it was the work of Bolsheviks, members of the International Workers of the World, or some other brand of Communist. The first Red Scare began that very night, and John Edgar Hoover was quick to catch the wave. Within two months Palmer appointed him head of the General Intelligence Division, and in the weeks that followed Hoover expanded the division's scope and powers to include radical activities at home and abroad and "economic and industrial disturbances." Young Mr. Hoover was not only a defender of democracy but a strikebreaker in defense of capitalism as well.

As the fear and hysteria built, whipped up by right-wing politicians, Hoover orchestrated hundreds of raids around the country, rounding up at least 3,600 men and women deemed to be threats to America. Unfortunately, many of the agents making those selections were in fact anti-Communist zealots donating their efforts as dollar-a-year men. Some of those arrested were deported immediately; most eventually were released when cooler heads prevailed. But apparently no one saw the real red flag waving amid the hysteria. It was buried in a confidential memo from Hoover to Frank Burke, assistant chief of the Bureau of Investigation, in which Hoover admitted there was "no authority under the law per-

mitting this Department to take any action in deportation proceedings relative to radical activities."

No legal foundation. And he knew it. But that hadn't stopped
him. J. Edgar Hoover was on his way.

■   ■   ■

Curt Gentry, in his extraordinary biography *J. Edgar Hoover: The
Man and the Secrets*, called the Justice Department in the early
twentieth century "the Department of Easy Virtue." If so, surely
there were no greater whores than the agents of the department's
Bureau of Investigation. Most were payrollers in the political sense
of the term, men who were expected to do little or nothing except
maintain allegiance to the man who gave them the job.

When Harlan Fiske Stone, who later became a distinguished Associate Justice of the Supreme Court, first took over the Department of Justice as attorney general in April of 1924, he said that "the
Bureau of Investigation was . . . in exceedingly bad odor." Stone's
notes, according to Gentry, included such references as "filled with
men with bad records . . . many convicted of crimes . . . organization lawless . . . many activities without any authority in federal
statutes . . . agents engaged in many practices which are brutal and
tyrannical in the extreme."

It wasn't supposed to be that way. When the Bureau of Investigation was conceived, Charles Joseph Bonaparte, the American-
born nephew of Napoleon I and the U.S. attorney general in 1908,
just wanted a "small permanent detective force" within the Department of Justice, mostly because the department had no investigators of its own and hated borrowing agents from the Treasury
Department's Secret Service. Yet Congress officially said "no" twice
before Bonaparte started the small unit on his own authority. Eventually President Theodore Roosevelt approved the idea, making the
bastard unit legitimate—and quality started downhill at about the
same rate that manpower and budget increased.

Stone knew the Bureau of Investigation he inherited in 1924 was rotten. But he also knew what it ought to be. He laid all that out clearly in a public statement when he fired BI director William J. Burns.

There is always the possibility that a secret police may become a menace to free governments and free institutions because it carries with it the possibility of abuses of power which are not always quickly apprehended or understood. The enormous expansion of Federal legislation, both civil and criminal, in recent years, however, has made a Bureau of Investigation a necessary instrument of law enforcement. But it is important that its activities be strictly limited to the performance of those functions for which it was created and that its agents themselves be not above the law or beyond its reach.

The Bureau of Investigation is not concerned with political or other opinions of individuals. It is concerned only with their conduct and then only with such conduct as is forbidden by the laws of the United States. When a police system passes beyond those limits, it is dangerous to the proper administration of justice and to human liberty, which it should be our first concern to cherish. Within them it should rightly be a terror to the wrongdoer.

Burns's BI had become just about everything Stone thought bad for the country. It suffered from virtually all the possible ills he listed. So he sent Burns packing, back to his famous detective agency, and looked around for new leadership.

J. Edgar Hoover was close at hand, almost too close. As assistant chief to Burns for the last couple of years, he was not untainted by the Bureau's image or overlooked by the Bureau's enemies. But he made a great impression on Harlan Fiske Stone and so was named acting director of the Bureau of Investigation on May 10, 1924. He was only twenty-nine years old.

Within a few days, Hoover began the cleanup Stone wanted, even adding his own idea of raising "employment qualifications so as to exclude from consideration any applicant without legal training or a knowledge of accounting." Over the years that notion would be elevated to an official requirement that all agents be lawyers or certified public accountants, though, in truth, Hoover kept a core of hired guns, flamboyant and tough lawmen of the old school, through much of the 1930s.

J. Edgar Hoover did not become an immediate legend. In fact, during the first ten years his job as director was never very secure nor was his Bureau very distinguished. And there were humiliations that stayed with him the rest of his days. One of the worst came a year and a half after his appointment when Agent Edwin Shanahan walked up to a suspected car thief in a Chicago garage.

Agents were not legally allowed to carry guns, and Shanahan, unlike some of his fellow officers, followed that rule. So when car thief Martin Durkin reached for his own weapon, there was nothing Shanahan could do. Durkin shot him in the chest at point-blank range, making Edwin Shanahan the first special agent of the Bureau of Investigation to be killed in the line of duty during its entire seventeen-year history.

Hoover was incensed. "We've got to get Durkin," he told his subordinates. "If one of our agents is killed and the killer is permitted to get away, it will be open season on all our agents. Get him."

By all accounts, agents volunteered their time all over the country, working days off and holidays for three months until they cornered Durkin in St. Louis. But then came the final indignity. The agents had to stand aside while local officers made the arrest and turned Durkin over to a state court for trial. After all, killing Shanahan was no federal crime, and virtually impotent federal agents couldn't have done much about it if it had been. Hoover vowed to change all that—someday.

But good things happened too. Hoover systematically transformed the lax and lazy outfit into a unit, instituting new procedures, higher expectations, inspections, a sense of mission, and manuals, always manuals. And, finally, in early 1932, the high-profile Lindbergh kidnapping case brought the Bureau into the national spotlight. For weeks the entire nation agonized over the whereabouts of Charles Lindbergh Jr., the nearly two-year-old son of the famous transatlantic flyer and Anne Morrow Lindbergh. With no jurisdiction at all, Hoover's Bureau was not just on the sidelines but on the back row of the bleachers, hardly even a player until the boy's body was found. But at that point President Herbert Hoover ordered all federal agents, from the BI to Treasury to the Coast Guard, into the case.

Deservedly or not, the BI scored major points with the public during the long Lindbergh investigation, more because of Hoover's high visibility than the Bureau's achievements. In fact, the Bureau's actual performance was sometimes comical. At one point, for example, Hoover's agents "found" the baby boy, only to discover at the last moment that beneath the diaper was irrefutable evidence of their mistake. And another time Hoover himself spotted an ordinary pigeon at the Lindbergh house and excitedly declared it a messenger from the kidnappers, apparently forgetting that homing pigeons require extensive on-site training before they can carry ransom notes.

Nonetheless, Hoover's agents were everywhere, and the director managed to appear to the public to have full command of the federal effort, though in fact that was not yet the case. And years later, when Bruno Richard Hauptmann was charged, convicted, and executed, Hoover was quick to take credit for solving the case, though Treasury Department agents were mostly responsible.

However, none of that secured Hoover's job in the early thirties. At least twice in the first months of 1933, he was on the verge of being sacked, and twice fate came to his rescue. The first brush was very close indeed.

Thomas J. Walsh, an old and outspoken enemy, was the clear favorite to become attorney general when President-elect Franklin D. Roosevelt took the oath of office in March 1933, following his landslide victory the previous November. That was terrible news for young Mr. Hoover. He and Walsh had clashed over the Teapot

Dome Scandal in the Harding administration and fought repeatedly during the years since. The mutual hatred was public and well documented. Once installed as attorney general, Walsh could fire Hoover, and it was generally accepted that throwing Hoover out would be Walsh's first official act.

He didn't get the chance. On March 3, 1933, en route to Roosevelt's inauguration, Walsh died quite unexpectedly. His new wife awakened to find him on the floor beside their bed on the train that was taking them to Washington. The official diagnosis was coronary thrombosis, though Hoover's staunchest enemies always have suspected that he (and a BI agent who happened to be riding the train) might have had something to do with the death. Others simply saw fate smiling on the young director.

But the threat wasn't over. Homer S. Cummings, quickly chosen to fill the job of attorney general, did not encourage FDR to move quickly on Hoover's reappointment. In fact, Cummings was known to favor someone else entirely, a former Justice Department official named Wallace Foster. But fate intervened on young John Edgar's behalf again when Foster died, quite as unexpectedly as Walsh.

FDR was still mulling over Hoover's future when the nation was shocked and sickened by the bloody massacre in Kansas City's Union Station Plaza. On July 29, 1933, just over a month after the massacre, as he launched a high-profile campaign to rid the heartland of the scourge of murderous bank robbers, John Edgar Hoover, already nine years in office, was reappointed director of the Bureau of Investigation. He would live thirty-nine more years, holding that office until the day he died.

■　■　■

In retrospect, perhaps we should have seen where Hoover was headed with his redefined, reshaped, retooled Bureau. Certainly the massive Union Station Massacre file marks some of those early compass points. Today, with 20/20 hindsight, we see clearly, thanks to Gentry and others who have documented the deeds and misdeeds, high crimes, and misdirections of the latter-day Federal Bureau of Investigation.

Wiretapping, for instance, clearly was a Hoover addiction from the beginning. Massacre investigators tapped any phone they wanted, any time they wanted, though Hoover demanded to know about each tap and its yield. When the wives of Francis Keating and Tommy Holden, imprisoned former Frank Nash associates, took a cross-country trip in the fall of 1933, agents routinely tapped the women's phones and bugged their rooms on the chance they might say something of interest about the massacre. Mostly, however, the agents heard bedsprings, since the two women had many male friends and loved to entertain. The agents dutifully reported it all, relevant or not, to Hoover, including a cast of characters, a thorough explanation of sleeping arrangements, and all the intimate details.

When Pretty Boy Floyd's wife took her son to St. Louis, her room was bugged and her phone line tapped. Virtually everyone who was related to anyone who was a suspect was tapped or bugged or both, and watched, and their mail opened and read. It wasn't exceptional, it was routine.

We now know this systematic intrusion into private lives was the Hoover norm, despite oft-repeated public statements to the contrary. Back in 1924 when Attorney General Stone officially banned wiretapping the first time, Hoover chimed in that such tapping was unethical. And Hoover said in 1932 that the FBI only used wiretaps in cases involving kidnapping, white slavery (prostitution) investigations, and national security. Yet nothing in the massacre case involved any of that, and the taps and bugs were everywhere.

Then there's the whole idea of organized crime. As most Americans now know, Hoover long maintained that there was no national criminal organization, no nationwide Mafia. Yet the thousands of pages of the Union Station Massacre file are replete with references to the "national crime operation" and the national web of Italian-led crime gangs. In fact, Hoover's agents had a pretty good understanding of who was who in the underworld. When Hoover wanted to put pressure on a particular gang, he knew how to do it. He knew quite well how to send a message along the network, even if he would spend a lifetime denying that such a network even existed.

Hoover's public refusal to investigate or even recognize the existence of organized crime has been thoroughly examined elsewhere, usually ending with the conclusion that the Mafia had something big and bad on J. Edgar Hoover, perhaps something involving his sex life, that he did not want and probably could not afford to see made public. Some authors have speculated that the "something" involved compromising pictures of himself and Clyde Tolson, his friend, companion, and, eventually, associate director of the FBI.

The massacre file offers nothing in that regard, and that aspect of FBI history is well beyond the scope of this inquiry. But Tolson's rise within the organization can be clearly plotted during the decade the file covers. In mid-1933, Tolson's name is far down on the memo circulation list. Within a year he has moved up considerably. By 1937 he is near the top, behind only Hoover and Harold "Pop" Nathan, the assistant director who served twenty-eight years in the Bureau, forty-two years in overall government service, and finally retired in 1945. Only then did Tolson become the official number two, complete with the new title of associate director, the only one in the Bureau's history.

There are other hints of the future, too. For instance, the director's marks are everywhere on the documents: notes in margins, comments, criticisms. Though the photocopies do not show it, those marks are always in blue ink—because Hoover was the only person in the FBI ever allowed to use blue ink. The standard joke was that Tolson always wrote in pencil—so that his remarks could be changed to match the director's. But laugh as they might, no agent ever used blue ink.

Most chilling, in retrospect, is the agents' fierce determination, evident on every page, to please "Mr. Hoover." Just as evident is the swift retribution taken by Hoover on those of whom he disapproved. Agents come and go, reassigned at whim, reflective even then of Hoover's success at keeping the FBI forever outside any civil service laws. Agents always knew they served at his pleasure and could be fired at any moment or, much worse, be exiled to agent obscurity.

Author Gentry and others have shown us vividly the product of that atmosphere. By now it is hard to imagine how any agent in Hoover's FBI could have avoided committing crimes. Burglary, for instance, was a routine and thoroughly illegal activity. When the Senate's Church Committee asked about the long history of break-ins during hearings in the 1970s, the FBI responded, "Since there exists no precise record of entries, we are unable to retrieve an accurate accounting of their number," adding that "at least fourteen domestic subversive targets were subject of at least 238 entries from 1942 to April 1968."

That statement prompted a sarcastic retort from a former agent. "I myself actually participated in more than 238 while assigned to the Chicago office," said M. Wesley Swearingen, a twenty-five-year FBI veteran. "The Chicago office committed thousands of bag jobs." So, he said, did every other FBI office.

Hoover's FBI went downhill from there. By the time he died, he had blackmailed presidents, civil rights leaders, politicians, actors, publishers, and housewives. His best agents had saluted (or the FBI equivalent) and gone along. The hard fact is that Hoover could not have survived without the support, often illegal, of his men.

But most of that stayed well out of the public eye until Hoover's final days. During his lifetime, the combination of private fear and public honor kept him safe. Even in the days after his death, the essential elements of the legend remained secure.

Jack Anderson, the columnist who had been Hoover's friend and then his bitter enemy, and who won a Pulitzer Prize by taking on the Bureau, could still issue this statement after the old man died in 1972.

J. Edgar Hoover transformed the FBI from a collection of hacks, misfits, and courthouse hangers-on into one of the world's most effective and formidable law enforcement organizations. Under his reign, not a single FBI man ever tried to fix a case, defraud the taxpayers, or sell out his country.

Hoover was also scrupulous at first not to step beyond the bounds of a policeman. But I would be hypocritical not to point that in his fading years he sometimes stepped across those bounds.

But Jack Anderson never read the Union Station Massacre file. He never was allowed to look closely at the birth of the modern FBI.

And he never met special agents Joe Lackey, Frank Smith, and Reed Vetterli.

CHAPTER THREE

THE PRETTY BOY

Friday, June 16, 1933

THE Pretty Boy's timing couldn't have been worse.

Fresh from a family visit in the clannish isolation of Oklahoma's Cookson Hills, he rolled into Missouri the day before the massacre completely unaware that a herd of lawmen, backed up by two companies of National Guardsmen, were hot on what they thought was his trail. Unfortunately, they were at that moment dead ahead, stomping over much of south and central Missouri. Convinced the infamous Pretty Boy had killed a state trooper and a county sheriff near Columbia the day before, they were determined to bring home his scalp.

Charles Arthur Floyd would never have waltzed knowingly into that kind of mess. He was much too careful. Sure, he wanted to get to Kansas City. Yes, he looked forward to a quick romp or two with some lady friends. But Pretty Boy Floyd had proven time after time that, given the choice, he'd rather run than fight. After all, he was a thief, not a fool.

The man beside him in the stolen Pontiac that morning was another matter entirely. Adam Richetti, twenty-four, was neither bright nor balanced. Worse, he was a hopeless alcoholic, known to drink a case of beer a day and seldom on the road without a stash of whiskey. His virtues, from Floyd's point of view, were that he idolized Floyd, who was only two years his senior, and he did what he was told—most of the time.

Both were killers, with few of the redeeming features Hollywood later would bestow. It was rumored that Pretty Boy tore up mortgages when he pillaged country banks, but there is no evidence he ever did any such thing. And there weren't even rumors of anything good about Adam Richetti.

That morning Floyd would have spun around and headed quite literally for the hills had he known what lay ahead. As one of America's most wanted fugitives, his face was well known to millions from Wanted posters in post offices from coast to coast. So getting around was hard even when he could stay in the shadows. Now he was driving into a full-scale, if misdirected, manhunt. And, though he did not yet know it, much worse.

His immediate problem, however, was the stolen Pontiac, coughing and choking for miles, then gasping into silence on a gravel stretch of Missouri Highway 13 not far north of Springfield. Luckily, Richetti's brother Joe lived only twenty miles up the road in Bolivar; better yet, he was a mechanic. So Floyd flagged down a passing farmer and negotiated a tow into town.

Since daybreak Adam Richetti had been hitting the sauce, this time a supply of corn whiskey in quart mason jars. By the time they arrived at the Bitzer Chevrolet Garage where Joe worked, Adam already was drunk—and it wasn't yet 7 A.M. Joe turned to Floyd and asked pointedly whether his brother now did this often, getting drunk so early in the day. Pretty Boy only shrugged.

Joe knew Floyd well enough to get away with such a suggestion of criticism. After all, Adam and "Choc," as Floyd was called by friends, dropped by Joe Richetti's house from time to time, usually arriving after dark and leaving before sunrise. Not that the timing made much difference in the little town. Anybody who cared knew when the outlaws were visiting at 317 East Summit Street.

"We used to stand across the road and watch them, sitting there on the porch, talking," recalled Paul Butler, who lived a few houses away in those days. "We could see their cigarettes glowing in the dark. It was the most exciting thing that ever happened. 'Course, our mothers had told us to stay away from there, especially when a strange car was around. But we knew. We always knew."

So did everybody else. But there was more at work in the small towns of middle America than just minding one's own business. There was danger in curiosity, especially for law officers.

"My dad was a deputy sheriff in those days," explained an old-timer who grew up near Joplin, Missouri, the crossroads for a slew of the period's robbers and killers. "He said he thought he saw Floyd on the road one time—so he turned around and went the other direction."

Not an uncommon reaction. When local lawmen did give chase —after a bank robbery, for instance—the chase probably stopped at the county line. That's where jurisdiction, and often interest, ended. State police were few, and federal police were all but non-existent. When the common man's resentment of the banks that took their farms and of the law that made it possible was mixed in, the country's cat roads, the farm-to-market network of dirt and gravel, became the outlaw's friend. Folks out there, if not exactly welcoming, were not likely to be the bank robber's bitter enemies either.

It didn't take a criminal mastermind to figure all this out, as proven by the short-lived success in the early thirties of a string of society's underachievers. Bonnie Parker, a sexually adventurous nineteen-year-old "bored crapless" in a little town, and Clyde Barrow, a sexually confused saxophone player with little talent and no money, ran totally amok until law officers ambushed them in 1934. Bonnie and Clyde killed readily, especially lawmen, but their biggest robbery garnered less than $3,500. Mostly, they hit grocery stores and filling stations before moving up to small-town banks. And for most of the period they kept a little apartment in Joplin, coming and going pretty much as they wished.

The notoriously dysfunctional Barker family, Ma and her four boys, came out of grinding Ozark poverty to rob banks all over the heartland, kidnapping businessmen for ransom and skipping vir-tually unmolested along the cat roads for years.

And Machine Gun Kelly, whose reputation was more the product of a bragging wife's ambitions and J. Edgar Hoover's rage than of any demonstrated competence with the weapon, had a thriving sideline business, running a fugitive farm in Texas for fellow crooks too hot to travel. His neighbors never complained.

When John Dillinger, by far the smartest of them all, came along in 1933, it was obvious he'd done his homework. He just about turned his Public Enemy label into Public Idol, actually telling bank patrons more than once to keep their money, that he only wanted the bank's money. The master of escape was, in fact, as much a master of public relations.

They all profited from a conflicted public that was angry, disappointed, afraid, suspicious—and sorely in need of popular heroes. Contrary to logic, the more the gunmen broke society's laws, the more the back roads seemed to tolerate, even accept, them. Jesse James would have understood.

Though no one ever quite admitted it, something along those lines was probably at work that morning at the Bitzer Chevrolet Garage in Bolivar. Pretty Boy Floyd and Adam Richetti jawed comfortably with a half-dozen salesmen and mechanics who later claimed they had strolled in to see Floyd's powerful Pontiac. Since everyone in town knew Joe (though they pronounced his last name *Rach*-etti), knew about his brother Adam, and knew about Adam's famous partner, it's unlikely the car was the only attraction.

In any case, all went well until Jack Killingsworth, a former car salesman himself, slipped through a side door to join the boys for morning coffee and to see about getting some work done on his automobile. When he offered an innocuous comment about the Pontiac, Adam's head snapped up. Amazingly quickly for a man in his condition, he reached into the car's backseat, threw back a blanket, and leveled a Thompson submachine gun at Killingsworth's belly.

"There's the law now!" Adam shouted at the Pretty Boy.

Adam ordered everybody up against the wall and then turned his machine gun and an evil eye on Killingsworth, who was only six months into his job as Polk County sheriff. Joe knew the look. Quickly wedging himself between the sheriff and the gun barrel, he told his brother, "If you kill him, you're going to have to kill me."

Floyd didn't give his drunken partner a chance to decide. He grabbed Killingsworth and pulled him aside, his own .45 pistol against the sheriff's temple. Adam, suddenly enraged, turned his machine gun toward the others, screaming and threatening mayhem.

"That liquor is getting the best of you," Floyd barked, and Adam immediately settled down. Floyd turned to Ernest Bitzer, owner of the garage, apologized for the threatening tactics, and then added, "This is life and death for us."

Killingsworth could do nothing even if he had had a gun, which he didn't. It was in his car half a block away. He didn't need it much in Polk County. Even his badge stayed in his shirt pocket most of the time. Now, only a block from the center of town and the Polk County courthouse, he thought he was facing death. When he heard what Floyd had in mind, he was sure of it. Floyd wanted a hostage.

"Why take me?" Killingsworth asked Floyd.

"You know all the roads, and you can keep me off the highways," Floyd said, shoving the sheriff out the door toward Joe Richetti's car, soon to become the most famous vehicle in Bolivar's history. Floyd held everyone at gunpoint while Adam moved their belongings out of the ailing Pontiac and into Joe's brand-new Chevrolet.

"I still remember that car," Paul Butler, Joe's neighbor, recalled six decades later. "It was beige over brown with beautiful wheels. It was some car."

Adam got behind the wheel, Floyd and the sheriff in the rear seat. Floyd held the machine gun on his lap, the barrel toward Killingsworth.

"You can have my car, Joe," he shouted over his shoulder. It was a great gift, considering the Pontiac was probably driven to death and definitely stolen.

As Joe Richetti's car wheeled away from the curb, word spread through Bitzer's front door that the sheriff had been kidnapped by Pretty Boy Floyd. Within minutes, police departments in every direction got the call, including the small army of lawmen who already thought they were on Floyd's trail several miles to the northeast. This wasn't just another bank robbery. Jack Killingsworth was a friend.

"You know the roads," Adam shouted at Killingsworth as they roared west, away from the town's center. "Get us out of here."

"Where do you want to go?" the sheriff yelled.

"Kansas City," Floyd said.

"Turn north."

Decades later, Killingsworth's recollection of the first couple of hours of that ride was still terrifying. At one point, he said, a state patrol vehicle pulled alongside them, and Adam, driving erratically, wanted to open fire. Floyd, however, told the sheriff to wave the officer away.

"I stuck my Panama hat out the window and waved as hard as I could," Killingsworth said. "He finally got the idea."

A few miles farther down the road, several members of a posse began to close in on the outlaws. That really frightened Killingsworth. "I sure hoped they wouldn't surround us completely, because there sure would have been bloodshed," he said, thinking it would start with his own.

Convinced his life depended on getting the fugitives away from the law, Sheriff Killingsworth led them on a convoluted route over the cat roads, doubling back, heading the wrong direction sometimes, near Bentonville and Fairfield and Mount Zion and Bronington.

"We missed those towns," Killingsworth would later testify. "We went in that direction."

They took country roads and lanes, guided by Killingsworth's knowledge and the names on water towers in the distance, meandering generally northwest toward Kansas City. And the sheriff worried more every mile about Joe's flamboyant car.

"I told them they would have to get another car if they hoped to get away," he recalled. But he had another agenda, too. Adam had told him he could take Joe's car back home when they found a replacement. So he kept talking about the danger of driving this flashy car.

Finally, they took his advice. About a mile and a half south of Deepwater, Missouri, on Highway 52, they slowed to a stop and waited. Several cars passed, none of them what Floyd wanted. Then, about 11 A.M, Walter Griffith, who supervised several farms for the Mutual Benefit Life Insurance Company, came along in his brand-new Pontiac, just the sort of car Floyd liked.

Richetti raced up beside him, and both he and Floyd motioned for Griffith to pull over. Thinking at first they had mistaken him for someone else, Griffith drove on. So Richetti crowded him off the road. Griffith saw three men jump out of the car, one with a machine gun and another with two large pistols. When they ordered him to slide over in the seat, he couldn't move.

"He was too scared," Killingsworth testified later. "Any man would be."

What Griffith saw next didn't help. As the men transferred their stuff from Joe's car to the Pontiac, he counted two .45s on Floyd, another in Richetti's belt, and the machine gun. One of the first things they moved was a woman's stocking heavy with .45 ammunition that would fit the pistols and the machine gun. Then came an army trunk, heavy and clunking, which they stood on end in the middle of the backseat. Finally, Richetti grabbed another quart mason jar of moonshine, but the lid slipped loose and the jar shattered on the pavement. Richetti was furious.

Neither outlaw offered to make good on Richetti's promise that Killingsworth would be released when a fresh car was found. And the sheriff wisely did not press the point.

Floyd took the wheel, Griffith beside him. In the rear, Killingsworth sat behind Griffith and Richetti sat behind Floyd, with the machine gun propped atop the army trunk, the barrel pointed in the general direction of Griffith's left ear. Richetti didn't even lower it when they met cars. Floyd, meanwhile, laid one of his .45s on his right thigh, his hand often resting on the handle. Every time a car passed, he released the safety.

Montrose ... Appleton City ... Ballard. Then across Highway 71, up a short stretch of the Missouri Pacific tracks, through the edge of Archie, and into Kansas.

Griffith had a lot of time to stare at that .45 on Floyd's thigh. He wondered what the strange addition to the hammer was all about, but he didn't ask. He said as little as possible.

They stopped only three times, the first to fill up the gas tank. Richetti paid the teenage girl, and they moved on. Then they stopped near a farmer hitching up his horses to go to the field. Floyd asked if they could get some water from the windmill, and the old man nodded. When the team and its master were gone, Richetti climbed out of the car, walked to the well 250 feet away, hauled up the water by an old rope tied to a bucket, and made three trips back to the car to bring a dipper of water to the others. When the last man drank, Richetti returned the dipper to the well for the next thirsty traveler. He was, after all, a country boy.

The heat of the day and the liquor, which he continued to knock down from time to time, left Richetti "dauncey," in Griffith's words. He napped in the car. When Floyd pulled into a ravine late in the day, Richetti slept hard under a tree nearby. Griffith, still terrified, never left the front seat.

Killingsworth and Floyd, however, almost became friends. Over the next three hours, they talked about family and outlaws and lawmen. And Floyd let himself get personal. When Killingsworth said he already missed his young son, Floyd flashed angry.

"You shouldn't kick about one day," Floyd spat. "How would you like to be hunted night and day, day and night? How would you like to sleep every night with this [machine gun] across your knees?"

Then the anger turned maudlin.

"I have a son too. Maybe you think I wouldn't like to see him. When you get home, you can have your son with you every day and sit and talk with him," Floyd said softly. "All I ever get to do is see mine once in a long while. Then all I can do is to stand off and look at him for a minute."

Years later, Killingsworth still felt the tenderness of that moment.

As the hours passed, the two walked along a nearby creek, then sat under the shade of a tree while Floyd cleaned his .45 pistol. At one point, Floyd took out the machine gun's magazine and let Killingsworth look the gun over thoroughly. The sheriff noticed the serial number had been rubbed away, but he made no comment.

The mood was broken when a plane flew low overhead. Floyd scrambled to get the Pontiac under cover, deeper in the ravine, but he relaxed when the plane did not return. In a few minutes he announced it was time to move on, shook Richetti awake, and told everybody to get back in the car. Out on the road, Killingsworth became the cop again, working the conversation around to the Missouri state trooper and the county sheriff murdered the day before near Columbia. He knew, though Floyd did not, that Floyd and Richetti were prime suspects and subjects of the massive manhunt.

"You're not going to try to put that one on us, are you?" Floyd asked.

"I am not putting anything on you," Killingsworth said. "I just merely asked you."

But Richetti couldn't leave it there.

"Guess those two won't be stopping any more cars, will they?" he sneered.

Floyd took the Pontiac on a long, meandering route, almost to Ottawa, Kansas, then well west of Kansas City, Kansas. They finally came at the city from the west, though they had started the day to the southeast. Even in Kansas City, Kansas, Floyd avoided the main streets, driving back and forth across the major downtown thoroughfare, Minnesota Avenue, several times before heading across the intercity viaduct toward Kansas City, Missouri. But before they could reach the city and its high bluffs, Floyd wheeled the Pontiac down a side ramp into the industrial West Bottoms at Ninth Street.

At one time, a strip of Ninth Street near the Kansas–Missouri line claimed the title of Wettest Block in the World. The block had twenty-four buildings, and twenty-three of them housed saloons. (The other was probably a whorehouse, though the prostitutes were more likely to work the streets and alleys.) By 1933 it was still a rough-and-tumble place that the law usually left alone, just right for two killers on the run.

At about 10:45 P.M., Floyd pulled to a stop at the northwest corner of Ninth and Hickory. He got out, leaving Richetti in charge of the two hostages. Killingsworth asked if he could stretch his legs, and Richetti, fondling the machine gun, said he should not go far. He didn't. Standing on the corner, he watched Floyd disappear into a building about a block and a half away.

Less than five minutes later, Floyd was back. He made very clear what he expected of everyone. In a few minutes, he said, a car would arrive for him and Richetti. When the car came, Killingsworth and Griffith were to get out of the Pontiac and stand quietly on the corner. He and Richetti would drive the Pontiac to a loading dock about a block away, take their stuff out, and leave.

"He told us before he left to come on up there when they stopped and the motor would be turned off and the lights would be left on; for us to come and get the car, my car," Griffith later would testify at Richetti's trial. "While we was standing there watching him, there was some traffic there, several cars, there was a car drove up to the side of my car and they transferred that [army] trunk to this other car and drove on around the corner to the left."

The second car then disappeared down St. Louis Street, leaving Killingsworth and Griffith alone and relieved, though not yet relaxed. They'd been told, after all, that they would be watched. The two walked quickly to Griffith's car, started the engine, and headed out of the West Bottoms. When they stopped for gas a few minutes later, they assessed their situation.

"Mr. Griffith and I talked about whether we would report it or whether we would take a chance on it or not," Killingsworth said.

It wasn't a long debate. Choosing to follow another of the Pretty Boy's suggestions, they drove straight to Lee's Summit, a small town southeast of Kansas City, for an early breakfast. Killingsworth thought they were followed for a while, but he didn't check too closely, not really wanting to know. They ate a hearty meal, called their families, and started home.

"Floyd told me not to make any report of this, [that] it would be too bad for me if I did," Griffith would say later.

The sheriff agreed. He just wanted the long, trying day behind him. It was done and, he thought, best forgotten. So he had not been impressed when Floyd offered him a souvenir—the golf clubs he had left at the garage back in Bolivar.

"They will be something to remember me by," Floyd told him at the last minute.

The sheriff had declined. "I won't need anything to remember you by," he had said.

He couldn't know, at that moment, that Charles Arthur "Pretty Boy" Floyd's greatest fame was still eight hours away.

CHAPTER FOUR

THE CONVERGENCE

Friday, June 16, 1933

THEY WERE commandos, really, on their own in hostile territory: two federal agents and an Oklahoma police chief, not much to impress a collection of robbers, thieves, and killers in a "safe" town deep within a state that pretty much specialized in looking the other way.

But Bureau of Investigation agents Joe Lackey and Frank Smith were determined to pull off this operation, and they would use a few pages from the age-old manual of behind-the-lines operations to do it: Get in, do the job, get out fast.

The agents knew well that they were skating very close to the edge in several ways. For one thing, they were grossly outnumbered. Outlaws from all over the country hung out in Hot Springs, Arkansas, in the early 1930s, enjoying the waters, licking their wounds, and planning their next adventures. The biggest names passed through, including some of the Italians from the big cities to the north and east. Everyone relaxed in the glow of official protection.

Hot Springs, after all, was about as notorious as its clientele. When crime boss Richard Galatas and his main man, Chief of Detectives Herbert A. "Dutch" Akers, promised a quiet stay in their homey little town, they meant to keep that promise. They were paid well for their consideration, and disturbances were bad for business.

Yet manpower wasn't the agents' only problem. They also were skating close to the edge of their legal authority. That's why Chief Otto Reed, Ott to his friends, was along. Though several counties and one state away from his McAlester, Oklahoma, home, Reed's claim to jurisdiction for this little caper was still stronger than the Bureau of Investigation could muster in those days. And Ott had a personal stake. He hated Frank Nash, had hated him for years. So the chief willingly came along when the agents invited him in on the grab.

For his part, Frank Nash, the lawmen's target, just wanted to get away for a while from the helter-skelter of bank robbing, hiding out, and general life on the lam. It seemed somebody was always looking for him, whether for the old train robberies, the more recent bank robberies with the Barker Gang, or that old unfinished business with the Leavenworth Federal Penitentiary. Besides, he had a new "wife" named Frances, who was way too pretty for him, some fresh money in his pocket, and a little time to enjoy both.

Frances was indeed a looker. He'd picked her up in Chicago, where he'd found her working as a cook in an old friend's tavern. The fact that they'd never really taken any vows and he'd never really told her much about his past, especially the bit involving Leavenworth, didn't seem to stand in their way. Of course, she hadn't been exactly straight about her past either, like the part about her first husband leaving her to marry her sister and how she had him shot for the insult.

But they were happy, trying to build a family for her daughter, Danella, about eight years old. This vacation was a chance for them all to be together, which wasn't easy with Frank on the road so much and Danella spending a lot of time with Frances's parents in Minnesota. In only a couple of days, they had rented a small house not far from downtown, made contact with some old friends, and settled into the vacation atmosphere. That morning Jelly, as Frances called Nash, told her he was going to the White Front for some cigars and maybe a game or two of pool. She and Danella, playing on the porch, watched him drive away.

She would never again see him alive.

The lawmen, at that moment, had been in Hot Springs only a few hours. They had arrived between 3 and 4 A.M. and checked into the Como Hotel after driving from their Oklahoma City base, through McAlester to pick up Chief Reed, and across half of Arkansas. After only a couple of hours of sleep, Frank Smith was on the phone to his informant, the man who had told him Frank Nash was in Hot Springs, triggering the entire operation. That morning Smith got a description of Nash's car, his Illinois license tag number, and the tip that Nash liked to hang out at Galatas's White Front Cigar Store. In fact, the store was more of a mini-mart for tobacco, liquor, prostitutes, con games, gambling, pool hustling, police payoffs, and general gangland networking.

Lackey and Reed left Smith at the hotel and cruised up and down the town's main streets in search of Nash's car. They found it near the White Front. Lackey left Reed to watch from across the street and went back for Smith. When they returned, Reed pointed out Nash just inside the door. The two agents drove on by, made a U-turn at the corner, and stopped their car smack in the middle of the street in front of the cigar store. They wanted to move quickly.

Lackey walked in first, striding to the counter to buy a cigar. Smith and Reed were close behind. The front part of the store was partitioned off, separating it from the pool tables in the rear. About a dozen men sat or stood around the café tables; the lawmen did not know how many were back in the poolroom.

At that moment, Nash started toward the front entrance, pushing past the two agents. Both Lackey and Smith pulled sidearms and stepped toward him. Chief Reed quickly turned his back to the agents, drew his own long-barreled revolver, and leveled it at the other men in the hall. No one moved.

"Frank Nash," Smith said to his prisoner, "stick up your hands."

Nash, unarmed and confused, unsure whether he was being arrested, abducted, or assassinated, pleaded not to be shot. Lackey, after searching Nash for weapons, turned to join Reed in covering the others as Smith hustled Nash outside, across the street, and into the front seat of the waiting car. Lackey and Reed backed out of the cigar store together and ran to the car. Lackey drove; Reed and Smith sat behind Nash. The chief quickly and graphically made clear to Nash what would result from any hint of escape. Lackey gunned the engine and headed north toward Little Rock. The grab had taken fewer than five minutes. They were on their way out of Hot Springs a little after noon.

They didn't make it far. At Benton, not twenty miles up the road, three men with rifles and sawed-off shotguns motioned them off the road and into a gas station. They announced they were in search of a man with a black mustache who had been kidnapped from Hot Springs. Lackey could only show his credentials and hope. It's still unclear whether Lackey told the truth or pretended the men in the car were all lawmen while Reed or Smith persuaded Nash to remain silent. In any event, they were on the road again in minutes, careening around corners and flying over hilltops on the tough mountain road. In fifty-five minutes, by Lackey's watch, they had covered the fifty-eight miles to the outskirts of Little Rock.

And they were in trouble again. Two local policemen, each armed with a riot gun, stopped Lackey's car for a second time, again reporting they were in search of a Hot Springs kidnap victim. But this time the policemen not only let them go, they offered an escort through Little Rock. At the other side, they asked where the agents were headed.

"Joplin," Lackey answered, knowing the road forked not far ahead.

In fact, they were bound for Fort Smith, Arkansas, due west, not north toward Joplin, Missouri. And they were beginning to believe they might make it. Convinced that any pursuit from Hot Springs was now futile, encouraged by twice talking their way past road-blocks, and invigorated by the open road, the lawmen began to relax. At one point Reed suddenly reached forward, gripped Nash's tuft of red hair, and pulled hard. It came off in his hand.

"I knew you was bald, Frank," the chief roared, shaking the wig a bit before returning it to Nash, who carefully refit it to his smooth, shiny head.

They stopped to eat in Russellville and called R. H. Colvin, their boss in charge of the Oklahoma City office, which also covered Arkansas. Colvin was glad they had Nash in custody, but he wanted them to get rid of him as quickly as possible. He told them to proceed to Fort Smith and call again for instructions. Meanwhile, he would work things out, make all the arrangements.

Colvin first checked the train schedules. The Missouri Pacific would leave Fort Smith about 8:30 P.M. and get into Kansas City at 7 A.M. the following morning. But it was supposed to lay over in Kansas City for a full hour before going on to Leavenworth. That wouldn't do. So Colvin called Reed Vetterli, the agent in charge of the Kansas City office, quickly explained what was happening, and asked for help. Vetterli was eager to do whatever he could. Anything.

"They'll arrive on the Missouri Pacific tomorrow morning at seven o'clock," Colvin said. "Can you meet them? Get them on to Leavenworth by car?"

"I'll take care of it," Vetterli answered. "Leave everything to me."

Vetterli immediately called the Kansas City Police Department and made arrangements to have the two men in charge of the Hot Shot, the department's riot car, be at Union Station to meet the agents, though he later said he did not offer anyone any details. But he would need Bureau help, too. So he called one of his own trusted agents and alerted him for action.

Back in Fort Smith, Lackey took no chances with his prisoner. Even though they planned to be in town only a couple of hours, he locked Nash securely in the county jail, telling the jailer and the sheriff the prisoner's identity but admonishing them to keep quiet. Both would later claim to investigators that they followed those instructions and kept their mouths shut. The two agents likewise would claim they said nothing, strictly according to standard Bureau procedure and Colvin's direct orders of the day.

One of the two agents stayed with Nash every moment. Lackey again talked to Colvin in Oklahoma City and was told in detail about the arrangements. Everything seemed to be in order.

"You'll be met in Kansas City," Colvin said.

Colvin also had another suggestion. He told Lackey to ask Reed to accompany the two agents to Kansas City and on to Leavenworth rather than head across Oklahoma to his home in McAlester. Reed agreed, thus sealing his own fate.

The three waited nervously until 8:15 P.M., when they were taken by a deputy sheriff to the train station only a few blocks away. Unfortunately, the train was late, leaving the lawmen to stand in the depot for more than fifteen minutes, hardly inconspicuous with their manacled prisoner.

A young Associated Press reporter saw them and marched up to Lackey, asking for details about the prisoner. Who was he? What had he done? Where were they taking him? Lackey always told Hoover that he answered none of the reporter's questions, that he gave away nothing about their planned movements to Kansas City and on to Leavenworth. Despite the excitement of the moment, the glow of success, the adrenaline pumping through his body, Lackey maintained he told the reporter nothing at all. However, if that young AP reporter relied only on guesswork, he managed to be remarkably accurate and detailed in the report he filed a few minutes later.

> *FT. SMITH, ARK. July 16 (AP)—Frank Nash, one of the last surviving members of the notorious Al Spencer gang of bank and train robbers that operated a decade ago, was recaptured today at Hot Springs, Ark., by three Department of Justice*

agents—who "kidnapped" him on the streets of the resort city.

Nash had been at liberty since his escape from the federal penitentiary at Leavenworth, Kansas, in October 1930. He was serving a 25-year term for robbing a mail train at Okesa, Okla., with Spencer and five others of the gang.

The Department of Justice men moved with utmost secrecy after rushing Nash out of Hot Springs in their automobile. They revealed the identity of the prisoner for the first time here, although they were stopped by officers at Little Rock following a report from Hot Springs that three men had kidnapped a man known there as "Doc."

The agents left their automobile here and boarded a train for Leavenworth shortly after their arrival here from Little Rock tonight, in an effort, they said, to balk a possible attempt at rescue by Nash's confederates. Nash was heavily manacled and the agents were armed with rifles.

The secret service men refused to discuss details of how Nash was trailed to Hot Springs. They said they "kidnapped" him because of the danger of a clash with Nash's men in making an open capture.

It was indicated the agents had been "shadowing" Nash for some time, waiting for an opportunity to capture him when he was alone.

In fact, the reporter appears to have had extensive knowledge of details that could have come only from the agents or Chief Reed. So despite his later claims, it's likely that Lackey bought the age-old reporter gambit—"It won't be in any papers until tomorrow morning"—and gave the reporter the story.

It *wasn't* in any papers until morning—until the morning editions, that is, which began hitting city streets not long after midnight. Also, the sensitive information passed quickly through AP to the Hot Springs newspaper office, which was not an unfamiliar place to Galatas and his boys. In short, any hope of the federal agents entering Kansas City in secrecy was destroyed well before midnight. An AP message for clients even announced what train, complete with Kansas City arrival time, the agents and the prisoner had boarded.

But Galatas didn't have to wait for all that. A gangland connection, just hanging around and listening in the Fort Smith train station, had passed the information to Hot Springs before the train crossed into Oklahoma.

Lackey, Smith, and Reed knew none of this as the Missouri Pacific left Arkansas just before 9 P.M. to meander its way across Oklahoma and Kansas on its way north. In fact, they thought they had handled everything quite well. When the train finally had arrived in Fort Smith, they had followed the rest of Colvin's instructions to the letter, going directly to Drawing Room A, Car 11. Lackey even had asked agent R. N. Butterworth, who just happened to be getting off the train as they were boarding, to come to Drawing Room A and hang around until departure. It all went without incident.

Lackey also bought a ticket for lower berth number 12, which was right beside the door to the drawing room. He knew there would not be enough space in the drawing room for all four of them over so many hours. Before long, all had settled into place. Nash lay in the upper berth, handcuffed to the bed. The three lawmen were exhausted, having been up almost all the previous night and throughout the tense day. Now they could rest. Lackey took the lower berth outside from about midnight until 2 A.M., then switched with Smith until 6:30 A.M. Reed took the lower in the drawing room.

But if the lawmen wanted to sleep, Nash did not. He preferred to chat, to entertain. He talked about his wife, books, anything. To their surprise, he was a glib and affable traveling companion, chattering to whichever lawman would stay awake and listen.

It was a pleasant enough evening, considering that, for half of them, it was their last.

CHAPTER FIVE

THE CITY

Kansas City in the 1930s has been called a wide-open, anything-goes town, but that description could not be further from the truth. In fact, the city was firmly in the grip of a few determined men who ran it to the benefit of a decidedly larger group. And that larger group included political, business, and civic leaders, doctors and lawyers, butchers and bakers, and one famous failed haberdasher named Harry.

Time has cast bossism in a dark and sinister light, but it didn't seem that way at the time, at least not to those like young Harry Truman, who got a leg up from the tough-minded, iron-willed boys at the top. The Pendergasts, for all that has been written about them since, could hardly have built their powerful political machine in Kansas City without, at some level, the support and consent of the people they bossed.

Like most dictatorships, the Pendergast machine's operations were a model of efficiency. Only the democratic aspects, those pesky periodic elections, got sloppy from time to time. But for the most part Boss Tom, following in the footsteps of his older brother, Jim, kept things from getting out of hand. His Goat faction of the Democratic Party might fight like hell with Joe Shannon's Rabbit faction, but for many years the two found ways to share power and its perks once the voting was done.

There are lots of ways to define the Goat and Rabbit factions, by philosophy or geography or lifestyle. None works very well. It was said, for instance, that old Jim Pendergast's followers had to be goats to climb over the city's high bluff from their base in the West Bottoms near the confluence of the Kansas and Missouri rivers. And, likewise, it was said that Shannon's men were so stupid they scampered (and reproduced) like the rabbits with whom they shared the environs of O.K. Creek.

Or you could make the distinction that Pendergast's army originally was based around Boss Jim's North Side tavern and all that sprang from it, while Shannon's centered around family and friends in the Ninth Ward on the city's southeast.

Or, if you were really in a bind, you could argue that the Pendergasts were Jacksonian Democrats and Shannon was a Jeffersonian Democrat. But you would have found few on the streets who would have understood or cared much about that.

In Kansas City, like most other boss-run cities, it was about jobs and favors—and money above and under the table. And it was about the political control that would keep all those things coming your way. For Boss Tom Pendergast, that meant sliding out of the tavern business as the nation turned to Prohibition and sliding into the ready-mix concrete business as the Depression's public works projects got under way. So when the city dug out and then paved miles of Brush Creek, using thousands of men in the place of heavy machinery and laying down thousands of tons of concrete, it was Boss Tom's Democratic workers holding the shovels and Boss Tom's trucks pouring Boss Tom's concrete.

From Kansas City's beginnings, crime and politics were intertwined, in large part because Kansas Citians didn't always share the rest of the country's definitions about what was political and what was criminal. Passing out jobs and favors was political, not criminal, because it gave the people who had supported you what they needed. Rigging a bid or contract was political, not criminal, because it backed the people who had backed you. So why shouldn't that perspective bleed into other things that the people clearly wanted, especially if those people had helped you gain power and keep it?

Gambling has always been one of those other things in Kansas

City. In the first place, Boss Tom's family fortune was based on booze and betting. By the late 1920s, much of his political power was, too. And the citizenry seemed to approve. When a group of ministers calling themselves the Charter League and led by Rabbi Samuel S. Mayerberg rose to campaign against the rampant betting parlors, casinos, slot machines, and card games in the early 1930s, the good citizens of Kansas City paid little attention. On the contrary, Mayerberg was frequently threatened with assassination, his home was vandalized, and his family lived in fear.

By contrast, there's the story of Conrad H. Mann, president of the Kansas City Chamber of Commerce, who went to Washington to try to convince the new occupant of the White House that gambling was a good thing. Before he could get home, however, this man, ironically called Con Mann, was indicted by a federal grand jury in New York City of violating federal lottery laws. In consternation, thousands of Kansas City citizens turned out at Union Station to welcome him home, carrying signs declaring their support. He was met and escorted by the city manager and other political leaders, and the chamber presented him with a resolution pledging their unshaken faith in their president. William M. Reddig wrote in his book *Tom's Town* that there also would have been a brass band had not the Ministerial Alliance objected.

Kansas City was shouting as loud as it could that it did not consider gambling a crime. For Boss Tom that was an attitude both visceral and practical. After all, his power and Kansas City's stability in the early 1930s stood on four clearly identifiable legs, all rooted in gambling and official corruption.

The first, of course, was political. Beyond just the profits, liberally spread around, there were important promises made to business and civic leaders that the gambling scene would be kept under control, well regulated, and out of their upper-class neighborhoods. The upper crust, the old money, the insurance moguls and bankers all well knew what was going on, even participated themselves, though seldom openly and never anywhere near the mansions along Ward Parkway. William Rockhill Nelson, the wealthy publisher of the *Kansas City Star*, might squawk from time to time, but the unofficial gentlemen's agreement was well understood by all.

The second leg was the police. After years of trying, the Pendergasts had, by the early thirties, wrested home rule from the state, giving the city complete control of the police for the first time in decades. City Manager H. F. McElroy, called Judge by everyone in town, wasted no time. Rabbi Mayerberg charged in 1932 that there were seventy-five ex-convicts on the KCPD; Hoover's men estimated there were far more than that. In any case, the police department became a tool of the machine, enforcing the gentlemen's agreement: protecting gambling, keeping order among thieves, and taking its cut of the profits. There were good cops, though few and ever-diminishing in number, but you never knew who they were.

The third leg was never a formal part of the machine, but it was always important. Kansas City, after all, was and is a southern city, at least in attitude. The counties along the Missouri River, including Kansas City's Jackson County, had been as devoutly and heavily slave counties as any in Mississippi. Jesse James, who rode with the murderous Quantrill's Raiders during the Civil War and got his criminal start robbing northern banks and railroads, was from Kearney, just a few miles north of Kansas City in Clay County. His brother Frank James, in his older years, was a bouncer in one of Boss Tom's gambling dives. Even today Kansas City's deeply troubled school system is a monument to decades of racial prejudice, economic discrimination, spending disparities, and shattered neighborhoods.

So Kansas City's segregated blacks could be only an unofficial part of the Pendergast operation. None held significant public office, few voted, and they brought no real clout to the tables of power—except in gambling and crime. There Kansas City's black community had its own power structure, its own bosses, and its own special relationship with the police and Pendergast's machine. For the most part it was a simple arrangement: Do what you want but keep it quiet.

That same basic philosophy extended to the fourth and most important leg of the Pendergast power machine. With an operation parallel and not much subordinate to Boss Tom's, organized crime in Kansas City was run by Johnny Lazia, an Italian-American son of immigrants, who fought his way to power from the Market Square area where Kansas City's northernmost points touched the Missouri River.

Lazia differed from most other crime bosses only in looks. With his soft features, wireless glasses, and gentle voice, he could be mistaken for a decent human being. In fact, he was a bloody killer who wouldn't hesitate to order the murder of a close friend. The record is clear that Lazia and Pendergast worked hand in glove to control Kansas City, Lazia reaching over to deliver the vote on election day and Pendergast, in turn, using the police to help Lazia with his various criminal operations. Gambling was their common ground, and the rest grew from there.

It's rumored that Johnny once pulled a knife on Boss Tom, but we don't know that. More likely, they never let their relationship deteriorate that far because they needed each other too much. And they both had enemies enough of their own. Boss Tom had to fight off periodic impulses of good citizenship from the folks of Kansas City, worry about the situation in the rest of the state, often dominated by Republicans, and increasingly keep an eye on the threats and promises of the growing federal government.

And Johnny Lazia had to fight every day to preserve the place he'd carved for himself. There were always young amateurs who saw what he'd done and wanted to do the same. A quick hit, the body left as an example, would usually handle that. Then there were the other organized local gangs, most of them Italian, always trying to knock him down and move into the primary seat of power. The Lusco gang was the most troublesome of these; it even had allied itself with a small faction of the local Democratic Party.

But Lazia's big threat was always from outsiders who saw the sweet deal home rule and bossism had brought to Kansas City and wanted to muscle in. Gangster elements from the Chicago, St.

Louis, and New York mobs, among others, periodically showed up to look around and make everybody nervous. But by gentle persuasion and ruthless action, Lazia kept them all out.

In fact, by 1933 it was a well-established rule that all underworld visitors checked in with Johnny Lazia when they came to town. It was just a courtesy, but the implications were clear. Nothing criminal of any consequence happened in Kansas City without the knowledge and consent of Johnny Lazia. If you wanted to relax out of the law's reach, you didn't plan to do any night work on the side. If there were conflicts among crooks, Lazia would sit in judgment. If operations were to reach outside criminal circles, he would say yes or no. It was just another clause in the gentlemen's agreement.

Upstart outsiders began to threaten that criminal balance in the early 1930s. Encouraged by quick and easy profits, a rash of sloppy and sometimes deadly kidnappings tormented the heartland. Worse, they often were pulled off by amateurs who didn't know or care about the rules. One kidnapping took place on Ward Parkway, not more than a block from Boss Tom's home. That's when Boss Tom is rumored to have taken a poke at the knife-wielding Lazia because, for a few minutes, it was thought the Boss's son was the victim. But the victim turned out to be Michael Katz, owner of a large drugstore chain in town, who was later released unharmed.

Then, just a month before the Union Station Massacre in 1933, it all hit entirely too close to home. Mary McElroy, the spirited and some would say slightly nutty daughter of City Manager Judge McElroy, was whisked out of her bubble bath by a quartet of nobodies. Later she would proclaim undying love, kindled in captivity, for one of the kidnappers and beg for his life, writing in her suicide note, "My four kidnappers are probably the only people on earth who do not consider me an utter fool." But at the time her kidnapping was an affront to all that the machine and its various alliances stood for in Kansas City.

In short, this was exactly the sort of thing the machine-police-mobster arrangement was supposed to prevent.

So, only one month before the Union Station Massacre, Johnny Lazia's pride was hurt and his reputation sullied among the people he most wanted and needed to impress. After all, a large part of McElroy and Pendergast's sales job to the public was that police should ignore "minor infractions" such as gambling so they could concentrate on major crimes. And, unofficially, keeping both the reality and the public perception of major crime in check was Lazia's job.

The rash of kidnappings in and around Kansas City had been like small stones tossed into the citizenry's apparent sea of tranquillity. Then Mary McElroy's abduction from her own Ward Parkway bathroom hit with the splat of a big, flat rock.

But no one could guess that a virtual boulder was teetering in the parking lot at Union Station. And none could know that, when it finally fell, Kansas City's perception of itself would never be the same again.

CHAPTER SIX

THE MASSACRE

VOLUME ONE, page one, of the Bureau's massive Union Station Massacre file offers stark Western Union testimony to what happened the morning of June 17, 1933.

DIRECTOR, UNITED STATES BUREAU OF INVESTIGATION,
WASHDC= OTT REED CHIEF POLICE MCALESTER OKLAHOMA
SPECIAL AGENTS FRANK SMITH AND LACKEY WITH FRANK
NASH WERE MET UNION STATION THIS MORNING SEVEN
FIFTEEN AM BY AGENTS VETTERLI AND CAFFREY AND TWO
LOCAL DETECTIVES. NASH WAS TAKEN TO CAFFREYS AUTOMO-
BILE IN FRONT UNION STATION WHEN UNKNOWN PARTIES
BELIEVED FOUR ALTHO DEFINITE NUMBER UNKNOWN OPENED
UP WITH SUBMACHINE GUNS KILLING TWO LOCAL POLICE
OFFICERS CHIEF REED FRANK NASH AND SHOOTING AGENTS
CAFFREY IN HEAD FATALLY LACKEY SHOT RIGHT SIDE NOT
BELIEVED FATAL FRANK SMITH ESCAPED UNINJURED VETTERLI
NIPPED IN LEFT ARM LICENSE NUMBER OF SHOOTING CAR
OBTAINED DOING EVERYTHING POSSIBLE. VETTERLI.

But that telegram didn't even begin to tell the story. Those who rushed to the agents' car in the moments after the shooting found battlefield carnage of the worst kind. Police officers Bill Grooms and Frank Hermanson lay almost arm in arm beside the front fender, an angelic pose except for the thick rivers of blood still oozing from their heads and congealing in a small lake around their bodies. The curious repeatedly fell into the gore, losing their footing in the rich red slime. A young UPI reporter would retell for years how her new white shoes were stained a permanent red by the time she returned to the office.

Agent Ray Caffrey lay near the other front fender, trying to talk but managing nothing anyone understood. Within a few hours, he too would be dead. Inside the car, Frank Nash's head was mangled, a huge part of the rear skull missing. In the backseat, Chief Reed's lifeless head had flopped forward on his chest. When Agent Frank Smith recovered his wits enough to climb out of the rear seat, he found Kansas City police officer Mike Fanning's gun jammed into his chest.

"I'm a federal officer," the badly shaken Smith mumbled. "I'm a federal officer."

Fanning finally believed Smith, let him go, and turned to help Lackey out of the rear seat and onto the pavement. Lackey had three wounds in his back.

Within hours of the attack, John Edgar Hoover knew all this—knew his men had been butchered and his Bureau humiliated—and his furious response set the tone for the long months ahead.

> Confirming my several telephonic conversations with you today [he wrote Vetterli before day's end], it is my desire that every effort and resource of this Bureau be utilized to bring about the apprehension of the parties responsible for the killing of Special Agent R. J. Caffrey and the injuring of Special Agent Lackey and yourself, as well as the killing of the police officers who were assisting us in this assignment. I cannot too strongly emphasize the imperative necessity of concentrating upon this matter, without any let-up in the same until the parties are taken . . .

Most important of all were the final three words, clearly typed, then overstruck with x's. But even on a copy of a copy six decades later, the words are as clear as they would have been to Vetterli and the other supervising agents who got Hoover's message and their own marching orders: "dead or alive."

To lead the charge Hoover turned to Gus T. Jones, one of the old-style lawmen Hoover kept on hand in remote places despite the lawyers-and-accountants public image the Bureau already was cultivating. Jones was of the old school, a former Texas Ranger who believed wholeheartedly in the Rangers' frontier motto: One riot, one Ranger. He favored cowboy hats and long-barreled six-shooters. And he still played hunches in an age when scientific evidence was quickly coming into style. Officially, Jones came up from San Antonio to use his several contacts with Leavenworth prisoners, many of whom he had put away himself, and he was to assist Vetterli. Unofficially, he was to do what he did best.

The younger agents in Kansas City immediately threw themselves into the chaos at Union Station, extracting dozens of eyewitness accounts from the eager and fearful, from sincere citizens and publicity seekers. Samuel Link, who identified himself as a local manufacturer, provided a detailed account that looked like the first big break.

> I was driving my Hupmobile sedan . . . and by accident had gotten on the wrong side of the buttons [lane markers] at the east end of the Union Station Plaza Drive. I heard a voice say, "Duck, you blankety-blankety, duck!" I looked up and saw a man coming out of the left rear door of a Reo sedan. I recognized him as Harvey Bailey, the notorious criminal.

Bailey knocked his hat off as he got out of the car, Link said, revealing his distinctive curly hair. But even more distinctive was the machine gun he carried in his right hand. Link pulled his car to the curb, directly in front of Union Station, to see what was up.

A few seconds later he saw a formation of officers come out of the station with a prisoner, cross to the parking lot, and begin to climb into the car. That's when Bailey went into action. In coordination with another man who had arrived in a separate car from the other direction, Bailey approached the officers' car. The other man also had "a big gun" in his hands.

"I observed Bailey lift his gun to his shoulder" and fire into the officers, Link told the agents. He assumed the other man fired too, but by then he had ducked sensibly behind his Hupmobile.

And there was more. Link said he probably could identify, if he saw him again, a man who stood by the door and gave the signal when the agents emerged from the station. And Link positively identified the driver of Bailey's car as Wilbur Underhill, a killer who had escaped along with Bailey and others from the Kansas State Prison in Lansing just weeks before.

Finally, a major bonus. "I wish to advise," Link said in his official statement,

> that during 1926 and early part of '27, I was a deputy constable in Kansas City, at which time it was my duty to serve attachment papers on a woman, whose name I do not recall, living in the south part of Kansas City on Brooklyn Street, the exact address not recalled, in about the 4400 block. At the time of the attachment proceedings, I was confronted with Harvey Bailey, who was then using the name of "Morris." Bailey, alias Morris, and I had an encounter at this time by virtue of which fact I have a very vivid recollection of him.

There were other identifications too. Lottie West, the Travelers Aid attendant, told the agents she was sure Pretty Boy Floyd had been sitting at her desk when she arrived just before 7 A.M. When she asked if she could help him, he walked away. The picture they showed her was a dead ringer for the man she'd seen.

By then the agents knew Floyd had come into town the night before. Western Missouri was full of tales about the kidnapping of Sheriff Killingsworth. West's story could fit, but Jones doubted it. He knew of no prior connection between Floyd and Frank Nash. And Floyd wasn't the type to hire out, especially for danger.

All leads were checked, even the observations of a "colored" woman named Margaret Turner, though every agent knew Hoover's feelings about "colored" people, especially as witnesses. Yet Turner told a fascinating tale about sitting in a car in the parking lot throughout the night and watching several men and a woman in a white dress circle the lot and check out the doorway many times over several hours. She said she got a very good look at two of the men and identified them from photographs as Harvey Bailey and Wilbur Underhill. Bailey, she said, had walked in and out of the station at least twice during the night.

Bailey's name just kept coming up. J. D. "Red" Jameson, a porter at Union Station, told Agent J. R. Calhoun that Bailey, identified from a photograph, had asked him about the time of the Missouri Pacific's arrival because "he and some friends would like to go down to the platform to pick up an invalid who was arriving on the train." Jameson told them they would have to see the stationmaster.

Later, Jameson said, he watched from the sidewalk as that same man raised a machine gun and fired into the federal agents' car, "and he later ran around to the rear of the car and fired again." It would be noted later that Jameson said the man was walking with a cane during their brief verbal exchange.

Such vivid eyewitness accounts were crucial, especially since the agent's fellow officers, potentially the best eyewitnesses, were of virtually no help at all. Lackey, speaking from his hospital bed, and Smith, still badly rattled, could tell chapter and verse about bringing the prisoner to town, about arriving at the station, and about loading Nash and the officers into the car. But the attack, they said, was little more than a blur.

In fact, in reports filed to Hoover within hours of the incident, the agents were very clear about what they did *not* see that morning. Lackey's first hint of danger was when he saw two men about thirty-five feet away, behind the Plymouth parked to the right of Caffrey's car.

"Agent saw these men through the window glass on the windshield of the Plymouth, which was none too clean, and therefore a clear view could not be obtained by agent," Lackey wrote, or dictated for his boss. At another point he added,

> Agent did not at any time see but two of the attackers, but judged from the shooting, there were at least four and possibly more men shooting, as the shots were coming from nearly all directions. Agent got such a hurried glance at these two men and this glance was through a none too clean window and windshield of the Plymouth, that he is not sure that he could identify either of these men, nor is he positive that he could identify the voice of the man who commented that Nash was dead.

Smith was even more precise.

> At the first volley . . . the writer dropped his head down below the front end as if shot and remained in that position until the firing ceased. While the writer observed by a glance a man behind the machine gun pointed and shooting in his direction, he was unable to obtain any kind of a description of him and was unable to see anyone else who did the shooting.

Vetterli could help a little. "I saw but one man, who was operating the machine gun from my right," he reported. After looking through photographs, he was able to offer something, at least. "I am convinced that the man who first opened fire from our right, with a machine gun, is Bob Brady."

It fit. Robert Brady was another Kansas convict, killer, and member of Harvey Bailey's gang. And he had escaped from Lansing along with Bailey and Underhill.

Hoover and his men were angry, in large part because their fellow agents had been so badly outgunned. So the director turned that weakness into a weapon. He quickly played up the underdog role, accentuating to the Washington press corps that his agents could only carry pistols in extreme circumstances, certainly not machine guns. But when he admonished Gus Jones to pull all stops in going after the killers, Hoover got it back in his face.

"What with?" Jones asked the director, "these peashooters?"

Hoover knew Jones was right, but hearing it from the old Ranger could not have sat well with him. Hoover called Clyde Tolson into his office and told him to order two machine guns while Hoover stormed into the attorney general's office. Two days later, Tolson wired Jones that two machine guns were on their way, along with bulletproof vests.

Hoover's war on crime had begun. And so had the propaganda campaign. So successfully did the Bureau portray its men as under-armed that virtually nobody realized Lackey and Chief Reed had carried riot guns, shotguns with sawed-off barrels. In truth, Reed carried a sidearm and a shotgun, Lackey carried a sidearm and a shotgun, Smith carried two pistols, and Caffrey carried a pistol. Both Kansas City detectives carried sidearms. Vetterli was the only lawman unarmed that morning; the file shows that clearly and de-finitively.

Yet the myth dies hard. Fifty years after the massacre, former agent and massacre investigator Ray Suran still held to the Bureau line. "We only had one pistol in the office," he said. "They both couldn't have been carrying it. And I'm sure they weren't carrying shotguns."

Back in 1933, however, the agents were more incensed about what *wasn't* there that morning. Kansas City police officers Grooms and Hermanson, after all, should have arrived with a machine gun of their own. Their Hot Shot riot car was routinely outfitted with one. That morning, however, the machine gun had been mysteriously missing when they picked up the Hot Shot at police headquarters. An administrative mistake, police officials said later.

Fat chance, the agents muttered. Their guys had been set up by the corrupt Kansas City Police Department, and they knew it. The already strained relations with the KCPD completely unraveled in the hours after the massacre. First the department wouldn't share information—any leads or witness accounts. Then Eugene C. Rep-pert, director of the Kansas City police, told the world that, in effect, the massacre was the Bureau's problem. According to a later federal perjury indictment, Reppert privately told his officers, "This is not a police matter. Hands off. Have nothing to do with it."

In any event, the Kansas City Police Department backed out of the investigation completely. Officials would later claim this wasn't so, but nothing ever came of any KCPD efforts. Thomas Higgins, the chief of detectives, claimed from time to time that he had explosive evidence locked in his safe. If so, he never revealed it.

And that left Hoover and his Bureau in a nearly impossible situation. Undermanned, underequipped, overextended, ill-trained—and on America's center stage.

CHAPTER SEVEN

THE CONSPIRACY

WHILE THE AGENTS at Union Station tried to sort out who did the killing, others immediately tackled the question of how the massacre could have been pulled off at all. Frank Nash's would-be rescuers, after all, had little time, not more than nineteen hours from the time Nash was grabbed off the street over four hundred miles away in Arkansas. And the roads between Little Rock and Kansas City were some of the worst in the country, demanding at least twelve hours at the best of times.

Obviously, the killers had relied on more than fast cars and hot guns, and that's how Hoover's men would track them. The key came that first night when Agent Colvin called from Oklahoma City. His agents, checking records of all long-distance calls out of Hot Springs, had found a call from the residence of a Mrs. E. B. Conner to a Joplin, Missouri, telephone number: 1541-W-2. In fact, they'd found three calls, one made at 4:30 P.M, another at 10 P.M., and the third at 9:51 A.M. that Saturday, not long after the massacre.

Agents Hal Bray and W. F. Trainor were in Joplin by Sunday morning, tracking down Chief of Detectives Ed Portley to ask some pointed questions about the people at 1541-W-2. But Portley, acting on instinct, was way ahead of them. That number belonged to Herb Farmer, and Herb Farmer had been the first person Portley thought of that Saturday morning when he heard about the massacre in Kansas City. By noon Saturday, the chief had taken it on himself, with questionable legality, to raid Farmer's place seven miles southeast of Joplin. Unfortunately, he found nothing—no Herb Farmer, no evidence of any crime, just a caretaker who seemed to know nothing at all.

Herb "Deafy" Farmer was hardly a stranger to the Joplin police or to several other departments around the country. He'd been arrested several times for confidence games and more than once for beating someone up when things didn't go his way. At six feet and 210 pounds, he got his way a lot.

And he made some strange friends. Neighbors were quick to tell Bray and Trainor that the Farmers had quite a lot of sporadic company, and it seemed the visitors' cars always went into the sheds and barns, even though Farmer's Cadillac sat outside in the weather. One neighbor said he was convinced Farmer ran a sort of way station for outlaws on the run.

The neighbor was right. It later became clear that Herb and his wife, Esther, ran the best crook motel in the region. It was beautifully located in the southwest corner of Missouri, able to accommodate those going to or from the Oklahoma hill country or the deep ravines of the Ozarks. Little Rock, Kansas City, St. Louis, and Oklahoma City were all within a day's drive. And the farm itself was at once remote, accessible, on the way, and out of the way. It was perfect.

So Herb built a flourishing business in being accommodating. He hid cars and traded them, patched up wounds, ran an extensive mail system, and served as a communications service for friends and clients. And he wasn't above using muscle and mayhem to help out a friend in need. Buck and Clyde Barrow stopped by from time to time with their ladies, Blanche and Bonnie. The Barkers were regulars. Harvey Bailey and the Underhill brothers were old friends of Deafy's. Frank Nash had passed through several times. But the agents didn't know all that yet.

They did know the calls from Hot Springs to the Farmers just hours before the massacre were very suspicious. And they wanted to know who the Farmers might have called in response. But the tickets for calls going out of Joplin on Friday the sixteenth already had been sent to the phone company's St. Louis headquarters. Only the more recent weekend call records were still available in the Joplin office, and they showed nothing of interest.

That's when Agent Reed Vetterli made a mistake that prolonged the case by months, if not years, and gave the fog time to settle in. When Agent Bray reported by phone from Joplin on Sunday that he couldn't get those outgoing call records but wanted them badly, Vetterli waited until Monday before sitting down at his Kansas City desk and writing a letter to the Bureau's St. Louis office. The letter hardly had an urgent tone:

> In connection with the recent shooting at Kansas City, will you please check the records of the St. Louis Accounting Division of the telephone company for Friday, June 16th, and Saturday, June 17th, for all long-distance calls placed from Joplin 4271 and 1541-W-2 to any long-distance point. I understand all the records are at St. Louis.

The phone company's response would be days in coming.

"He should have called and gotten the information within minutes," Bray said of Vetterli in 1983, the anger still evident after all those years. "I'll never forget that. It made all the difference in the world. It gave [the killers] the chance to get away."

If Vetterli had acted decisively, agents could have tracked an amazing series of events, a web of phone calls between Hot Springs, Joplin, Chicago, and Kansas City that led to the massacre at Union Station.

It all began with pride, friendship, and a woman's love.

■   ■   ■

Dick Galatas was furious that anyone would take a protected guest from his town. Even before the agents' car pulled away from the White Front—his own establishment, by the way—Galatas was on the phone to Dutch Akers at Hot Springs police headquarters.

"Stop them! Now!" Galatas demanded.

Akers knew that his job—and his cut of future protection payments—was on the line. He grabbed the phone and frantically began calling police departments up the highway. When an incoming call interrupted (Officer Joe Scott trying to report the kidnapping), Akers roared into the receiver, "For Christ's sake get off this line and stay off!"

Galatas, meanwhile, worried about Frank Nash's wife, Frances. A frail thing, or so he thought, she would be frantic at the news. He rushed across town to the tourist camp where Nash had been staying and found Frances at home with her daughter. He told her Frank had been arrested but said he would use his considerable power and influence to get him back.

Galatas took Frances to the home of Mrs. E. B. Conner, Lou to her friends. Lou looked after Frances while Galatas worked the phones in the other room. Within two hours, Akers called to tell Galatas that Little Rock police, who briefly stopped the fleeing car, had confirmed the agents were on their way to Joplin, Missouri.

That's when Galatas placed a call, duly recorded by phone company operators, to Joplin, Missouri, number 1541-W-2. When he hung up, he told Frances there was no longer any reason to worry.

"This is all going to be taken care of," he said. "You can meet Frank at Joplin."

Galatas arranged for a Ryan monoplane owned by one John Stover to pick up Frances and her daughter, Danella, at the small Hot Springs airport and take them to Joplin. But Frances hated to fly—in fact was terrified by the thought—and Galatas could not get her on board. Finally, in exasperation, he climbed aboard with them.

Frances Nash, however, was never entirely the cream puff she seemed. Back in Hot Springs, she had set in motion her own chain of phone calls, trying to locate an old friend of Frank's who she was sure would help. She knew he was in Kansas City, but only Frank knew the telephone number and the phony name he was using. She never knew stuff like that. She later would claim to agents that she didn't even know Frank's real name was Nash until after he was dead.

So she had turned to Louis "Doc" Stacci, who owned the O.P. Inn in Melrose Park, just outside Chicago, placing the call in midafternoon. Stacci was an old friend, her former boss and, though she kept it to herself, the guy she had talked into shooting her first husband. Maybe he would help again.

A confirmed crook, a fixer in the world of thieves and killers, Stacci made his O.P. Inn a center for all sorts of activity, almost all of it illegal. Want a gun? Go to the O.P. Inn. Want to put out a contract? See Stacci. Want a place to hide out? Stacci could arrange it. Want a woman? Well, Frances probably could have shed a little light on that aspect.

Stacci knew the guy Frances wanted to find, but he only had a contact number in Kansas City, a go-between named Frank "Fritz" Mulloy, friend of bank robbers, killers, and politicians, who hung out and took calls at the Horseshoe Tavern. Stacci made the call. Mulloy then made more calls.

Meanwhile, Herb Farmer was a busy man. Neighbors later would report seeing several cars racing up and down the long lane and along the road toward Joplin. Those neighbors said the party-line telephone was busy too, ringing often for the Farmers. There was activity enough that no one noticed when one neighbor cautiously picked up the receiver and listened in on an early evening phone call. Though he didn't understand what he heard, the federal agents would later have little trouble making sense of it.

"We watched from three different angles, but they got through with the papers," a man's voice told someone in the Farmer household.

Deafy was supposed to meet Galatas and Frances at the airport, but through some confusion they all ended up at the Midway Drug Store at 1512 Main Street, a notorious gangland hangout and a popular speakeasy. He took them home, where Esther was waiting with warm food, cold drink, and little cordiality.

Esther wasn't thrilled with all this in the first place. Now she had to deal with this frantic woman, moaning about her Jelly being lost. Frances, who had expected to meet Frank when she arrived in Joplin, appeared to be rapidly coming unglued.

It was worse at 10:09 P.M., when Galatas got a phone call from Lou Conner in Hot Springs. When Galatas hung up, he announced that things had changed, and not for the better.

"They're taking Frank by train to Kansas City," he said. "They left Fort Smith an hour ago."

Eight minutes later, at 10:17 P.M., a pivotal phone call was made from the Farmer house. Frances always swore it was made by Esther Farmer from a little book she consulted. Esther always swore it was placed by Frances. In either case, the caller reached a house at 6612 Edgevale Road in Kansas City, phone number Jackson 7073. It was listed to Vincent C. Moore, but the man who answered was Vernon C. Miller. He was the man Frances had been trying to reach through Doc Stacci, and he was an old friend, running mate, and frequent client of Deafy and Esther Farmer. He was about to become the most hunted man in America.

Verne Miller was a lawman gone bad, a former sheriff from South Dakota who got elected on his puffed-up war record and then got caught with his hand in the county treasury. He claimed he got his demonstrated skill with a machine gun from military experience. But then he also claimed heroism, though the army recorded nothing at all outstanding about his service. He was never decorated for bravery, or wounded, or gassed, nor did he participate in any battles.

Out of prison, he quickly turned to robbery and murder, operating from time to time with several gangs, most closely with the

Barkers—and Frank Nash. But he also took time to hire out as a gunman for eastern outfits. All told, Verne Miller, thirty-seven years old, was a very bad man.

He did, however, have a soft spot for the ladies. Some would later say he was deferential to them; others even called him a bit effeminate because of his charm and good manners. Miller didn't seem to care. His demeanor made him much in demand by women. His current girlfriend, Vi Mathias, was a knockout.

Miller was a loyal friend, too. He willingly shared money with other crooks, often including Frank Nash. When he had fresh money, everybody had a good time. He didn't waver that evening when the gang in Joplin told him Frank Nash was being brought to Kansas City. In fact, he had already received the message through Stacci in Chicago. He told Frances not to worry, he would take care of Frank, but Frances was not sure.

"What shall I do? What shall I do?" she moaned. Abruptly, she held out the receiver to Galatas. "He wants to speak to you."

Galatas listened and then asked one question: "Could I be of any help to you in any way?" After a pause, he said, "If that's the case, I'll be going back to Hot Springs right away by airplane."

He hung up the phone.

They talked for a while, all of them too excited to sleep, and before long Esther was telling Frances about the Farmers' long friendship with Frank Nash. She even brought out a present Nash had given them. It was a one-volume collection of the complete works of Shakespeare, with a marred spot on the spine where a number had been. The number, Esther proudly explained, was the one assigned to Frank Nash when he was in Leavenworth Federal Penitentiary. She did not say and probably did not know that the "gift" was, in fact, the same thick volume Nash had stolen from the prison library when he escaped—and the marred spot was where the book's library call number once had been.

They finally went to bed, Danella and Frances in the main bedroom, Esther in the living room, and Galatas and Herb Farmer in the second bedroom. Two hours later, just a few minutes into June 17, the phone rang.

"Let me answer it," Esther later quoted Frances as saying. "I know it must be for me."

"This is Verne," the caller said. "I'm down at the [Union] station."

Miller assured Frances everything would be all right. But he was worried about where she was going to go when she left Joplin, and he made several suggestions: friends in Oak Park, Illinois; her relatives. Frances said she'd had enough of friends and saloons. And she didn't really want to see her family. Nothing suited her.

"What shall I do? Where can I get in touch with you? I can't go home. I have no place to go," she sobbed into the phone.

Miller tried to console her—again.

"Don't take it so hard," he said at one point. "You'll see your Jelly again."

But Frances continued to sob, until she suddenly looked up wide-eyed at Esther. The line had gone dead. "I apparently must have made him mad," she said.

The household was up by six o'clock in the morning, and Galatas was on his way back to Hot Springs in Stover's airplane by eight. By ten-thirty the Farmers, Frances, and Danella were sitting in the Joplin home of Frank Vaughn, an outlaw friend and until recently the owner of the Midway Drug Store, listening to his radio for news out of Kansas City. They'd heard flashes about trouble, about people being killed, but the news wasn't clear. They could only drink beer, listen, and wait. At about 1 P.M. the word came: Frank Nash and several law officers had been murdered outside Union Station.

Frances was shocked.

"I didn't think they would do that to him. I can't believe it's true. I can't believe it's true," she repeated.

She stayed at the Vaughns' house for a while, but Joplin was getting hot fast. Already, the Farmers' place had been raided by Joplin's chief of detectives, Ed Portley. Harvey Bean, Esther's grandfather, who had been mistaken for a caretaker, said everybody should stay away. Somehow, Verne Miller got a message to Frances: "Get out of there."

About the time agents Trainer and Bray were meeting Chief Portley in his office Sunday morning, Frances Nash and Danella were a few short blocks away catching a bus for Chicago. Once again, she would turn to Doc Stacci.

.　.　.

Thanks to Reed Vetterli's bad judgment and the chaos of the moment, it would take days for agents to unravel the conspiracy. Agent Bray already was convinced the Farmer household was somehow tied to the massacre. But, not yet in possession of records of the crucial outgoing Friday-night phone calls, he could only follow up suspicions based on the three known incoming calls from Hot Springs.

That meant listening and waiting. A small cabin in a nearby resort called Sloan's Park offered a good view, though from a half mile away, of the Farmer place. And the phone line ran close by. To add to his cover, Bray moved in with his wife, Margaret, and their children, and tapped the Farmer's party line.

"We sat there for two weeks and we didn't hear a thing," Bray recalled half a century later. "I know it was so hot we stripped to our underwear and sat in lawn chairs with all the windows open. But we got nothing."

Herb and Esther Farmer were on an extended trip. When they finally turned up on July 7, almost three weeks after the massacre, Portley promptly arrested them. Vetterli wanted to borrow an armored car to bring Farmer to Kansas City, but Washington vetoed that idea.

Vetterli was further embarrassed when Hoover finally realized on July 11 that agents never had searched the Farmer house. "It should have been done Saturday [the day of the massacre]," Hoover scrawled across a memo in his bold hand. "Find out why it was overlooked."

The next day Harold "Pop" Nathan, the Bureau's number-two man, who was by then in Kansas City, gently explained that "it was thought [by Vetterli in Kansas City] that Farmer and his wife being in custody there would be ample time for the search of their home during the period of their custody and that therefore every possible attention should be given to the prisoners rather than to the searching of their residence."

Hoover didn't buy it.

"This is absurd," he wrote back. "Other agents could have made the search. During the interim persons friendly to Farmer could have entered and done away with evidence."

The Farmer place was searched that very day. They found nothing, but, to Hoover, that wasn't the point.

By mid-July the agents had just about unraveled the conspiracy. The Farmers were in custody. Frances Nash was with her family in Wenona, Illinois, being interviewed by agents. Doc Stacci was being grilled by the Chicago office, and Fritz Mulloy was on the hot seat in Kansas City. Galatas and Lou Conner had disappeared, and no one seemed to know where they might be.

The Union Station Massacre case was quickly breaking into two parts: the conspiracy, and the search for the shooters. The first would provide an early triumph for the federal agents and their ambitious leader. The second would lead them into frustration and much, much worse.

CHAPTER EIGHT

THE MANHUNT

R<small>EED</small> V<small>ETTERLI</small>'s cavalier treatment of Agent Bray's tip about the telephone calls was disastrous. Though the conspiracy link from Hot Springs to Joplin was established within hours of the massacre and exploited immediately, the further link from Joplin to a bungalow on Kansas City's South Side was not solidified for five long days. That left the residents of 6612 Edgevale Road time to clear out and cover their tracks.

In fact, they didn't even move all that quickly. Verne Miller, after all, was rather fond of Vincent C. Moore, the man he had become in the quiet middle-class neighborhood, and he really didn't want to give it all up. He had joined a couple of golf clubs, his favorite being the Milburne, made some new friends, and let his old friends know they could stop by any time. He felt safe and at home with his "wife" Vi and her eleven-year-old daughter, Betty, something he had not felt often over the last few years.

Vi was much of the reason. The man who had known a lot of ladies was nonetheless head over heels in love with this twenty-seven-year-old farm girl from Brainerd, Minnesota. Of course, Vi Gibson, as she was born to John and Bertha Gibson, hadn't been a farm girl for a long time, but she still looked the part. Soft and sexy, sometimes confused and helpless, she had a way of making men want to take care of her.

In fact, she was a survivor. She had to be. A necessary marriage at sixteen, where she picked up the name Mathias and her precocious daughter, had ended quickly. She lived with Mathias only a couple of months before he was sent to prison for the murder of a South Dakota policeman. When, from behind bars, he tried to get her to get rid of their unborn child, she walked away and never went back. A year later she picked up her only jail time, ninety days for aborting a second pregnancy.

To support herself and her baby, she worked in a laundry, as a waitress, as a department store clerk in St. Louis: whatever it took. At nineteen, back in Huron, South Dakota, she met suave, softspoken, good-looking Verne Miller, fresh out of prison and headed for trouble. And she went along for the ride.

That had been almost seven years earlier, and it hadn't all been fun. After dozens of boardinghouses and apartments, saloons and tourist courts, the house on Edgevale had finally offered a chance to put down some semblance of roots. They'd even retrieved Betty from Vi's parents' farm, at least for the summer. For a while they were a family.

So even the horror and heat of the massacre at Union Station wasn't enough to make Verne Miller bolt. Unwisely, the little family stayed right there in the house on Saturday night after the massacre, even lingering until late afternoon Sunday. Finally, when Verne said it was time, they walked away.

Hoover's agents didn't arrive in the neighborhood until four days later, five days after the massacre, when Vetterli's letter to St. Louis finally got an answer, naming the bungalow at 6612 Edgevale Road as the next link in the telephone conspiracy. Seeing no activity inside, Agent George Harvey, along with one of the few city detectives that the agents trusted, nosed quietly around the neighborhood. Across the street, at 6623 Edgevale, they struck pay dirt.

Earl Smith and his wife were not only curious, they were thorough. And suspicious. Almost from the time this Vincent Moore person moved into the neighborhood six weeks earlier, they had thought something was amiss. A lot of cars with out-of-state license plates came and went, and the passengers were curious-looking characters, carrying things in and out of the house and leaving at odd times. And cabs arrived at all hours. And then there was the little girl who wouldn't talk.

Agent Harvey was interested, but he was more than a little scared. If Smith was right, it made the phone call from Joplin fit perfectly with the massacre. And it meant the people across the street would be a nervous lot, especially if two strange men lingered in the neighborhood too long. He arranged for Smith to come to the Bureau's office the next day and left Edgevale Road.

The next day, with four agents lined up to listen, Smith recited an amazing knowledge of his "withdrawn and unfriendly" new neighbors. He gave detailed descriptions of Moore, his wife, and the little girl, and he said the child lived most of the time in Brainerd, Minnesota, with her mother's parents. He knew where the Moores shopped, who delivered their groceries, and who the little girl's friends were. He knew where Moore played golf and what state license plates had been represented on the various cars. And he knew the Moores' habits: no sitting on the porch, no uncovered windows in the summer heat. He even knew where they took their film for developing.

The agents were so taken with Smith's thoroughness that they all but deputized him on the spot. Though the phone number, Jackson 7073, was tapped by agents, the assignment of watching the Edgevale bungalow fell to Smith and his wife. Incredibly, after telling Smith to give them a call if anything happened, the agents turned their attention to other things.

Four days later, on June 26, Smith's wife frantically called the Bureau office in the Kansas City Federal Reserve Bank. A moving van was hauling everything away, she said. Still, the agents waited.

Finally, on June 28, eleven days after the massacre, with the house on Edgevale emptied of the former tenants' possessions, they asked the landlord to let them inside. Suspicions were heightened immediately. In the cellar they found a two-gallon milk can half full of roofing nails with flat heads, about one inch long. These were the type, agents knew, that were often carried by bank robbers and dumped in the path of pursuing police vehicles.

It got better. In the attic they found a bedpan and a syringe. On the floor were marks indicating beds had been rolled about. There was an electric heater that the landlord said did not belong to the furnished house. And there were bloody rags. A wounded person, the agents quickly concluded, had been harbored in this attic.

Still the agents took it excruciatingly slow. The following day, the twenty-ninth of June, twelve days after the massacre, they sent a fingerprint man inside. Luckily, they had a full-fledged expert of their own available, temporarily on loan from the St. Louis office. John E. Brennan, at thirty-three, had been an agent fourteen years, but he'd been studying fingerprints for almost twenty. After all, his father was a true fingerprint pioneer, establishing the print classification system for the St. Louis Police Department back in 1904. For the younger Brennan, therefore, fingerprint analysis was more than a lifelong hobby and now a career; it was a family legacy.

Brennan went after the house on Edgevale with his father's zeal. He found prints on all sorts of common objects but also on the uncommon, such as the bucket of nails. And in the cellar Brennan found prints on dusty beer bottles piled in a corner. In all, he found at least forty full or partial prints.

Assistant Director Pop Nathan, by now heading up the massacre investigation with Vetterli as second in command, was on the phone to Washington that very evening, asking Bureau headquarters for photographic copies of the file prints of sixteen men and women on a growing suspect list. Though the Bureau photographer had gone home, headquarters didn't wait.

FORWARDING TONIGHT VIA AIRMAIL PHOTOSTATIC COPIES OF PRINTS REQUESTED AND AVAILABLE PHOTOGRAPHS ADVISE IN MORNING IF PHOTOGRAPHIC COPIES NECESSARY. HOOVER.

Soon after the file prints arrived, Brennan made the match. Vincent C. Moore was, or had been, Vernon C. Miller, killer, bank robber, and now the most wanted man in America.

Too late, the agents began to piece together what had happened on Edgevale Road in the hours before and after the massacre. With Miller, Vi, and young Betty on the lam, they had just one lead left—Fritz Mulloy.

Mulloy was the Kansas City connection, first because he had taken calls from Doc Stacci in Chicago in the hours before the massacre, then because he admitted seeing "Vincent Moore" and babysitting Betty off and on over the crucial weekend, and finally because he took delivery of "Moore's" personal effects when the moving van pulled away from Edgevale Road. When proof turned up that Mulloy had sent a money order to Frank and Frances Nash in Hot Springs in early May, the circle was complete. Mulloy was in it up to his neck.

But Fritz Mulloy was a professional friend, the confidant of crooks and pols and cops and hookers. You didn't get that way in Kansas City by being mouthy or stupid. And he was neither. When agents asked about Verne Miller, he said as little as he had to. When they asked about Vi, he described her as an old friend and occasional dinner companion. He played dumb. Maybe that wouldn't keep him out of jail, but it might keep him alive.

It would be months before agents would figure out that Mulloy, in fact, had tracked Miller down at a golf course that Friday afternoon, dutifully passing along Stacci's urgent message about Nash's arrest in Hot Springs. And neither they nor anyone else would ever know the true role Mulloy played in Miller's dealings with Johnny Lazia's Kansas City underworld and the corrupt KCPD.

Until Mulloy cracked or they found Miller, it seemed, the Edgevale trail led nowhere.

■　■　■

But there were other questions—and leads aplenty to go with them. Who, for instance, were the other shooters that morning at

Union Station? Witnesses reported as many as seven or as few as two, though the number soon settled around four or five. Assuming Verne Miller was at the center, the organizer, that still left at least three or four killers hiding out somewhere.

The agents looked first to Nash's links, then to Miller's, and finally to the common ground. Harvey Bailey's name came up again and again. From the first days of the investigation, Gus Jones, who had chased Bailey for years, was convinced Bailey and his gang were responsible, and he would take that conviction to his grave many years later.

It made sense. All three men—Nash, Miller, and Bailey—were alumni of the old Keating-Holden Gang out of St. Paul, and the attack in Union Station bore more than a hint of that gang's trademark, brazen and a little bit daffy.

And brutal. Francis Keating and Tommy Holden never wanted any softies around. They specialized in kidnapping and bank robbery, neither of which would allow for indecision. They wanted their victims to be afraid, so they cultivated the worst in their gang members. When Verne Miller, the former sheriff, sought membership, for instance, Keating and Holden sent him out to prove his mettle by intimidating a fellow gangster they didn't much like. Miller found the guy, took him to a dark and lonely place—and broke all his fingers.

Keating and Holden were sent to Leavenworth's federal prison in the late twenties after conviction for a mail robbery, but they didn't stay long. On the last day of February in 1930, they walked out with two trusty passes supplied by a young up-and-comer named George Kelly, who would later substitute "Machine Gun" for his first name.

By mid-1932, Keating and Holden had discovered the joys of relaxation in Kansas City between jobs around the region. They and their wives, like Miller and Vi to follow, discovered a comfortable social environment where recreation and good food were always available. Then, on July 7, 1932, while playing golf on the famous

Old Mission course, Keating and Holden were nabbed by federal agents. Harvey Bailey was arrested with them. Agents learned later that Frank Nash, playing well behind the rest of the foursome, slipped off into the bushes and got away.

By 1933, Holden and Keating were tucked into Leavenworth, but former members of their gang were terrorizing the nation's heartland. Forming and re-forming into new gangs or floating from one gang to another for a particular job, they comprised the nucleus of the reign of terror J. Edgar Hoover would decry. Among these alumni were Fred Barker, Alvin "Creepy" Karpis, Nash, Miller, Bailey, Shotgun Ziegler, Machine Gun Kelly, and Wilbur Underhill.

Harvey Bailey was never quite like the rest. Smart and a meticulous planner, he often drove the back roads around a town for days to be sure he knew all the escape routes that could be used after a bank robbery. And he'd call off a job if it didn't smell right. He was a businessman, and this was his chosen business. He liked success.

He had not started out with any. Born on the West Fork of the Monongahela River near Weston, West Virginia, one of seven children, he was fourteen when the family moved to a farm near Green City, Missouri, in 1902. Soon his father was a deacon in the New Zion Baptist Church and Harvey was a student in the Dudley Rural School, another poor kid in a poor county in a poor state.

At age nineteen he followed two brothers to Omaha, and a few years later Harvey began to run beer and liquor to German farmers in the vicinity of Council Bluffs, Iowa. He liked the easy money, so he never looked back, moving into train and bank robbery as his skill and appetites increased. Through it all, he provided well for his family, buying at least two farms in Wisconsin for his wife and children.

Bailey's criminal activities ranged over the heartland. He knew most of the major players, and they knew he was an old hand at evading the law. He had a string of hideouts, including his mother's farm in Sullivan County, Missouri, south of the Iowa line, and he didn't mind sharing with a friend. So when Fred "Killer" Burke needed someplace to go after his role as a shooter in Chicago's St. Valentine's Day Massacre in 1929, Bailey sent him to his mom's place. That's where police caught Burke after a nearby filling station attendant recognized his picture and raised the alarm.

By the 1930s Bailey was the old man, well over forty and well respected. But something went wrong with the Citizens National Bank job in Fort Scott, Kansas, in June of 1932, and witnesses were able to identify him after he was caught on that Kansas City golf course with Keating and Holden. The courts sent him to the Kansas State Penitentiary in Lansing to serve ten to fifty years.

Bailey didn't like that very much, so he vowed not to stay long. On Memorial Day of 1933, less than three weeks before the massacre at Union Station, Bailey was ready to take his leave.

The escape had all the earmarks of a Bailey bank job, including planning down to the last detail. Clearly the hard part was already done when Bailey gathered his boys under the bleachers during the annual Memorial Day baseball game. Bob Brady, a trusted friend, passed out the guns, six Navy Colt automatics: one each for Bailey, Brady, Jim Clark, Ed Davis, Wilbur Underhill, and Frank Sawyer, a genuine rogues' gallery of killers. Underhill, especially, was little more than a vicious animal.

Their timing was a bit off. Warden Kirk Prather, who always showed up for the game, was late, and he was an integral part of Bailey's escape plan. Prather was to be their shield out of prison and their hostage during the race to the Oklahoma hills. Finally, just before 11 A.M., Prather walked out of the administration building and around the backstop. Brady and his men moved out from under the bleachers to meet him.

Jim Clark quickly threw a short wire around Prather's neck and pulled it tight, threatening without words to slice the warden's throat if he did not cooperate. At the same time, Bailey and the others shoved guns into the backs of two guards walking with the warden. Hardly inconspicuous, the little gaggle began the long walk down the first base line toward the yard's corner watchtower.

Their plan to use a wagon and a ladder to get over the wall quickly fell apart; the wagon was chained and the ladder was missing. So they shuffled on toward the watchtower, a little knot of men where none should be. Within minutes everybody in the stands knew what was happening. A cheer went up from their fellow convicts in the third-base bleachers.

"Can we come along?" one of the prisoners yelled. Underhill, nearly frantic with excitement, waved them on. Only five made the run.

The tower guards threw down their weapons as the warden demanded, but that didn't get anyone through the gate. Instead, with the whole prison watching, they climbed the tower, threw down a rope, and lowered themselves, one by one, down the outside of the prison wall, even the grossly overweight Prather. The weird psychological paralysis suddenly ended when Bailey was halfway down the rope. A single shot rang out, the bullet hitting Bailey in his right leg just above the knee. Blood spurted from the wound.

Once outside, Bailey took full charge despite his obvious pain. He told the five hangers-on—Sonny Payton, Billie Woods, Kenneth Conn, Lew Bechtel, and Cliff Dopson—to get lost, waving his gun at them for emphasis. More shots were fired, but the unlikely group of six prisoners, their hostage warden, and two terrified guards made their way to a big Dodge touring car parked nearby. Bailey, now all but carried by Brady, ordered everybody inside, and they were away. They hijacked a fresh car, a Chevrolet coach, a few miles south of Lansing and headed for Oklahoma.

"We'll let you go later," Bailey promised his hostages several times during the long, fast drive. "You won't be hurt."

Once inside Oklahoma, the guards., L. A. Laws and J. H. Sherman, suggested it was about time they be turned loose, maybe at that filling station up ahead. Bailey responded with a short laugh and a sincere word of caution. He knew the people at that station.

"Then you better take off that cap," he told the uniformed guard. "They'll kill you for sure if they see that."

But Bailey kept his word. He let the hostages out at the side of a secluded road, and he and his gang sped into the Cookson Hills. Sawyer was picked up a few days later in Siloam Springs, Arkansas. The others just disappeared.

.　.　.

Now Bailey was a prime target of the federal agents in Kansas City. Witnesses at Union Station had identified him, sometimes without even the suggestion of a name or a picture. All the connections were there: friendship with Nash and Miller, use in the past of the Farmers' hideout in Joplin, the Keating-Holden Gang membership.

Then Colvin in Oklahoma City, citing "an absolutely reliable source," told them it had been Frank Nash who engineered the Lansing escape, Frank Nash who smuggled the guns inside, Frank Nash to whom Bailey and the others owed their freedom.

Could Bailey have been trying to repay the favor at Union Station?

"Yes!" Gus Jones said, and he would not entertain any other theories. When Hoover wanted to add Pretty Boy Floyd, who clearly had been in town about that time, to the five still-at-large Lansing inmates in a new round of wanted posters, Jones bristled.

"I have no doubt that the shooting was done by the Lansing escapees," he told headquarters by phone even before the Miller connection was established, "and I don't believe that Pretty Boy Floyd had anything to do with it."

Nonetheless, when the new posters, called identification orders by the Bureau, were mailed out on June 26, Floyd's name was on the list. Miller's would soon follow.

The pieces kept fitting together. One more turned up when a little boy named Wallace Eugene Williams, who lived at 6643 Edgevale, not far from the Moore house, brought agents a slip of paper with a list of addresses. He said he found it on the sidewalk right after the Moore people moved away. It read:

Mrs. B's address, 422 North B. Street, Wellington, Kansas
Fred Martin, Route 1. Richmond, Illinois
Mrs. Brown, Twin Lakes, Wisconsin

Agents knew Bailey often used the name Brown and that his wife lived at Twin Lakes, Wisconsin. They knew Fred Martin was Bailey's brother-in-law and that Martin received his mail at Richmond, Illinois. So the Miller-Bailey link wasn't an old one. It was as current as that slip of paper.

Taken together, it built a case. Three weeks into the investigation, Hoover's men were sure they were on the right track. So was their boss in Washington. Sure enough to start making brags and promises. Sure enough to launch a war he knew he could win.

■　　■　　■

The guns had barely cooled before the political heat turned toward Washington. John Edgar Hoover felt it coming and welcomed it. When the powerful *Kansas City Star* sent its correspondent, Theodore C. Alford, that first Saturday morning to pound on the attorney general's desk and demand action, Hoover took the appointment. When Alford roared about rampaging criminals, Hoover talked pointedly about jurisdiction and power. He had not enough, he said, of either.

When calls from the media came in over the next week, he took them too. When politicians wrote the Bureau in praise or sorrow or encouragement, he answered every one. He never missed a chance. Even his condolence letter to the wife of slain KCPD detective Frank Hermanson held to the drumbeat.

"I trust that his death will not have been in vain," Clyde Tolson wrote over Hoover's signature, "and that it will result in the awakening of the public conscience to its responsibility to demand more effective laws and more effective enforcement of the laws in dealing with the criminal element in this country."

An outraged America was demanding action, and Hoover wanted to harness those demands. Already lawmakers were talking about major new legislation and important new powers for federal police. And already Hoover was finding receptive ears on Capitol Hill to his requests for more money, more resources, more, more, more. If his Bureau was to thrive, he had to seize the moment.

Hoover's relentless message to a fearful, worried citizenry was simple, clear, and reassuring: Give me the tools, and I'll do the job for you.

But it all hung on the Union Station Massacre case. Union Station was the symbol, the challenge, the mutual focal point of America's impotent fear and gangland's ruthless power, and Hoover knew it. A month into the investigation, he was ready to make his promise.

"Those who participated in this cold-blooded murder will be hunted down," Hoover swore to a convention of the International Association of Chiefs of Police. "Sooner or later, the penalty which is their due will be paid."

To his men, the order was crystal clear. His words to the wounded Joe Lackey were not long reaching every office and every agent in the Bureau network.

"[The Union Station Massacre killers] must be exterminated, and they must be exterminated by us," Hoover wrote, "and to this we are dedicating ourselves."

A theme was struck. A chord was touched. The War on Crime was under way.

The outlaws helped, keeping the public pot at a constant boil, especially in the heartland. Only a month after the massacre, Bonnie Parker and Clyde Barrow, backed up by Clyde's brother, Buck, and Buck's wife, Blanche, shot up several lawmen and embarrassed a lot more in a tourist court between Kansas City and Platte City, about where Kansas City International Airport is today.

Bureau files show the lawmen were tipped that Bonnie and Clyde were there, and the police had time to assemble officers from several law enforcement agencies, led by the sheriff from Kansas City.

However, the overwhelming numbers surrounding the cabin did not impress the Barrows.

"A gun battle ensued and the individuals . . . escaped," according to Vetterli's report. "Gus T. Jones and Special Agents Dwight Brantley and L. G. Turrou are now in the process of making a complete investigation."

Another bloody shootout so close to Kansas City only turned up the heat, both on the Bureau and on the men they sought. Harvey Bailey, as the leading suspect along with Miller, was on every agent's mind every day, as they sorted repeatedly through the possibilities.

Bailey had been wounded above the right knee in the escape from the Kansas prison. Did that fit with porter Red Jameson's observation that the machine gunner at Union Station walked with a cane?

How about the bloody rags in Miller's attic on Edgevale Road? Could Bailey have been nursed back to health there in the days before the massacre?

Then there was KCPD officer Mike Fanning, who said he had rushed out of the station to see a man running toward an automobile to the south of the agents' car. "I took a shot at him, and he stumbled or spun around or was hit," Fanning said.

That would fit with a report from an Edward Shoptaw, an attendant at a service station on State Avenue in Kansas City, Kansas. Shoptaw said three men roared in for gas at about ten-fifteen on the morning of the massacre, one of them not moving much in the rear seat. That man's left shoulder appeared to be injured. When Shoptaw looked closely, he saw a bandage and noticed that the man's left arm was out of the coat sleeve. They asked how far it was to Topeka.

From the moment those bloody rags were found in the attic on Edgevale, there was a lot of talk about wounds, and, oddly, it worked both for and against Harvey Bailey. Agent D. O. Smith of the Chicago office argued that Bailey could not have been involved in the massacre precisely because of the leg wound. "A confidential informant . . . has received information that Harvey Bailey . . . is now in Bartlesville, Oklahoma, where he is receiving medical aid for a broken leg," Smith wrote.

But Bailey's most dramatic—and most bizarre—defense came from Harvey J. Bailey himself. Feeling the heat of the massive manhunt, he tried to convince agents that he couldn't possibly have committed the massacre because he and his fellow escapees were busy at the time robbing a bank in Black Rock, Arkansas.

"This is to certify that we, the undersigned, of lawful age, make the following statements of facts of our own free will and accord, and submit fingerprints as a testimonial of the affiants' identity," the gang wrote on an aged typewriter that stopped spacing between words after the first few lines.

"It is apparent that the Oklahoma officers have been misled to believe that certain innocent parties (some of whom are now being detained in jail) are guilty of participating in the robbery of the Black Rock, Arkansas, Bank on June 16, 1933, at about 8:45 A.M. o'clock," they continued. "We the undersigned are the perpetrators of the robbery."

The letter was signed by Harvey Bailey, Wilbur Underhill, Bob Brady, Ed Davis, and Jim Clark. To prove their identities, each placed a clearly labeled fingerprint on the letter.

The escapees claimed they only wanted to be sure nobody else got blamed for their misdeeds, something none of them had ever worried much about in the past. And the letter never once mentioned the massacre in Kansas City. But it was sent to the Bureau's office in Oklahoma City. The import was obvious.

The letter offered intricate details of the stolen money, including a complaint that bank officials were overstating their loss. It listed the currency, money orders, and coins and described a botched getaway that forced the robbers to abandon in Black Rock the same car they'd stolen during the prison break at Lansing. That, they said, left them walking through the woods of northeast Arkansas all day long on the sixteenth. They didn't catch a ride until after dark, according to the letter, and then went to Batesville, Arkansas.

If true, that would have put them 350 very difficult miles away from Kansas City only seven or eight hours before the massacre, out of range and beyond suspicion by virtually any measure.

Though it was probable that at least one of the signatories either participated in the Black Rock robbery or had intimate knowledge of what happened there, the federal agents did not buy the letter or the robbery as an alibi for Bailey and all his friends. In fact, the letter immediately worked against Bailey when Charles Appel, the soon-to-become-legendary head of Hoover's new crime laboratory, identified the typewriter as the same type if not the same instrument used in the Urschel kidnapping case.

Charley Urschel, a millionaire oilman, had been playing cards with neighbors in Oklahoma City when two men armed with machine guns burst in, demanding to know which of the men was Urschel. When no one would tell them, the gunners checked wallet identifications until they found their man, even though one of the card players was an accomplice and had set Urschel up for the kidnapping. The two gunmen were Machine Gun Kelly and Albert Bates, and their destination that night was Kelly's in-laws' ranch in Texas. With Urschel blindfolded, bound, and frightened, they were convinced he could never find the place again.

Unfortunately, they were wrong. Urschel proved to have a fine memory and a great sense of direction. After his family paid the $200,000 ransom and he was released, Urschel was able to tell agents just enough to lead them back to the general area of the ranch. Using cars, horses, and airplanes, agents scoured the area, looking for some hint of where Urschel had been held. When they showed the oilman a likely place, he confirmed it: That was the hideout.

"In the early morning of August 12, Special Agents of the Division of Investigation of the United States Department of Justice closed in upon a house in a remote section of Texas, about seven miles south of the town of Paradise," Hoover reported to the attorney general, "coming upon the occupants before they had time to awaken."

Inside the shack, they got a major bonus. They caught Harvey Bailey sleeping, a machine gun and two automatic pistols lying on the floor beside his bed. He didn't even reach for them.

The agents fired questions at Bailey about the massacre, then about Urschel, and Bailey maintained from the beginning that he knew nothing at all about either case. He hadn't been close to Kansas City at the time of the massacre, he said, and he was just unlucky to be hiding out at the Shannon place when the agents stopped by.

However, his argument was hardly bolstered by the $700 in identifiable Urschel ransom money found in his pocket. That was just money paid by a friend to settle a debt, Bailey explained, though he didn't much want to name that friend.

Bailey's arrest triggered celebration in the Bureau's Kansas City office and the Washington headquarters. Agents saw it as a giant step toward solving the massacre case. They'd spent two intense months, after all, trying to put Harvey Bailey behind bars.

Yet a closer look wasn't so encouraging. Aside from some witness identifications, based on pictures, and a lot of circumstances surrounding the Miller-Bailey relationship, they didn't have much hard evidence. What they needed was a fingerprint or a ballistics match, something rock solid.

Merle A. Gill was working on that. In the days before police departments had crime laboratories, Merle Gill was another pioneer. He called himself a ballistician, and he had testified in hundreds of cases in and around Kansas City. The KCPD turned to him regularly. So did the sheriff of Jackson County. And so did the Kansas City office of the Bureau of Investigation.

It was a strange relationship, primed for trouble. After all, the federal agents didn't trust the KCPD at all. Sheriff Thomas Bash, by all accounts an honest man, tried to work with the federals but keep some links to the locals. And Merle Gill played all sides of the political street while claiming impartiality in what should have been the most purely scientific, unbiased aspect of the investigation.

But he also was the only game in town. Hoover's lab in Washington, established only the previous year, was nothing of what it would become. In 1933, Bureau offices still routinely farmed out analysis jobs locally that would never be allowed out of Bureau's own hands even five years later. So almost all scientific aspects of the Union Station Massacre case went to Merle Gill and his private laboratory operation in Kansas City.

During the summer of 1933, Merle Gill was a very busy man. Bullets, shell casings, and guns of all descriptions came through his door almost daily. When Harvey Bailey was arrested in Texas, specimens from Bailey's two automatic pistols and his machine gun were sent to Gill. He did what he'd been doing all summer: He tried to match them to the few similar specimens picked up at the massacre.

By modern standards, the Union Station Massacre scene had been a forensics nightmare. No one blocked off the area. No one protected the evidence. News photographers moved clothing and even bodies to arrange the shots they wanted. Of the hundreds of gunshots allegedly fired that morning, only a few slugs and shell casings ever found their way to Gill's laboratory, and those trickled in over several days as lawmen remembered they had them in their pockets. Most of what would be evidence today just spread out through Kansas City and the nation, picked up as souvenirs by travelers, gapers, reporters, and cops.

What Gill had, so far, amounted to nothing at all. Every time a gangster was captured, almost anywhere, Gill would try to make a match to the massacre, just as he tried with Bailey's guns. Nothing. He tried after the Bonnie and Clyde shootout at Platte City. Nothing. After every bank robbery. Nothing.

Nonetheless, Hoover pushed local prosecutors to bring an immediate murder indictment against Harvey Bailey, and he grew furious when they dragged their feet.

"I want Bailey tried for the massacre immediately," Hoover told Pop Nathan by phone nine days after Bailey's arrest. "I want a commitment from the local prosecutors now. If there's any doubt about it, tell Keenan to call me."

Keenan was, in fact, Joseph B. Keenan, special assistant to the attorney general and not, on paper, someone to whom Hoover could give orders. Besides, the decision to prosecute murder in the state courts would not be Keenan's or Hoover's to make. And the locals had real doubts about the case. When they voiced them, Hoover climbed all over his own agents.

"I have been somewhat disturbed since receiving telephonic advice from Mr. Keenan, at Kansas City, that while he felt the state would secure a conviction in the Bailey case, at the same time he thought that some further investigation should be conducted in so far as the identification is concerned," Hoover wrote the Kansas City office. "I wish that you would promptly advise me in what respect the investigation is lacking and as to what was overlooked by the agents."

On September 13, 1933, a federal grand jury returned a string of indictments against Harvey Bailey, Esther Farmer, Fritz Mulloy, Frances Nash, Wilbur Underhill, Robert Brady, Herbert Farmer, Richard Galatas, Vernon C. Miller, Lou Conner, and Doc Stacci. But all the indictments were for obstruction of justice. No one is executed for obstructing justice. Hoover knew that. The American citizenry knew that.

If John Edgar Hoover was going to keep his promise of bloody retribution, he had to do better.

CHAPTER NINE

VERNE MILLER

IF THERE WERE serious doubts about Harvey Bailey, there were none at all about Verne Miller. First, phone records put him in the conspiracy loop; then the Farmers and Frances Nash confirmed his call from a Union Station pay phone about midnight that Friday, placing Miller at the scene of the crime just hours before the massacre. Only one witness could identify Miller's picture, unfortunately the same man who named Bailey, but along with everything else that was enough.

Enough, at least, to launch the biggest, broadest, hottest search in Bureau history. From Chicago to Detroit to New York, Miller's known contacts were rousted, questioned, and not so gently warned that harboring their old friend would not be taken lightly by Mr. Hoover. Gangsters soon were whining to each other that Verne had put them all on the spot. George "Machine Gun" Kelly, never as tough as his name anyway, growled about it to his wife not long before she was arrested by agents in the Urschel kidnapping case.

"George came back from Chicago incensed over how this had brought the heat on everybody," Kathryn Kelly told the agents who arrested her. "George said Harvey Bailey was furious at Miller and didn't want Miller to contact him or know where he was. Bailey told George he had been robbing a bank in Arkansas when the massacre happened, but he was getting the blame anyway. Because of Miller."

As the days passed, it only got hotter. Friends in Chicago who had taken Miller in immediately after his flight from Kansas City weren't so glad to see him come around a second time. Without much ceremony, Verne had Vi dump Betty at Vi's parents' Minnesota farm. This was not going to be a fun romp, and it was no place for a kid.

Hoover's agents had tried to keep the discovery of the Edgevale house and the search for Miller to themselves. But the climate in Kansas City didn't allow for cooperation; if anything, the various law enforcement agencies were more into sabotage. Hoover's issuance of the identification orders on the Lansing escapees and Pretty Boy Floyd, for instance, was upstaged by the KCPD. Local police first announced that they had solved the case, and then they shouted from coast to coast that Miller was the killer.

Though the local police had had nothing to do with establishing the Edgevale connection, Director of Police Eugene C. Reppert told assembled reporters he and his department were positive the massacre had been perpetrated by Miller and William Weissman, a local gangster. Now the whole world, not just the underworld, knew about the heat that followed Vernon C. Miller.

Maybe distance would bring some cooling off. Miller had friends in New York, after all, and Vi was always popular on the party circuit. A guy like Miller could always find work.

But it wasn't that easy. Miller had done some favors for Louis "Lepke" Buchalter, already a power among New York mobsters and one day to be the leader of Murder, Incorporated. Specifically, Miller had murdered several members of rival Irving "Waxey" Gordon's gang, during a dispute over booze and territory earlier in 1933. So Buchalter owed Miller. But taking on the man who had pulled the Union Station Massacre wasn't Buchalter's idea of good business, any owed favors notwithstanding.

However, looking after Vi Mathias was another matter. Both Buchalter and his wife liked the vivacious, beautiful farm girl and welcomed her to stay with them as long as she liked. Vi, who had changed her hair color from blond to red for her New York visit, brightened every room, made every party livelier. Beneath the lovely open surface, the Buchalters knew, was a girl with powerful appetites and a real zest for life. A deal was struck. They would take care of Vi, but Verne had to stay away.

They all led Hoover's agents on a not-so-merry chase that summer and fall, the agents always a step or two behind: Vi and the Buchalters whooping it up in Montreal, Verne at the famous Greenbriar Hotel in West Virginia; Vi and Mrs. Buchalter shopping on Fifth Avenue and lunching at the Waldorf-Astoria, Verne at Miami's Hialeah Racetrack.

By fall, nerves inside the Bureau were wearing thin. Hoover was willing to play a few long shots.

"With reference to the above entitled subject [Verne Miller]," he wrote the New York office, "you are requested to advise police officials on duty at the Giant Stadium Baseball Park in New York City, during the coming World Series, to watch for this subject, who has always been interested in baseball and in frequent attendance at baseball games. It may be well to arrange for the distribution of a sufficient number of identification orders."

The *Kansas City Star*, spurred by police gossip about bloody rags at the Edgevale bungalow, reported that Miller had been wounded in the left arm during the massacre. Likewise, Hoover's agents themselves, obsessed by the idea of a telltale wound on one of the killers, thought Miller might be injured. In fact, he was physically fine, though increasingly weary of the endless moving and discouraged by the snubs he was getting from old friends in the East.

Things had been great back in Kansas City. The house on Edgevale had been a social way station for the slick and dangerous. The Barker boys used to stop by, sometimes with their ma, to enjoy the town and maybe stay overnight. And there were people to eat with every evening, the Mulloys or the Nashes or Alvin Karpis. Now

Miller did all that alone, usually in a different place every night, and he hated it.

He needed Vi. Even those who loathed Verne Miller later would remark on the deep and abiding love he felt for his lady. But the heat of the manhunt made any visit impossible. If he planned to see her at all, he couldn't be Verne Miller. He had to become somebody else.

For help Miller turned to Al Silvers, a sort of traveling representative of Abe "Longy" Zwillman. Zwillman ran most mob operations in New Jersey and would one day be one of the top mob bosses in the nation. Silvers, unlike Miller's other mob-connected friends, was willing to lend a hand, undoubtedly for a price.

Knowing how hot Miller was, Silvers did not turn to gangland contacts for help. Rather, he kept this job within his own family, taking Miller to the offices of Dr. Irwin R. Silvers, an optometrist at 237 Main Street, Orange, New Jersey. Irwin was Al's brother, primarily straight but not above making an extra buck from time to time. Irwin would tell investigators later that he never had an inkling anything was amiss with the man brother Al introduced to him as Stephen J. Gross Jr.

Mr. Gross, brother Al is said to have explained, was a businessman, business unspecified, who was going on the road and wanted a second business as a sideline. Al thought Mr. Gross might sell eyeglasses for the Mason Optical Service and asked Irwin's help in setting him up.

Though it was a Friday, well into the afternoon, and Mr. Gross wanted to hit the road that same night, Irwin said he saw no reason to suspect anything. However, he explained, he couldn't get the materials together until the next day.

By noon Saturday, Mr. Gross and brother Al were back in Irwin's office. The doctor turned over two sample cases of frames and mountings from the Bertram line, which he had picked up from the Mason Optical Service the afternoon before. Dr. Silvers also gave Mr. Gross a stack of business cards, fresh from the Eagle Printing Company, attesting to the fact that Stephen J. Gross Jr. was a full-fledged traveling representative of the Mason Optical Service. Finally, the doctor provided an assortment of letterhead, blank prescription forms, and envelopes and four more sample cases from his own stocks.

Verne Miller, sporting a full mustache for the first time in his life and wearing eyeglasses to mask his distinctive gray eyes, walked out of Dr. Irwin Silvers's office a new man. On the street he loaded his ample business materials into a beautiful new car, a Ford coupe purchased by Al Silvers and registered to Al Silvers.

It was October 24, 1933. Verne Miller was going to Chicago. Going to see Vi.

■   ■   ■

Vi was no happier than Verne. After frolicking over much of the Eastern Seaboard with the Buchalters, she was tired of restaurants and trains and hotels. Tired of being entertained and of being the entertainment.

She turned for help to her friend Bobbie Moore, a slightly plump live wire who worked as a nightclub hostess in Chicago. Bobbie's friendship went back a long way, actually further with Verne than Vi. If Vi ever realized just how far, she either ignored it or accepted it. When agents would one day crudely suggest that Bobbie's kids, ages fourteen and twelve, were also Verne's kids, both women would look them square in the eye and tell them to mind their own business.

In fact, Hoover's men got that wrong. Bobbie's children sprang from a bad first marriage, though Bobbie apparently contributed most of the bad. She eventually hooked up with a gangster named Jack Harris, and when the courts gave her first husband custody of little Phyllis and John in 1929, Bobbie and Harris simply kidnapped them.

Eventually, however, Bobbie got tired of Harris, so she took out a big insurance policy on him and had a chat with her new friend Verne. Harris's body was found in New York City in early 1932. Though agents could never prove it, the accepted version in files and correspondence was that Bobbie set him up and Verne pulled the trigger.

In any case, Bobbie's loyalty to both Verne and Vi was total. When Vi contacted her that fall in Chicago for help in finding a place to live, Bobbie didn't hesitate.

"There's a place coming available in my building," she told her friend. "I'll see if I can get it for you."

The two women became neighbors in the Sherone Apartments, upscale buildings near Lake Michigan, Vi in 211 and Bobbie in 101. Vi registered as Mrs. Clare T. Hays, telling the management that her husband would be joining her soon.

Vi lived quietly in Chicago, waiting for Verne to come to her. She had no doubt he could track her down when he was ready. Until then, she would relax and try to put New York and Kansas City behind her. With Bobbie's help she got to know some of the people in the building, and, perhaps missing her daughter, Betty, she put together a Halloween party in her apartment for some neighborhood children. They were barely finished with the refreshments when Bobbie showed up at the door, yelling excitedly.

"He's here, Vi, he's here!" she screamed.

"Where is he, Bobbie?" Vi asked, nearly breathless. "Tell me, where is he?"

"He's downstairs," Bobbie said, meaning her own apartment. "I told him you had a lot of children in your apartment and that you would be downstairs just as soon as you could get rid of the kids."

"How does he look, Bobbie?" Vi asked.

"He looks just grand," her friend assured her. "I told him you had been blue and crying all day."

"Tell him I'll be down in a few minutes," Vi said, closing the door and turning toward the children.

Bobbie hurried back up the hallway. Verne was walking toward her. She threw her arms around his neck, kissed him, and told him she was very glad to see him.

"Vi's been crying all day," she told him again. "She hasn't heard from you for a very long time."

They walked back toward Bobbie's apartment, her arms still around his neck. In a few minutes, they would all be together. It was perfect.

■   ■   ■

Not quite. The little scene outside Vi's door was watched closely, and not just by a nosy neighbor. One of J. Edgar Hoover's agents had scribbled down every word.

Unfortunately for the women and their visitor, a snitch had alerted the Bureau's Chicago office to Bobbie's association with the Miller gang within a few hours after the massacre at Union Station. Through sheer coincidence the agents had finally gotten around to following up the tip only three days before the scene in the hallway.

When the agents had talked at length with Mrs. Pollachek, manager of the Sherone Apartments, on October 28, she hadn't been at all surprised at what they told her about Bobbie Moore, but the agents had been startled when Mrs. Pollachek responded with a rundown on her new tenant, Mrs. Clare T. Hays. It took little imagination to recognize Vi Mathias.

However, the manager suggested that the agents keep a very low profile in and around her building. She explained that Mrs. James Bidderman, her assistant manager, had arranged the lease to Mrs. Hays with the help of Bobbie Moore. And not only was Bobbie quite friendly with most of the building's staff, she was sleeping from time to time with Mrs. Bidderman's son, Lawrence. The agents could look for no allies in the Sherone Apartments. No one could be trusted to work against Bobbie.

So the agents had brought in their own cover. That very evening Agent John Madala and his young wife moved into apartment 207,

just down the hall from Vi's place, and began the business of settling in. They registered as Mr. and Mrs. John L. Malleck of Buffalo, New York. One of their corner apartment's nicer features was
a small service door off the kitchen that opened to the hall—and
offered a straight shot fifty or sixty feet down the hallway to the
door of 211, three apartments away. If Verne Miller showed up,
they'd know it.

Washington was notified of the break immediately. A message
pounded out so quickly that it was never signed or initialed by the
supervisor who wrote it arrived on Hoover's desk before he left the
office that day. It outlined the Chicago situation and asked for help.

"All calls go through the switchboard, which would make it difficult to do any tapping," the memorandum said in part; ". . . in this
connection they may need the services of Agent Nichols."

"Watch this carefully," Hoover scrawled across the bottom.

The next day Agent Lou Nichols, a wiretapping expert (not the
same Lou Nichols who would later become famous as Hoover's
publicity and propaganda chief), arrived on the scene. Before dark
the phones in both women's apartments were tapped. Everything
was in place—just in time.

Agent Madala witnessed the excitement in the hallway in the late
afternoon on Halloween. He thought the man had to be Verne
Miller, but he couldn't be positive. This guy's hair was different,
longer. And he had a thick brown mustache and wore dark horn-
rimmed glasses. With his gaze lowered under a brown snap brim
hat, his features were obscured most of the time. But the build was
right. Madala only got a look through the ventilator of a door as
the man walked away; still, the agent sent out the alarm.

"I think we've got Miller," Madala told D. O. Smith, a senior agent
in the Chicago office.

Smith wasn't about to take any chances on letting Miller slip
away. Every available agent plus two squads of Chicago policemen
descended on the apartment complex. The entrances were covered,

and agents joined the Madalas in apartment 207 for a long night of watching and waiting. At least fifteen lawmen were in and around the building, several in parked cars on the streets outside.

However, some didn't exactly stay undercover. By the next day, Chicago police dispatchers were getting citizen complaints of suspicious characters loitering on the streets, some of them with big ugly machine guns on their laps. The agents' top secret operation was fast becoming the talk of the uptown neighborhood.

Reluctantly, Agent E. P. Guinane, who was directing the operation, ordered his men to back off, into vacant apartments and onto side streets. This less optimal positioning brought communications problems, so a system of signals was worked out, including the big one. If Miller was positively identified and on the move, a shirt would be waved from the Sheridan Road window of the tactical operations center in apartment 207. At that signal, everybody would descend on the Sherone Apartments, ready for anything. Guinane laid out what would today be called the rules of engagement: "Take Miller, and do not hesitate to shoot him if he makes the slightest move."

The long afternoon of November 1 wore at the agents' nerves, especially those of the men in apartment 207. Like runners at the starting block, several of them huddled for hours close to the apartment's door, heavily armed and waiting in line to rush out and pounce on the killer from Kansas City as soon as he showed his face. The slightest sound from the hallway set their adrenaline pumping.

The problem was identification, or rather the lack of it. No one was absolutely certain beyond any doubt that the man now in 211 was Vernon C. Miller. And Washington was insisting on a positive identification. That's why Doris Rogers, a stenographer in the Bureau's Chicago office, had been brought to 207, and why Agent E. N. Notesteen had flown in from the St. Paul office. Both had grown up in Huron, South Dakota. Both knew Verne Miller by sight.

There were plenty of indications they had the right man. For one thing, Bobbie had called her friend Vi, not using the alias on the apartment's registration forms. And Agent Nichols, the wiretap specialist, had overheard Vi passing along instructions by phone from one apartment to the other. "Verne wants you to put away the Auburn," she said, referring to his car but indiscreetly using his real name.

All day long Rogers and Notesteen hovered around the service door, opened just a crack to allow an uncomfortable but effective view of whoever came down the hallway from Vi's room. Their nerves were the most frayed of all.

It didn't help that, shortly after the man disappeared into the apartment, Bobbie Moore walked out to his car and returned with a very heavy valise. That, the agents guessed, was Miller's arsenal, including a machine gun. They had to assume that any confrontation would start a deadly gun battle.

All afternoon Guinane, backed by most of the other agents on the scene, pressed Washington to approve a raid on apartment 211. Agents could simply call Vi's apartment, announce their presence and intentions, and see what happened, he reasoned. If the man came out, okay. If not, tear gas would go through the window and bullets through the doors. Plans were made to go in at 5 P.M.

Guinane's negotiations with Washington were made all the more difficult because of Nichols's unorthodox wiretapping technique. He had diverted the lines in Bobbie's and Vi's apartments into the agents' command post in 207. But that somehow had left the tactical commanders unable to make outgoing calls or receive any incoming calls. And that meant Guinane, tied to the Hoover umbilical, had to traipse in and out of the apartment numerous times in order to update Washington and the director.

Then, only forty-five minutes before the pumped-up agents were to make their 5 P.M. raid, word came from Washington: Mr. Hoover does not want the apartment crashed until we can make a positive identification.

Now there was no choice. Agents would wait for the man they were increasingly sure was Verne Miller to leave the apartment at the end of the hall. If Agent Notesteen could positively identify him, arresting agents would rush into the hallway, confront the man, and open fire if he made any move for his gun.

The plan was simple enough. The way the apartment was configured, the door to their own apartment 207 was at the end of the long hall, opposite the point where the man would have to turn away toward the elevators. Notesteen's perch in the kitchenette looked straight down the hall. Actually, Notesteen and the assault squad were within a few feet of each other, yet three rooms apart.

Therefore, the signal would have to be passed. So Guinane stood in the doorway between the kitchenette and the dining room where he could see both Notesteen and Agent Earl Van Wagoner, who stood in the living room. Van Wagoner stood where he could see both Guinane and Madala at the head of the assault team. If or when Notesteen made the positive visual identification he would give a chop signal, Guinane would pass it to Van Wagoner, and Van Wagoner would pass it to Madala, who would charge out the door. Someone else would wave a shirt in the window signaling the ground teams to move in.

As to the assault team, Madala was to go first, followed by Agents J. J. Keating, Nichols, and Van Wagoner, Chicago policemen Frank Fremuth and Sergeant Thomas Curtin, and Illinois State Police Sergeant O. W. (Buck) Kempster. Most were armed with machine guns or riot guns.

Everything was planned. And nothing worked.

At about 8:30 P.M. Bobbie Moore left the building, heading toward the Auburn in the parking garage across the street and alerting agents to the strong possibility that the game was afoot. The exhausted Notesteen, who had gone to bed only minutes before, was roused and put back on watch, his pants and shoes still in the bedroom. Suddenly, Guinane decided to send Agent W. A. Smith downstairs to tell the ground teams something might be up. Smith was then to come back to the lobby and watch the stairwell. That order triggered a revolt from the assault team at the door. What if Smith is in the hall when Miller comes out? Or if he meets Bobbie on the way?

He should wait.

He should go.

He should wait.

Finally he went, under Guinane's direct order.

Seconds later, the door to 211 swung open. A man and a woman emerged.

"That's Miller," Mrs. Rogers said at first glance. "I know that's Miller."

"You can't tell from this distance!" Notesteen barked.

"That's Miller! That's Miller!" she repeated as the couple came closer.

Still Notesteen's hand gave no chopping signal. Suddenly, he heard Madala at the front door taking up Mrs. Rogers's chant, "It's Miller! It's Miller!" But Notesteen knew that Madala, from his angle, could not see anything.

The assault team jostled, fidgeted, leaned toward the door like Thoroughbreds straining at the gate. Closer now, Notesteen could almost see. . . .

As Miller stepped under the hallway light, Notesteen at last was sure of the face and the man. But the man was also sure, spooked by something he saw or heard. Already three long paces ahead of Vi, Miller broke into a dead run.

Notesteen's hand dropped in the distinctive chop just as Miller bolted. But Guinane wasn't there to see it. His timing horrible, Guinane had stepped into the other room to quiet the assault team.

"It's him! It's him!" Notesteen shouted as he ran in his underwear through the apartment.

The assault team moved, but Miller had moved quicker.

They had planned for something like this. Now the killer would be trapped in the three-sided box of the elevator foyer. They had him.

Unfortunately, Miller didn't follow the plan. And he wasn't about to wait for an elevator. Unlike the agents, he knew exactly where the emergency stairwell led out of the hall, downstairs, and into the lobby. Without one second's hesitation, he was through that door and gone.

The assault team followed, but not nearly at Miller's speed. Somehow police officer Fremuth got in the lead. A big man with a big machine gun in hand, he seemed in no great hurry to round the stairwell's corners on his way to the lobby. Agents would complain later that he wouldn't move and they couldn't get around him.

Once in the lobby, Fremuth shoved his machine gun into the side of a man standing by the desk: the wrong man. Nichols, followed by Sergeant Kempster, ran past Fremuth and into the street.

The ground teams were nowhere close. Smith had not yet had time to alert them, and nobody remembered to give the shirt signal from the window of 207. Miller, walking briskly but not running, made his way to the Auburn at the curb near the Sherone's side entrance. The engine was running and Bobbie Moore was at the wheel. They were almost away when Lou Nichols ran across the grass and jumped onto the running board.

"Stick 'em up!" Nichols shouted, poking his revolver through the window.

Bobbie screamed and shoved the accelerator to the floor. Verne Miller answered with two rapid shots that whistled close enough to Nichols's head to scare him off the running board. Kempster, armed with a machine gun, leveled it twice at Miller, twice unable to shoot because of civilians in the line of fire on the busy street. Finally, with a clear shot, he let go at the rear of the fleeing car.

Bobbie screamed again as bullets shattered the glass. The windshield fell away in front of her. Slugs passed through the front seat, but none found blood or bone.

Agents J. H. Rice and A. E. Lockerman, who were supposed to be covering that exit from their on-street location, saw what was happening and tried to react. But they'd had to create a parking place in just the right observation spot by pushing other cars forward and backward in order to wedge their own into place. Now they found themselves boxed in—and facing the wrong direction on the narrow side street. They never did get turned around.

Bobbie Moore and Verne Miller disappeared around a corner. Of the nearly twenty officers by then on the scene, none was in effective pursuit.

■   ■   ■

Bobbie fought the big Auburn, but she knew she was losing. The left rear tire was flat, blown to shreds. Her face dripped blood from the shattered glass of the windshield, and her mind reeled. Verne shouted instructions in her ear, but she hardly heard them.

The Auburn made it only six blocks before Bobbie braked to a stop in a blind end of Buena Vista Terrace, only yards from Lake Michigan. Verne was out of the car in an instant, vaulting over a fence and into the backyard of a nearby apartment house. He headed toward Clarendon Road without even a glance over his shoulder. Bobbie, more than a bit disoriented by the whole affair, reacted, quite unintentionally, like a seasoned warrior. She got out of the car, closed the door, and walked at a normal pace around the corner and onto the busy street nearby. In seconds she disappeared into the crowd. By the time she came out of her daze, she was blocks away and well out of danger.

For over two weeks she would elude police. When she did decide to come in, it wasn't because of fear. It was because she missed her kids. But they already were on their way back to their father in Ohio.

Back in the Sherone, Vi listened in horror to the machine-gun fire from Sheridan Road and wailed only slightly louder than Agent Madala's terrified young wife. Both were convinced their men were killing each other down below. Madala soon comforted his wife. Vi cried alone.

Vi was taken to the Bureau's Loop office and questioned all night and then for days on end. But she said nothing, told the agents nothing about Kansas City. She even insisted for several days that she was Clare Hays, just as the Sherone's registration papers said. Her rough, rough road was just beginning.

■　　■　　■

Fifteen minutes after the shooting stopped, agents caught up with the Auburn. But fifteen minutes is a lifetime for a person on foot in that uptown neighborhood. The trail already was cold. Lawmen counted seven definite bullet paths through various parts of the car but found only the slightest trace of blood, Bobbie's.

"The position of the bullet holes," Smith later wrote to Hoover, "would indicate that it was by miraculous luck that these bullets did not hit Miller directly in the head."

But hit him they did not. And Smith, as the man ultimately in charge of the operation, could only order a massive manhunt throughout the Chicago area. In the hope that Miller had been wounded, the agents checked all hospitals. Jefferson Park Hospital, sometimes known to harbor fugitives under false names, was visited personally. Miller's friends were turned out of beds and bars all night, but agents found no hint of a trail.

Verne Miller had pulled off an incredible escape, and no one was more incredulous than John Edgar Hoover. The director raged at his underlings in Washington, who promptly sent forth a string of demands for explanation and blame-fixing in Chicago. Hoover wanted detailed accounts from every agent involved, no matter what his role. Twenty-four hours later, he reminded them that he meant it.

HAVE NOT YET RECEIVED WRITTEN STATEMENTS REQUESTED
OF YOU CONCERNING ESCAPE OF VERNE MILLER. PROCURE
THESE STATEMENTS IMMEDIATELY FROM ALL AGENTS IN-
VOLVED AND FORWARD BY AIR MAIL. HOOVER.

Everyone ran for cover, and for good reason. Hoover's anger already was legendary, and no one wanted to face his retribution. To
be fixed with blame and become the focus of the director's rage
meant a career in obscurity, if indeed the offender would be allowed to remain in the Bureau at all. Each agent scrambled to put
the best face on everything he had done that weekend.

"Even if I had been armed at the service door, which I was not,
having been placed there by Special Agent Guinane only for purposes of identification," Notesteen reported, "I could not have shot
MILLER from the service door inasmuch as MILLER was running
and less than a second elapsed between identification and disappearance from sight."

Madala said he certainly wasn't at fault. "I was positive of his
identification," he wrote. "However, no action was taken."

The fear and self-preservation quickly degenerated into an orgy
of finger-pointing:

■ Nichols said the escape was Chicago Police Officer Fremuth's fault. Fremuth opened the door to the emergency stairwell "very slowly" and then would not get out of the allegedly
eager agent's path of pursuit.

■ Notesteen said Guinane was out of position at the critical
moment, unable to pass on the all-important chop signal of
positive identification. And, he said, the assault team, especially
Madala, was "talking and making noise" enough to spook Miller
out in the hall.

■ Mrs. Rogers, the stenographer, said Notesteen was too slow
in making the identification and then the agents were even
slower in starting the chase. She said Miller entered the hallway
a full fifteen seconds ahead of the agents.

■ Guinane said the outside agents were out of place because W. A. Smith was too slow alerting them.

■ W. A. Smith said he was delayed because of indecision at the door of apartment 207.

■ D. O. Smith said Rice and Lockerman were out of position.

■ Rice and Lockerman said the shirt signal wasn't given, so they had no alert.

And so on and so on. But the booby prize for second-guessing and tail-covering went to V. W. Hughes, the Washington supervisor appointed by Hoover to fix blame in the episode. Hughes wrote:

> If Miller had been intercepted by a squad of law enforcement officials as he came out of the door of apartment 211 he could have been held up without much fear of his retaliating or shooting first when he saw a squad of men with machine guns. If by any possible chance it was not Miller, no harm would have been done as there would have been no shooting unless the man had fired first.

In fact, nothing about the actual operation, including Hoover's own demand for a positive identification, was ever geared toward such a quiet arrest and gentle surrender as Hughes envisioned. Rather, all the decisions on the scene and all the directives from Washington focused upon the inevitability of violent confrontation, whether in a surprise raid or an assault in the hallway. The orders were never "alive if possible." They were always "dead if necessary."

In retrospect, Hughes concluded, the agents probably had "enough assurance of the identity of Miller to proceed without a dangerous delay in awaiting an identification [by Notesteen and Rogers] at close quarters." This he said, was a "vital error" in this particular case.

Putting that analysis on record was a faux pas of the first degree. Hughes must have forgotten that the agents, including Guinane, had wanted to launch a raid on Miller's apartment earlier that afternoon. Therefore, if the "dangerous delay" did indeed allow Miller's escape, the cause of the delay was the order from Washington to wait for positive identification. And that order had come from John Edgar Hoover himself.

.　　.　　.

Verne Miller was on the run again, this time without any disguise to help. All his sample cases, stationery, and business cards had been left in the Ford, which was now in the hands of the federal agents. To even think of using that identity would be suicidal.

In fact, Verne Miller had few options and little time left. It's not clear where his flight took him through November of 1933, but there's no doubt where he ended up. Nude, wrapped in cheap blankets, and bound hand and foot with clothesline, his body was found in a drainage ditch at Cambridge and Harlow streets, then an isolated area about eleven miles from the heart of Detroit. He had dyed his hair and the mustache red. The last twenty feet or so of clothesline was left dangling at his feet.

He'd been beaten to death, killed by violent blows with a blunt instrument, probably a claw hammer. His forehead and the top of his head were pulp. Popular myth would later say he was stabbed in the face with an ice pick, but he was not.

The theory immediately circulated that Miller had run afoul of his old friends in Detroit's infamous Purple Gang, especially since gang warfare in that city had left several people dead in recent weeks. He was killed in retaliation, some said. Or to relieve the heat of Hoover's investigation, said others.

But Bureau files show Detroit and its internal warfare was more likely incidental than pivotal in Miller's death. Not much more than a week earlier another nude body had been found in Connecticut. It too had been tied with a clothesline and wrapped in cheap blankets. It had been beaten in the face and head with a blunt instrument, probably a hammer. And it too had about twenty feet of clothesline left dangling at its feet. All of it just like Miller.

The victim in Connecticut with so much in common was Al Silvers, the man who had helped Verne Miller with his phony identity and provided him with a car. Strange, said agents, that both men should die within a week under such similar circumstances.

In fact, it wasn't strange at all. Within days, informants told the New York office that Silvers's mob bosses had been angered that he helped Miller against their wishes, thus exposing their mobs to even more federal heat. According to that theory, the mob had first killed Silvers and then gone after Miller. Tying up loose ends.

It was just as likely, however, that Miller, again on the run, went back to Silvers for more help and was turned down. According to that theory, Miller killed Silvers, and the New York mob then sent hit men after Miller to even the score.

Hoover didn't much care. Though a file was opened on the Silvers killing, a much bigger file would start to close with the death of Vernon C. Miller. So the director wanted to be sure Miller was dead. When the word first landed on Hoover's desk, he wrote in bold script across the bottom of the memorandum, "Be absolutely certain it is Verne Miller. Do not merely accept the word of the police."

The Detroit office responded immediately, sending an agent after midnight to the city morgue. A full set of photographs and fingerprints was taken and air-mailed to Washington. Still, when over a month later a small South Dakota newspaper printed a story hinting that the man buried there might not be the real Verne Miller, the jittery Hoover again demanded proof.

"What about this?" he wrote. "Did we check the fingerprints?"

He was assured all had been checked. Miller was quite dead.

Unfortunately, Verne Miller had taken his secrets of the Union Station Massacre with him. And despite Hoover's other successes with the War on Crime in the heartland, the massacre's unsolved puzzle just would not go away.

CHAPTER TEN

THE NET

FROM THE OUTSIDE, during that fall of 1933, it looked like J. Edgar Hoover's pledge to avenge the massacre at Union Station was being fulfilled, even if some of the success actually had little to do with the efforts of his federal agents. When possible he simply ignored those pesky facts and took credit anyway. Miller's gangland murder in Detroit, for instance, was treated as a major Bureau victory. Likewise were the six-months-to-one-year prison sentences of Vi Mathias and Bobbie Moore for harboring Miller, even though the women's arrests came out of the major Bureau bungling at the Sherone Apartments.

But nowhere did Hoover reach higher or gain more from something his agents did not do than in the arrest of George "Machine Gun" Kelly in a boardinghouse in Memphis. In fact, his men were not even there, but that didn't stop the Bureau's publicists from circulating a highly theatrical piece of fiction.

According to Hoover's version, agents found Kelly cowering in a corner. With his hands thrown high, Kelly kept repeating, "Don't shoot, G-men. Don't shoot."

Though the story made famous the G-man name, which was later used in the Bureau's very popular radio show, there was no truth to any of it. In fact, the name had been around for years. Kelly was arrested by three Memphis city police officers, and Kelly's most memorable phrase at that crucial moment was something like, "I've been waiting for you."

Hoover got more help in early October when Sheriff Ira Allen in Tucumcari, New Mexico, landed a load of number-two buckshot in the liver and lungs of Bob Brady, one of the Lansing escapees being sought for the Union Station Massacre. Another escapee suspect, Jim Clark, was also taken into custody by Allen. First reports were that Clark was doing fine, but Brady probably wouldn't live. Eleven pellets of the 20-gauge shell had ripped into his body.

"If you want to talk to Brady," the sheriff told Hoover's man in El Paso, "you better hurry."

Brady had made a foolish attempt to escape after Allen and his deputies stopped them for questioning and a quick look inside their car. He made it only a few feet, as attested by the buckshot's concentration. Clark had wisely stood very still indeed.

Agent J. A. Street raced up through New Mexico, the Union Station Massacre uppermost in his mind. Washington clearly was hoping for a deathbed confession from Brady that would help lift the fog. It didn't happen.

"Agent attempted to interview Brady and soon detected that Brady was willing to discuss anything that had happened during his criminal career except the Kansas City massacre and to questions by agent regarding the Kansas City shooting he invariably answered: 'I do not know—I was not there' and would turn his head on his pillow and look the other way," Street reported, "and when the subject was changed he would turn and look agent in the face and discuss other things freely."

Worse yet, at first he and Clark clung to the story about robbing the Black Rock, Arkansas, bank the day before the massacre, just as the fingerprint-laden letter to the Bureau had alleged. However, Brady soon admitted that only he, Clark, and Ed Davis were involved in the bank job. Much later, when Davis was captured, he would confirm that.

"Wilbur Underhill was with Harvey Bailey at the time, nursing Bailey's wounded leg somewhere near Oklahoma City," Brady said. He wouldn't be more specific than that.

At first the disappointed agents believed none of it. "Agent Street and I are convinced that no manner of investigation will elicit any truthful information from either of these men," Agent F. J. Blake reported back to Washington in frustration. "Both are sentenced to life and both are so hardened in crime that we believed it to be a loss of time to further question them."

Though the agents had agreed to send a wire to Brady's wife, telling her he would probably die of his wounds, their mood had changed by the time she and Clark's wife arrived the next day.

"[I] proceeded to the hospital and told the guards that under no circumstances should these women be permitted to come up the stairway or talk to Brady," Street reported.

It turned out Brady wasn't dying after all. And Reed Vetterli, who had said early on that he thought one of the massacre shooters might be Brady, had time to get to New Mexico from his new assignment in San Francisco, hear the other agents' reports on Brady's interrogation, and take a good close look at the suspect. His report only added to the gloom.

"Please be advised that the necessary travel was made, and I talked with and viewed Bob Brady at Tucumcari," Vetterli wrote to Hoover, "and while he resembles somewhat the individual whom I saw operating the machine gun in connection with the Kansas City massacre, I am not at all convinced that he is the individual and, in fact, am quite doubtful. [Agent] Blake of the Dallas office will, no doubt, submit a comprehensive report on the interrogation of Brady and Jim Clark. I doubt if Brady had any connection with the Kansas City shooting."

It was the first in a string of waffles in Vetterli's identification of the shooter at Union Station. Each change came, like this one, when somebody seemed about to be marked off the suspect list or about to be put on it. Vetterli's perspective always followed the trend. He started with Brady, reporting to Hoover immediately after the shooting, "I am convinced that the man who first opened fire from our right, with a machine gun, is Bob Brady."

Then, in the same letter to Hoover that discounted Brady's involvement, Vetterli wrote about a new man in custody and suggested *he* might be the gunner.

"Frankly, [Machine Gun] Kelly resembles a great deal the individual whom I saw operating a machine gun in the Union Station shooting," he wrote. "I cannot be absolutely positive until I again see him when his hair and complexion are back to normal."

At one later point Vetterli even offered a reverse ID, reporting that the captured Harvey Bailey said to him, "I think I've seen you somewhere before."

And still later, when Pretty Boy Floyd moved to center stage, Vetterli would write to Hoover, "Frankly, I just have a hunch that if I am ever able to view Pretty Boy Floyd in person, I will be able to identify him as the wielder of one of the machine guns."

Perhaps not so coincidentally, Reed Vetterli had fallen out of Hoover's favor. Relieved of his Kansas City duties and shipped to San Francisco, he would come under criticism again and again over the next several months. Even before Vetterli left Kansas City, Hoover was questioning the "inadequacy" of the case prepared against Bailey. Vetterli would talk to the press when he shouldn't, trust people he shouldn't, be accused of negligence in the Nash transfer arrangements, and even be skewered for giving away Nash's bloodstained wig when Hoover wanted it for his trophy case. In short, Reed Vetterli was fighting to save his career. And he would take that fight a long, long way.

■　■　■

The massacre case lurched ahead, at least for the moment, when a snitch in rural Oklahoma, lured by a promise of a $500 reward from the federal government and another $350 from the state of Kansas, told massacre survivor Agent Frank Smith that he could put Wilbur Underhill, a prime massacre suspect, "on the spot." Smith wasted no time getting word to R. H. Colvin, the agent in charge of the Oklahoma City Bureau office.

Lawmen in Oklahoma hated Underhill, so Colvin had no trouble recruiting help. He soon led a fourteen-man posse—seven federal agents, four sheriff's deputies from Oklahoma City, and three Oklahoma City policemen. If Underhill hadn't done enough by robbing and killing civilians over the years, he was now virtually thumbing his nose at the lawmen themselves. Only two weeks earlier, using his own name, he had married Hazel Jarrett, sister of the notorious outlaw Jarrett brothers. And he'd had Bruce Brady, outlaw brother of Bob Brady, stand up with him.

In fact, Underhill was traveling Oklahoma as though he were not wanted by the law at all. Colvin received tips almost every day that he was here or there, but usually around the Shawnee area where Agent Smith lived. That's where they would run him to ground.

The posse arrived at 1:30 A.M. on December 30, talked with their informant, and headed to the house where the man said Underhill would be found, a small frame structure at 606 Dewey Street. Leaving their cars two blocks away, the small army of heavily armed officers approached on foot. Colvin split them into squads, he and five others to approach from the rear and the rest plus the local police chief to approach toward the front. Both squads were to come in at an angle to avoid killing each other in the gunfight they all expected. They were close to the house, but not yet in position, when a dog began barking savagely. All rushed at double time into place, acutely aware that the little house was fully lighted inside.

Though history, aided by Hoover's publicists, would record a thirty-minute gun battle, it didn't happen that way. Underhill was caught, quite literally, with his pants down.

"Underhill was seen standing inside dressed only in a long suit of underclothes and apparently just about to retire," Colvin reported to Hoover the next day. "Fearing that he would be alarmed by the barking of the dog, the writer accompanied by Lieutenant [Clarence] Hurt [of the Oklahoma City police] immediately rushed forward to the rear window, at which time Hurt shouted, 'Wilbur, throw up your hands. It is the law.'"

Surprised, Underhill seemed at first to comply, but he suddenly whirled "as if to pick up his guns." Hurt fired a tear gas shell through the window, and Colvin opened up with his Thompson submachine gun, three bursts, the second driving Underhill to the floor. The two lawmen backed away quickly, aware they were in the line of fire from other officers at the front of the house.

The firefight was on. Underhill got off one or two quick shots from the window as both police squads opened up with all they had. Underhill turned and sprinted through the house and out the front door, barefoot and wearing only his long johns. He ran head-long into a blaze of shotguns. Agent Birch fired six times from close range as the others tracked their target with lead across the small yard. Twice Underhill fell in the mud, recovered his footing, and ran again. He finally disappeared between two houses three doors south.

The firing didn't stop. Colvin, at the rear of the house, didn't know Underhill had run outside. Some of the officers in the front of the house had not seen him either. So shots continued to pour into the little frame structure from both directions. When agents finally shouted for those inside to come out, Raymond Rowe, a criminal friend of Underhill, yelled that he couldn't stand. Blinded by the gas, shot in the elbow and shoulder, paralyzed by fear and pain, he was no threat.

Eva May Nichols, a beauty parlor operator brought to the party by Rowe, ran screaming out of the house and fell on the front lawn. Shot in the stomach and abdomen, she would die a few hours later.

At the rear of the house, Hazel Underhill was miraculously un-scathed when she slowly stood upright in the lighted bedroom. Hurt called her by name and told her to come outside. She did. Overcome by the tear gas, she had lain semiconscious on the bed throughout the firefight.

Immediately, the search was on for the wounded Underhill, but they could find nothing. No trace. Colvin called for bloodhounds from the Oklahoma State Prison in McAlester, over a hundred miles away. When they arrived near daybreak, almost five hours later, Underhill was still on the loose in the rain and fog of the Oklahoma morning.

R. E. Owens found Wilbur Underhill, almost dead, in an old bed in the rear of Owens's secondhand furniture store at 509 East Main Street. Owens immediately called the local police, who rushed over, hauled Underhill away—and promptly announced to the world that they, not the federals, had made the sensational arrest.

That angered Hoover, who demanded an immediate explanation from Colvin. Yet that disappointment was minor compared to what the director would hear when Underhill refused to die. The killer had thirteen bullet wounds, as Colvin explained:

> One bullet struck him on the left corner of the forehead plowing a groove around his head and cutting off the top of his ear, apparently made by a machine gun slug. Another round entered right side just above the liver and apparently emerged through the spine tearing a jagged hole upon its exit, apparently a .45 machine gun bullet. Another wound through right forearm, apparently a .45 machine gun bullet. Several buckshot entered his back, one being now apparently lodged just inside the skin of the front of the stomach. Other buckshot struck him on the left arm while one entered the right leg below the thigh. Another struck him in the left leg on the inside above the knee. The doctor, J. A. Walker, in charge of the municipal hospital at Shawnee, at first stated that it would be impossible for Underhill to live, but today he appears somewhat improved, and the doctor is undecided as to the ultimate outcome. He states, however, that should it appear that Underhill might recover, he will tomorrow or the next day amputate Underhill's left arm.

Though nearly dead, Underhill could still talk, and his words were resolute.

"He thought he was dying and under such conditions positively asserted to Agent Frank Smith that neither he nor Harvey Bailey

Cops, reporters, and the curious stomped all over the Union Station Massacre scene almost before the gun smoke cleared, carrying away souvenir evidence that might have proven invaluable. Kansas City detectives Frank Hermanson and William "Red" Grooms lay in a huge pool of blood between two cars, Grooms's head cradled against Hermanson's chest. Agent Ray Caffrey's bullet-riddled Chevrolet (right, with Nebraska license plate) was the gunmen's target.

In the chaos of the moment, news photographers took over. In this picture, taken only seconds after the massacre's signature photo (above), a bloody straw hat with a hole blown through its front has been dramatically posed on the right front fender of the agents' car. Though the hat long was rumored to be Hermanson's, the position of the hole makes it more likely to have belonged to Agent Ray Caffrey, who also was killed.

Prisoner Frank Nash, much of his head blown away, was dead behind the steering wheel of the agents' car (foreground). Note that the windshield glass on both cars, Caffrey's and the neighboring Plymouth, is scattered outward across the hoods, indicating separate blasts coming *out* of the agents' car. Behind the gruesome scene, Union Station's traffic was already moving again.

A blowup of the neighboring Plymouth's windshield and door post clearly shows the direction of some of the gunfire. The metal is ripped forward, the side window glass is blown into the car, and the windshield glass is scattered outward over the hood. The reverse trajectory draws a straight line to the rear seat of the agents' car. A steel ball bearing like the one that ripped the Plymouth's door post was found on the floorboard beneath the steering wheel. It was crucial—but ignored—evidence of what really happened that morning.

Charles Arthur "Pretty Boy" Floyd, known as Choc to his friends, was popular and respected throughout the Oklahoma hill country, but to small-town bankers all over the Heartland he was just another thief and killer. And that was only the beginning of the Floyd contradictions. Among the poor he took on a sort of Robin Hood reputation as one who burned farmers' mortgages when he robbed their bankers, though there is no credible evidence he ever did any such thing. Likewise, he was reviled by J. Edgar Hoover and other lawmen as a brute who would kill for little or no reason. Yet those who knew him best never believed Floyd would have risked his neck to save anybody else's hide, let alone that of a prisoner in Kansas City whom he hardly knew.

The famous hole in the windshield of Caffrey's car is distorted by sun glare in many massacre photographs. This close-up, however, showing the concave holes and glass pulverized over the hood, leaves no doubt among forensics experts that someone in the rear seat, directly behind the steering wheel, fired straight ahead. That blast would have been exactly in line with the head of prisoner Frank Nash and in the general direction of Agent Ray Caffrey, who had left the passenger door and was walking in front of his car en route to the driver's door.

Frank Nash was a little bald guy with a big nose, a bad wig, and a beautiful wife. He was a mediocre bank robber who never got far ahead and landed in jail a bit too often. Then he would talk his way out—and maybe raid the classics section of the prison library as he left. He wasn't exceptionally smart, distinctively mean, or particularly talented. But he was likable. In the end his life and crimes meant little, but his death and friendship spawned the incident that created the modern FBI.

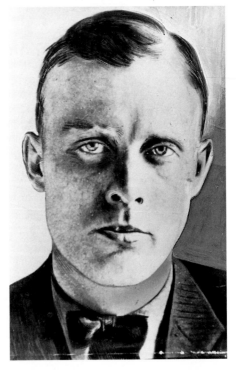

Vernon C. Miller was everything Nash wasn't—handsome, suave, brutal, bright, even a war hero, to hear him tell it. Yet Miller and Nash were the closest of friends. They worked together sometimes and played together a lot, sharing mostly the pride of beautiful women on their arms. When Frank got into trouble, Verne charged headlong into hell and history.

Adam Richetti now stands in the middle of the Union Station Massacre story, though in truth he was always on the edge. Born into crushing poverty and an alcoholic by his midteens, Richetti was a vicious, dangerous drunk held together by the powerful influence of his friend Choc Floyd. Later, with Floyd dead and no guns or liquor for courage, Richetti was no match for those who would take his life as the price for closure in the massacre case.

Francis Joseph Lackey, Joe to his fellow agents, emerged from the massacre a hero. Though badly wounded by machine gun bullets, he rallied within hours to give the Bureau a detailed account of the ambush. Then he stayed around to search out the villains and send one to his execution. In the end, no one sang Joe Lackey's praises louder than Joe Lackey. But evidence indicates Lackey was a liar, from that first day until his last day on earth. And he was anything but a hero at Union Station.

When disaster struck at Union Station in 1933, John Edgar Hoover was thirty-eight years old and already had headed what eventually would become the Federal Bureau of Investigation for nine years. No one knew better than he that his agents were poorly trained, legally impotent, unarmed, unrespected, politically appointed laughingstocks. And no one wanted that changed more than he and the cadre of ambitious youngsters surrounding him in the Washington headquarters. But they needed a cause and they needed a claim. The Union Station Massacre would be both.

Richetti's was one of the first major cases decided on fingerprint evidence, launching the Bureau's Single Fingerprint Section on the road to fame and reverence along with the rest of Hoover's vaunted crime laboratory. That evidence depended on a match of the 1934 print of Richetti's right index finger, taken when Richetti was captured in Ohio, with the 1933 print, taken off a beer bottle in the basement of Verne Miller's house. The match tied Richetti (and, by extension, Floyd) to the massacre.

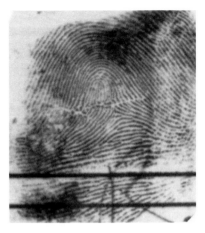

1932

The jury never saw the 1932 Richetti print, taken in Oklahoma and logged into Bureau records. But within days of the massacre a Bureau expert used that 1932 record print to seek a match with the 1933 bottle print. And he found no such match. Months later, the "match" was discovered in the Washington lab.

Yet the 1932, the 1933, and the 1934 prints all share the distinctive horizontal scar, raising serious questions about the Bureau's impressive and decisive "match":

1933

1. How did the Bureau expert miss a signpost so obvious as that scar within a sample of only sixteen suspects in the days after the massacre if the Bureau lab could find a "match" between the same two specimens months later among a sample of forty million?

2. If the Bureau expert saw no match in the days after the massacre because there *was* no match at that point, how did Richetti's print end up on that same beer bottle months later?

1934

A barmaid and prostitute turned devoted wife and mother, the lovely Frances Nash knew how to operate in her chosen world of men, muscle, and money. When her first husband went bad, she had her boyfriend shoot him. When she needed cash, she always found a friend. So when her beloved Frank was snatched off the streets by federal agents, she turned on the tears and pleaded for help. And, as always, men came running.

Too tough for tears and too smart to depend too much on anybody, Vivian Mathias kept herself a bit player in the Union Station Massacre story for over sixty years. In truth, she was in the middle of it all. She was Verne Miller's true love and confidante, adviser and partner. When Miller died, Vi cut a secret deal that gave her a new life, changed the course of history, and earned her the lifelong loyalty of Miller's hated nemesis—John Edgar Hoover himself.

Agent Raymond Caffrey, just transferred from the Omaha office, had a young wife, a new son, and a bright future that morning at Union Station. He was a good agent with a reputation for honor and honesty. Then he became the second Bureau man ever to die in the line of duty—and the undeserving repository of the Bureau's first Big Lie.

Detective William J. "Red" Grooms was a big man with a reputation to match in the Kansas City Police Department. But, stripped of his trusty machine gun by a department "error" that morning, he was no match for the fury at Union Station.

KCPD detective Frank Hermanson never really had a chance. He didn't see the gunmen coming, never turned to face them, and never knew what killed him. Or who.

The Bureau issued an Identification Order (Wanted poster), complete with fingerprint and arrest record, on Pretty Boy Floyd within a week of the massacre. However, even though Hoover and the Bureau knew Richetti was Floyd's partner and constant companion, no Richetti I.O. or fingerprint record ever was issued.

DESCRIPTION

Age, 26 years
Height, 5 feet, 8¼ inches
Weight, 155 pounds
Hair, dark
Eyes, gray
Complexion, medium
Nationality, American
Scars and marks, 1 Vac. cic.
1 tattoo (Nurse in Rose)

Chas A. Floyd

CRIMINAL RECORD

As Charles Arthur Floyd, No.
arrested police department
Louis, Missouri, September
1925; charge, highway robb

As Charles Floyd, No. 29078,
received S.P., Jefferson C
Missouri, December 18, 192
from St. Louis; crime, rob
first degree; sentence, 5

As Charles A. Floyd, No. 1695
arrested police department

Kansas City, Missouri, March 9, 1929; charge, investigation.
As Charles Floyd, No. 3999, arrested police department, Kansas City, Kansas, May 6, 1929; charge, vagrancy and
picion - highway robbery; released May 7, 1929.
As Charles Floyd, No. 887, arrested police department, Pueblo, Colorado, May 9, 1929; charge, vagrancy; fined
sentenced to serve 60 days in jail.
As Frank Mitchell, No. 19983, arrested police department, Akron, Ohio, March 8, 1930; charge, investigation.
As Charles Arthur Floyd, No. 21458, arrested police department, Toledo, Ohio, May 20, 1930; charge, suspicion.
As Charles Arthur Floyd, sentenced November 24, 1930, to serve from 12 to 15 years in Ohio State Penitentiary (b
robbery, Sylvania, Ohio); escaped enroute to penitentiary.

Agent Frank Smith, one of the older, pre-Hoover agents, led the Bureau to Nash's hideout in Arkansas and survived the massacre in Kansas City.

Otto Reed, the police chief in McAlester, Oklahoma, hated Frank Nash and had chased him off and on for over a decade. So when Reed was invited along to drag Nash out of the outlaw stronghold at Hot Springs, Arkansas, he jumped at the chance. But first the chief grabbed his best friend, a very special shotgun with a long barrel for game, a short barrel for men, and a special load for Frank Nash.

Reed Vetterli, agent in charge of the Bureau's Kansas City office, kept a squeaky clean life and a clear desk top in the days before the massacre. Just as obvious, to his fellow agents, was his compulsion to please the bosses in Washington. But he could neither tidy up after the massacre nor please his bosses, no matter how hard—and how often—he tried.

Louis "Doc" Stacci (left) owned the O.P. Inn outside Chicago and was friend to both Nash and Miller. When Frances put out the call for help and tried to reach Miller, she went through Stacci and his underworld connections.

Juanita Baird (left) and her younger sister Rose were Choc Floyd's friends from way back. Juanita even had taken a bullet meant for Floyd. So when the Pretty Boy and Richetti went into hiding after the massacre, the Baird sisters went along for the fun of it. The various relationships have never been completely clear, though Juanita was known as Floyd's girlfriend, Rose didn't much like Richetti, and both sisters claimed intimate knowledge of Floyd's scars—or lack of them—when agents inquired.

Long at the top of the Bureau's suspect list for the massacre, Harvey Bailey screamed his innocence from the beginning. He was a bank robber, not a killer, he argued.

Young and eager, Agent Mont Clair Spear stayed on the massacre case from the beginning and often ran the Kansas City office as Hoover shifted men in and out, trying to find someone who could jump-start the investigation. Spear's tenacity paid off. By the time the huge file closed in 1938, Spear was working in the D.C. headquarters, writing memos for the personal attention of the director.

Kenneth McIntire, like Spear, proved an exception to the incredible attrition rate among agents involved in the early investigation. Yet, unlike Spear, he stayed in the Bureau over the long haul, rising in later years to the top ranks of Hoover confidants.

Former Texas Ranger Gus Jones brought a can-do reputation into the massacre and left it badly bloodied. He never believed Floyd did it, and he said so, which sent him first into obscurity and then out of the Bureau.

Sent to Joplin to nail down the Hot Springs–Joplin connection, Agent Hal Bray spent much of a hot summer in a tourist camp south of town, stripped to his underwear and watching a gangland hangout across the valley. It could have been different, he remembered with bitterness fifty years later. His tip on the telephone traffic could have broken the case in the first few hours, if Vetterli hadn't muffed the lead.

Several times each year flowers show up on Adam Richetti's grave in Bolivar, Missouri. Who brings them and why are the massacre's final mysteries.

had anything to do with the Kansas City massacre," Colvin reported to Hoover. "He stated that at that time, he and Bailey were in Oklahoma City where he was attending Bailey's wounds received at the time of their escape from Lansing."

Colvin added this devastating summation: "This statement, made under such conditions, is believed to be true as he offered to produce credible witnesses to prove the fact."

The public relations coup of Underhill's capture had become a potentially devastating blow to the all-important Union Station investigation. Though agents were not broadcasting what Underhill had told them, they nonetheless wanted him well away from civilians and securely locked behind bars. However, the doctors refused, saying Underhill was in no shape to be moved. Only when hospital officials were peppered with a series of anonymous warnings that the Underhill "gang" was coming in to get their man did that stand change.

"The doctors would not say that Underhill could be moved although they were willing that we should move him if we desired," Washington supervisor V. W. Hughes reported to Hoover on January 2, 1934. "They stated confidentially . . . that if it weren't Underhill they would not permit his being moved as the move probably would be fatal to him."

That same afternoon, on Hoover's direct order, Underhill was loaded into a heavily guarded ambulance for the rough and rolling ninety-mile ride to McAlester. He survived the trip, barely, but his condition worsened steadily. On January 7, Hoover received the following terse wire from Colvin:

WILBUR UNDERHILL DIED AT ELEVEN FORTY FIVE TONIGHT IN MCALESTER PRISON.

Though the sensational thirty-minute gunfight had been a Bureau exaggeration, the house at 606 Dewey Street indeed had been riddled by the assault. The estimate of a thousand bullet holes, by most accounts, was probably accurate. But when the hapless owner of the house wrote J. Edgar Hoover, asking the Bureau to pay for the damages, he couldn't have known he was rubbing salt in an open wound.

"This unmitigated nerve," Hoover wrote on the bottom of the letter. "See that a thorough check is made to get all who can be charged with any knowledge of this, on harboring a fugitive from justice."

The director's foul mood was about to get worse.

■   ■   ■

Though no one, least of all the director, wanted to admit it, the Union Station Massacre case was coming apart at the seams. Truth and facts were whittling away at their list of suspects, and those names still on the list were threatened by an acute shortage of proof. Even the very root of the case, the legality of Nash's arrest and transport, was in serious doubt. Hoover wrote to the attorney general's special assistant on October 23, 1933:

> The reference letter of Special Agent in Charge E. E. Conroy states that Assistant United States Attorney Thomas J. Layson, at Kansas City, Missouri, has raised the question that successful prosecution might not be instituted, in view of the fact that no United States Marshal or Deputy United States Marshal had custody of the prisoner [Nash].
>
> The Division would appreciate an opinion from you containing citations of the law which would prove that Special Agents Lackey and Smith were legally acting as Agents of the Attorney General when transporting escaped Federal prisoner Nash.

It was the jurisdictional question come back to bite them. Despite the federal indictments, Hoover was having trouble getting the case into federal court. And if he did, there was a good chance it might be tossed right back out again, on the grounds that his agents shouldn't have been bothering Frank Nash in the first place.

State prosecutors were even more reluctant, complaining that things just weren't fitting together the way they were supposed to. For one thing, there were the autopsy reports showing that Agent Ray Caffrey had died from a wound to the head caused by a ball bearing ripping through his brain. There was no doubt about that. Doctors found the ball bearing "in or near" his head, which meant it may have fallen out of the gaping wound while he was dying on the stretcher. And KCPD Detective Frank Hermanson died from a wound that tore off much of his skull, consistent with a shotgun blast. Yet witnesses talked about machine guns and pistols being in the hands of the killers. No one mentioned a shotgun.

Hoover's best efforts to prod the local prosecutors just didn't work. They dragged their feet on a Bailey murder indictment through August, September, and into October. Yet despite Hoover's public drumbeat and private pressure, he did understand the situation. On September 22, in a memorandum for record of a phone conversation with Pop Nathan, his number two, Hoover at least privately faced up to the truth.

"Mr. Nathan stated that all the evidence we have in the Kansas City case is the telephone numbers, and an admission by Mrs. Nash that Verne Miller told her over the telephone the night of the massacre from the Kansas City Union Station that they would get her husband back," he wrote, without further comment.

And that was before Bob Brady's and later Wilbur Underhill's compelling denials that they or Harvey Bailey or others from the Lansing escape had anything to do with the massacre.

In truth, the ice under the Bailey gang's federal indictments and Hoover's case was even thinner than any of the prosecutors knew. Melvin Purvis, a powerhouse among field agents, had taken a close look at Samuel Link, the star witness against Harvey Bailey. It was Link who said he had seen Bailey clearly and had watched him get into position, raise a machine gun, and fire. Link's identification was extra solid because Link claimed to have known Bailey from Link's days as a process server in Kansas City. Purvis put all that into serious doubt.

"[Link] claims that he was with Teddy Roosevelt in South America and has personally met all the crown heads of Europe," Purvis wrote, quoting Link's Chicago business associates. Others called him "mentally deficient" and said Link was "a very erratic person and made many statements which could not be relied upon."

That report was filed on August 29. Yet throughout September and October, Link held his billing as the Bureau's star witness against Bailey. Even when other agents reported Link had served time in prison, that didn't change. On October 10, when Agent W. F. Trainor, the records expert on the massacre investigation, prepared a twenty-seven-page report designed to aid prosecutors in going forward with a state murder indictment against Bailey and the others, Link was still the linchpin in the Bureau's case.

Not everyone was comfortable with that. In a private letter from one agent to another, E. E. Conroy, by then running the Kansas City office, told Purvis in Chicago, "In addition, as you are possibly aware, the testimony of Link would be subject to severe attack on the part of the defense attorneys due to his apparent character."

Ultimately, even the diehards had to face the truth. Mont Clair Spear, Monty to other agents, was number two in Kansas City throughout that summer and autumn. He watched the case against Bailey build and then collapse.

"In the end, we just had nothing to connect Harvey Bailey and his gang to the massacre," Spear said, half a century after the massacre. "We had no proof."

As the pressure of the crumbling case mounted, things got a little bizarre that autumn of 1933. When Lillian Holden and Marge Keating, wives of the founders of the gang that spawned many of the massacre suspects, came to town they were treated like big-time gangsters themselves. Federal agents followed the women from Chicago to Kansas City, back to St. Louis, and on to Chicago through most of October. While the wives were in Kansas City, their every contact was recorded, the least of which being their trips to Leavenworth to visit their husbands. Hoover's men were far more interested in what the women did with their evenings.

To find out, they bugged the women's hotel telephone. Then they planted a Vactuphone, a crude listening device, in their room and eavesdropped from next door.

"The women spent most of their time during the nights of their stay in Kansas City at cabarets, according to their conversation as overheard on the following mornings," the agents reported to Washington. "It was also learned through their conversation, and other indications, that these women slept with the various escorts after their return from the cabarets on the occasions mentioned."

The agents knew who bedded down on which nights on the foldout couch and who got the bedroom at their Pickwick Hotel suite. They knew the women's most intimate secrets, learning to recognize their voices and other sounds. After stating near the top of their report that "these women carried on no conversation which would be indicative of the location of Miller, or other individuals sought in this case," the agents went on to file two detailed reports totaling twenty-four single-spaced typewritten pages.

The agents who followed the women out on the town had good duty. Hal Bray and Ray Suran spent many evenings at the Cotton Club with their spouses, watching the convicts' wives dance the night away. They were often out until dawn, when other agents would tune up their eavesdropping equipment. It seemed to irritate them especially that the women's taste ran toward Italian men.

Though the reports on the Keating and Holden wives may have appealed to the director's now well-known appetite for sexy secrets, they did nothing to advance the Union Station Massacre case. Little that autumn did. There were dead ends everywhere.

Miller was dead.

Bailey was no longer a serious suspect to most who knew the case.

Underhill was dead, all but cleared by his deathbed denials.

Without Bailey and Underhill, the likelihood of Brady, Clark, and Davis being involved was rather slim.

The phone conspiracy angle had about played itself out. When Lou Conner was arrested in Memphis in November, that left only

Richard Galatas, the Hot Springs protection man, still at large. Galatas had been especially elusive, reported gambling in Chicago, vacationing in Florida, and even traveling in Louisiana, dressed first as a priest and then as a woman. At year's end, he became a major focus of the case, primarily because there was little else.

All that left J. Edgar Hoover in a foul mood. And Hugh H. Clegg, a senior Bureau supervisor, reflected that mood in a memorandum for the director on the last day of January 1934.

> This morning I telephoned Acting Agent in Charge M. C. Spear, at Kansas City, and told him that the Division [meaning Hoover] was very much displeased with the reported lack of vigor in the investigation of the Kansas City massacre case; that it appeared that they had let this case fall by the wayside and it was being handled intermittently by any one of a number of agents and it was not being pursued vigorously toward a logical conclusion.

Clegg went on to quote Spear as responding that there "had arisen some friction in connection with the handling of the case," primarily because of conflicting theories about who conducted the massacre.

"I informed Spear that the various theories they might develop had no bearing on the case; that it was not the policy of agents of the division to get into disputes over theories; that we were seeking the facts, whatever they might be, and that he should not tolerate any friction in his office," Clegg reported to the director.

Hoover exploded, writing in a bold hand on the memorandum, complete with underlines and heavy marks for emphasis.

"This must stop *at once*," he wrote beside the part about friction among agents. Then, at the bottom: "See that a sharp letter is sent K.C. re such bickering. It must stop *at once*."

Whether Hoover liked it or not, the bickering in Kansas City was crucial to the direction of the massacre investigation. On one side was Agent W. F. Trainor, who had written all the comprehensive reports and was most familiar with the voluminous file. On the other side was Agent A. E. Farland, a newcomer to the investigation, who was convinced his interviews at the Kansas State Penitentiary in Lansing were leading toward the real killers.

Essentially, Farland believed the Barker Gang (brothers Doc and Fred plus Alvin "Creepy" Karpis) was responsible for the massacre. Trainor, supervisor of the case, thought that idea was simply wrongheaded. The debate sharpened when John M. Keith, one of Hoover's hired guns from the old days, came around on an inspection tour and sided with Farland against Trainor.

"It is my opinion that Special Agent Trainor has not sufficient administrative ability to supervise this case," Keith wrote, in a letter marked "personal and confidential" for the director. "It is my understanding that his original assignment was more or less in the nature of a recording secretary to receive and marshal the information obtained during those hectic days of our initial inquiries."

Keith wanted somebody else put in charge, with "Trainor acting as recorder under instructions not to attempt to supervise the development of the case and to permit free access to the existing file to any one of these . . . men."

Hoover agreed, opting for new blood in the investigation. He told Agent Harold Anderson, already in Kansas City but heretofore on special assignment, to take charge of the massacre investigation. Trainor would stay on, but only as Anderson's aide in finding his way through the files. Finally, Farland would follow his own leads. Confidentially, Clegg reminded Hoover that Farland had requested reassignment to New York City and suggested that this would be a good time to approve the transfer.

But Anderson was to be far more than a peacemaker. His charge from the director was to start from scratch, review every shred of evidence, and rebuild the stalled case from the ground up.

Perhaps, the director suggested, the other agents had overlooked something.

CHAPTER ELEVEN

THE PRINT

AGENT Harold Anderson took Hoover at his word, refusing to depend on Vetterli's and Trainor's summary reports but reaching back into raw agent narratives in the deepest drawers of the Union Station Massacre file. It was what would come to be called a bottom-up reappraisal of the entire operation, and Anderson wasn't the type to let personalities, even friendship, stand in his way.

When he first came across fingerprint evidence in one of these drawers, he didn't even know what it was. Trainor had to lay it all out for him.

Not long after the massacre, Trainor explained, agents tracked Miller to the house at 6612 Edgevale, but they were too late; Miller had fled with Vi and her daughter, Betty. All they could do at that point was to look for some fingerprints, but that hadn't gone far. The only match they came up with was Verne Miller himself.

But Anderson wanted to know what the rest of the stuff was, the beer bottles, the copies of fingerprints, the photographic negatives. All part of what John Brennan, out of the St. Louis office, did in trying to make a match, Trainor explained. The print cards, which were copies of criminals' fingerprints on file in the Washington headquarters, had been sent out for comparison purposes. It all came to nothing.

Anderson wasn't satisfied. What was all this stuff doing in a drawer? Why hadn't it been sent on to Washington to the new Bureau scientific laboratory?

The answers quit coming quite so easily as the resident agents realized where Anderson was heading. They could see their careers taking a sudden nosedive, and their first reaction, which Anderson dutifully reported to Hoover, was to look for some way to protect their hides. There was none. To delay would only make things worse. E. E. Conroy, the Kansas City office's agent in charge, sent the dreaded letter the next day, February 13, 1934. He didn't even send it airmail.

In the letter Conroy first explained that Agent John Brennan, along with Chief of Detectives Jack Jenkins of the Kansas City, Kansas, Police Department, had found some fingerprints at the Edgevale house in June 1933, not long after the massacre. Photographs of the latent fingerprints, he explained, were taken immediately upon the discovery of the prints. Then, in an offhand manner that fooled nobody, Conroy got to the point.

"The films, positive and negative, are now in the possession of this office and are being transmitted to the Division for analysis in the laboratory," he wrote. And, by the way, would the Bureau try to match the prints against those of eighty-one suspects on the attached list?

That triggered a fiery telegraphic rocket from the director, dated February 21.

REFER YOUR LETTER FEBRUARY THIRTEENTH WITH WHICH
TRANSMITTED EVIDENCE APPARENTLY AVAILABLE SINCE JUNE
DESIRE FULL IMMEDIATE EXPLANATION AIR MAIL WHY THIS
LATENT EVIDENCE NOT IMMEDIATELY TRANSMITTED UPON
DISCOVERY TO DIVISION AND WHERE HELD IN INTERIM ALSO
DESIRE DETAILED STATEMENT YOUR DESIRES FOR ANALYSIS AND
PURPOSES SUCH ANALYSIS. HOOVER.

The fat was in the fire, and a lot of people were about to get burned. In the first of what would become a series of explanation letters to Hoover, Conroy tried to keep it cool and businesslike with a simple restating of the facts—and a little contrition. "The Division is respectfully advised . . . " he began a second letter on February 21.

He then explained again how Brennan had been sent to 6612 Edgevale to look for prints, how he found them on several items, including dusty beer bottles in the cellar, and how he had a local photographer take pictures of all the latent prints. Brennan, Conroy said, had then told Nathan what he had.

> Mr. Harold Nathan, assistant director, telephoned the Division from the Kansas City field office requesting that photographs and fingerprints be immediately furnished the Kansas City division office of the suspects in this case. . . . Division telegram of that same date, June 29, reflects that photostatic copies of the fingerprints requested and available photographs were being forwarded to the Kansas City office via air mail.

When the copies of the sixteen requested fingerprints from Bureau records arrived from Washington, Conroy explained, comparisons were made "between the prints in question and the latent prints found at the above described residence" by Agent Brennan. "No identification other than Vernon C. Miller was made," he said, and that information was reported to Bureau headquarters. "The beer bottles containing latent prints have at all times, since their location on or about June 29, 1933, been carefully preserved in the Kansas City Division Field Office."

Conroy ended with an apology and an excuse.

> Undoubtedly photographic copies of this latent [fingerprint] evidence should have been transmitted to the Division for careful analysis there. However, it appears that in the excitement in connection with this investigation at that time shortly after the massacre happened, this was overlooked.
>
> At that time this case was being handled at the Kansas City office in the nature of a special assignment, numerous special agents being assigned to the Kansas City office specifically for investigation on this case.

That seemed to hold everyone off for the moment. At least the criticism from Washington let up over the first two weeks of March. Then, on March 14, all hell broke loose.

The day began with a routine letter written by Clegg for Hoover's signature saying the latent prints from Kansas City had yielded little in the Washington lab, only a few more matches with Verne Miller and twelve found to be identical with the prints of Vi Mathias. No surprise there.

But about noon the Union Station Massacre case took a dramatic, even decisive, turn when Conroy in Kansas City received an urgent coded telegram from the director:

ONE OF THE LATENT PRINTS SUBMITTED WITH YOUR LETTER FEBRUARY THIRTEENTH IDENTIFIED AS ADAM RICHETTI OKLAHOMA PENITENTIARY NUMBER TWENTY FIVE SEVEN SEVENTY THREE. HOOVER.

At that moment the focus of the massacre investigation shifted to a drunk named Adam Richetti and his much more famous partner, Pretty Boy Floyd. Though Floyd had been on the suspect list since the first day and had been indicted along with the Lansing escapees by the federal grand jury, he had never earned a top-level priority because nobody could even hint at any previous relationship between Floyd and Verne Miller, the acknowledged organizer of the failed Nash rescue attempt. The print found on a beer bottle in the cellar at 6612 Edgevale Road was "the connection between Richetti and the deceased Vernon C. Miller, which was heretofore not known to the Division offices," Spear would write to Bureau offices around the country a few days later.

Now, according to the file, Hoover was furious. A letter had already been written flaying just about everybody in Kansas City, chastising them for attempts to avoid criticism after Anderson "discovered" the prints, and demanding the names and statements of all those responsible. At the announcement of the print match, Hoover's lieutenants got Conroy on the phone and read that letter to him, along with much more. Six days later, on March 20, in a letter marked "personal and confidential" to the director, Conroy tried to defend himself and his men.

He first reminded Hoover that Brennan through Assistant Director Nathan had asked for prints of sixteen suspects, "among which, incidentally, were those of Adam Richetti, Oklahoma State Penitentiary Number 25773 (spelled Racchetti on the card furnished this office by the Division at that time).

"In connection with the above it appears that Special Agent J. E. Brennan, who made the comparisons at Kansas City, failed to make an identification of the latent fingerprints of Adam Richetti," Conroy continued. "In fairness to Agent Brennan, however, it may be noted that the same situation apparently existed at the division after the receipt of the February 13th letter from this office . . . which had the name Adam Racchetti . . . listed among the eighty-one suspects."

He pointed out that Hoover's own communications had said that "immediately after receipt [in D.C., the latent fingerprints were] compared with the fingerprints of all known suspects in this case, that search had been made without results, and that it then became necessary to begin routine examination of those latent prints against the records appearing in the Division's single fingerprint file."

In other words, Conroy was arguing, maybe our man Brennan didn't make the match, but your fancy lab didn't either.

And besides all that, Conroy continued, in the sort of burning defiance unheard of among Hoover's men, when all this happened in June of 1933 "the division had not yet established the single fingerprint section in the Identification Division."

That was too much. Hoover fired back a scorching rejoinder.

With regard to your statement the Division had not established a Single Fingerprint Section at the time of the commission of this crime, your attention is directed to Division letter dated February 16, 1933, addressed to all offices advising that a single fingerprint file had been inaugurated, and the division has noted your memorandum dated at Charlotte, North Carolina, February 18, 1933, advising your agents of this fact.

And as to Conroy's allegation that the Bureau lab had missed the match, just as Agent Brennan did,

> Your conclusion that the Division [laboratory] compared the latent prints submitted with the fingerprints of Adam Richetti and failed to effect an identification is erroneous. The Division letter of March 15, 1934, to which you refer, indicated that the more active suspects on the list which you submitted had been compared with negative results. These included those suspects most prominently mentioned during the course of your investigation, particularly those upon which identification orders had been issued.

The print identification process in Kansas City, Hoover concluded, had been "superficial."

Yet Hoover's scathing correspondence was at least as self-serving as it was accurate. His tirades disregarded the numerous mentions throughout the early volumes of the Union Station Massacre file of the latent prints from Edgevale Road. For example, one letter from the Kansas City office in 1933 referring to the latent prints was initialed by five Washington supervisors. In short, despite the elaborate 1934 paper trail of invective against the Kansas City office, the top brass in Hoover's headquarters, including the director, were a bit disingenuous in their elaborate protestations of surprise after the prints were "found" by Agent Anderson.

However, the bottom line is the same. Of the seventeen latent prints found by Agent John E. Brennan and eventually sent on to Washington by Agent Anderson, one was officially identified by the Bureau lab as that of Adam Richetti's right index finger. Had field agents known of such a match in June when the latent prints were found, it would have made a tremendous difference in the investigation.

Agent John Brennan had apparently bungled the biggest case in the Bureau's history. Yet Brennan was never criticized by name in any Washington correspondence, never reprimanded specifically by anyone in the paper fury, in fact never even mentioned by any of the Washington bosses.

Curious. But then everything about Brennan's role in the affair is very curious indeed.

■   ■   ■

John E. Brennan was no ordinary agent, and he did not take an ordinary background into 6612 Edgevale Road in June 1933. At age thirty-three, he already had been working with fingerprints at least two decades, most of the time under the wing of one of the Bureau's most renowned identification experts, Edward J. Brennan, his father.

In 1933 the senior Brennan already was a Bureau icon, "probably the most important man in Bureau history prior to the time that J. Edgar Hoover became the director in 1924," according to *The Grapevine*, the retired agents' newsletter. Edward had been one of eight Secret Service agents to come over when the Bureau was formed in 1908, and he is credited with helping to get the brand-new organization up and running.

But the elder Brennan's real specialty was always identification, first using the Bertillon system of body and head measurements and then applying the fingerprinting skills he brought from Scotland Yard by way of the St. Louis World's Fair after 1904. There Edward had learned British inspector Sir Edward Henry's new classification system, the same one still in use today. He implemented it at the St. Louis Police Department, and he took that knowledge and skill first to the Secret Service and then to the fledgling Bureau. Charles Appel, who would build Hoover's vaunted forensics laboratory and become an icon in his own right, studied at the feet of Edward Brennan before Edward retired in 1925.

John E. Brennan shared his father's interest, skill, and knowledge of fingerprints, as well as his devotion to the Bureau. He became an agent immediately after service in World War I, at only nineteen, already striding in his father's footsteps. In 1924 and 1925, when Edward, as agent in charge of the St. Louis office, directed the search for Martin Durkin, who killed the first Bureau agent to die in the line of duty, his son John was part of the team. When Durkin was run to ground, John Brennan was there.

So John E. Brennan brought a wealth of experience, training, and dedication to focus on the most important fingerprint in the history of his beloved Bureau. And, according to Hoover's files, he blew it.

How?

That question resonates even louder after a thorough inspection of the fingerprints themselves.

First of all, the Richetti latent print from the beer bottle is amazingly good. It is full, almost complete, not the partial that experts expect to get from rounded surfaces such as bottles. It is clear, unblemished by twelve days' worth of dust in the cellar or by smudges from any overlapping fingerprints.

But the real puzzle comes from the scar, a Y-shaped slash that cuts across the very center of the finger pad and dominates the fingerprint. The scar is there on the latent print from the beer bottle of 1933. It is there on the fingerprint taken from Richetti when he was finally captured in 1934.

Modern experts say they ignore all such scars and look only at the natural fingerprint features. But for the eyes, whether expert or amateur, to miss this Y-shaped scar would be like ignoring a sign that reads *x marks the spot*. For even the most untrained eye, the scar acts as a magnet.

Brennan sat down in Kansas City to match that scarred latent print against those of sixteen people. That means he had to compare that print to sixteen sets of ten fingerprints each, or 160 individual record prints—actually 159, since one of Verne Miller's fingers was missing at the first knuckle. And, according to the Bureau, Brennan failed to match one glaring Y to another glaring Y.

Even today, fingerprint experts form a close-knit little society, and they don't readily criticize each other, including those brothers long dead and buried. But when the top fingerprint expert of a major eastern city was asked by the author how any good print man could miss such a glaring feature from among so few samples, he acknowledged it was "most peculiar." Within the brotherhood, that's virtually an indictment.

The reason print identification specialists avoid depending on scars is that scars are not permanent features. For instance, if Richetti's record print sent from Oklahoma to D.C. and eventually on to Kansas City had not had the scar, if the cut had not yet been inflicted when that record print was taken in 1932, the 1932 record print and the 1933 latent print would not have shared the same Y-shaped mark.

Therefore, to be certain that the Y was a constant feature in all Richetti prints, the author asked the FBI for Richetti's original print record, the one taken in Oklahoma in 1932 and sent to Brennan in 1933. The FBI research department said there simply were no surviving records of Richetti's prints. They had been destroyed years ago. Yes, the print record sent to Brennan had come from the Oklahoma State Penitentiary, number 25773. But that record print was no longer in the Richetti file.

And it was no longer in the Oklahoma files.

And it was no longer in the files of the Johnston County, Oklahoma, sheriff's office, which had sent Richetti for "safekeeping" to the state prison after his 1932 arrest.

Even though the Richetti case long has been heralded by the FBI as one of the first important cases decided on fingerprint evidence, the crucial print record is not only *not* in a museum, it no longer exists anywhere.

Except in the dusty old Union Station Massacre file. In Volume 65, about 160 pages deep, where it has no logical reason to be, there is a copy of Richetti's original print record from Oklahoma. And there, clearly identifiable, is the Y-shaped scar.

So the scar *was* there on the record print to grab Brennan's eye in 1933, just as it still grabs the eye today. And Brennan missed it.

In the context of the Bureau and its vindictive director, who for decades believed in and practiced retribution, all that presents a natural question: How quickly was John E. Brennan drummed out of the corps?

Answer: He was not.

In fact, John E. Brennan went on to become a Bureau icon on only a slightly lesser scale than his father, Edward. John served until 1950, a total of thirty-one years, and he worked on "practically all of the big Bureau cases, in every state in the union except Alaska," according to *The Grapevine*. He became one of the top "sound" men, meaning an expert eavesdropper. And he was a firearms expert, credited in Bureau legend with killing two members of the Touhy Gang during a gunfight in Chicago with both Hoover and Tolson on the scene.

And the Brennan glory hasn't stopped yet. Another Edward J. Brennan, son and grandson of his predecessors, served in the Bureau for twenty-eight years during the fifties, sixties, and seventies. And John E. Brennan II is a serving agent today. Together they constitute a proud Bureau dynasty, four generations and counting.

Not exactly the stuff of disgrace.

■   ■   ■

There is another possible scenario, though it is far beyond proving at this point, and it runs contrary to the extensive paper trail. That scenario runs like this:

If it makes no sense that Brennan (1) muffed the biggest case up to that point in Bureau history and (2) went on to a long and illustrious career under J. Edgar Hoover, one must consider the possibility that Brennan *muffed* nothing at all and, in fact, did something to *earn* the favor he would enjoy for so many years.

And that could mean that the "match" was never a match at all. Not in July 1933, when Brennan said it was no match. And not in March 1934, when the Bureau said it was.

In short, under that scenario, the Richetti print was somehow faked, whether in Washington or Kansas City, in order to provide the missing link from Floyd and Richetti to Miller and the massacre. And Brennan either participated or simply knew the truth and went along with the lie.

The "Would they?" question at this point in history is hardly a question at all. In his excellent book on Hoover's FBI, Curt Gentry discussed how Hoover's agents for decades used break-ins to plant incriminating evidence that would then be "discovered" during a court-authorized search. Gentry's explanatory footnote, quoted in full from *J. Edgar Hoover: The Man and the Secrets*, reads as follows:

> Interviewed shortly before his death in a mysterious "hunting accident," the former assistant director William Sullivan admitted that he had "heard" that this "sometimes happened," but that he refused to discuss specific cases in which it had occurred. When asked if it had happened in the Rosenberg, Hiss, or Oswald cases, Sullivan responded, "I'm not going to answer that."
>
> Another former headquarters official, who does not wish to be identified, said simply, "It happened a lot oftener than anyone cares to admit."

The "Could they?" question is only slightly more involved. In a practical sense, any fingerprint subterfuge would not have had to be very sophisticated. With fingerprinting barely into its adolescence in the mid-1930s, the deck was heavily stacked in favor of the Bureau. There were few genuine nonpolice experts available to the defense, certainly not like there are today and absolutely not for indigents like Adam Richetti. When the Bureau's experts set up their charts and lectured juries about the whorls and ridges and bifurcating this and that, they were watched in awe and quiet acceptance. They were in a world few lawyers and almost no jurors understood. So to a degree far greater than today, expert testimony was unchallenged and unrefuted testimony.

This particular case sounded especially awesome to the layman. The Bureau kept to itself the fact that Brennan had missed in his search for one match among sixteen people. Rather, Hoover's publicists bragged to the world that the Richetti match came out of the D.C. laboratory's single fingerprint file. Bureau technicians, they claimed, had made the match from among four million people's prints. Given the technological awareness of the time, few could even conceive of that. But all were impressed by it.

Finally, it is no secret that Bureau laboratory scientists during those years were experimenting extensively with faking fingerprints. They admitted it in court during the Richetti trial. Some of their more intensive laboratory efforts had involved tape, powders, and glass surfaces. However, Bureau expert Jerry R. Murphy told Richetti's jury, "we were decidedly unsuccessful."

Did someone try again, with a little more success, in the Richetti case? The physical evidence is gone now. Neither of the original bottles has survived. The Union Station Massacre file does contain a picture of the Miller bottle, but there is none of the Richetti bottle.

There are few absolute certainties. Only reasonable doubts.

CHAPTER TWELVE

THE ASSASSINATION

THE RISE OF Adam Richetti and his buddy Pretty Boy Floyd to the top of the suspect list featured none of the fanfare and public promises that had accompanied Harvey Bailey and the Lansing escapees. Hoover had already dropped one joker. This time he would hold his cards close to his vest and demand that everyone else do the same.

So Adam Richetti, despite the print that broke the case, was never the subject of a Bureau identification order, the famous Wanted posters that have decorated post office walls for decades. In fact, the very existence of the fingerprint match was a closely held Bureau secret. When word of it appeared to leak out many months later, after Floyd was dead and Richetti was in custody, Hoover reacted like Bigfoot on a bug.

On November 6, 1934, Hoover wrote to the Kansas City office:

> Associated Press dispatches emanating from Kansas City, Missouri, indicate that Jack Jenkins, head of the Identification Bureau, Kansas City, Kansas, Police Department, has given out information to the effect that identifications were made by that Bureau from latent prints taken from beer bottles recovered at the residence of the late Vernon C. Miller, which implicates Miller, Floyd and Richetti. . . .
>
> Of course, the identification of the prints of Miller and Richetti were effected in the Technical Laboratory of the Division and this

information was being treated as confidential until such time as it became necessary to disclose the information at the trial of the case. I, therefore, desire that you make every effort to determine the source of Mr. Jenkins's information that the identifications had been effected.

In fact, without the fingerprint match, the case against Floyd and Richetti was even worse than the all-but-defunct case against Bailey. The only person who believed she'd seen Floyd at the massacre that morning was Lottie West, the Travelers Aid lady, and among agents that "identification" was little more than a joke.

> The Kansas City office was advised by Mrs. Lottie West of the Travelers Aid Society, stationed at the Union Railroad Station at Kansas City, immediately after the massacre that she positively identified a photograph of Charles Arthur Floyd, which was shown to her, as a likeness of one of the participants in the massacre, and also she stated that she had seen the same individual sitting in her chair at the front of the lobby in the Union Station about 7:00 A.M., which was about fifteen minutes before the massacre [Trainor wrote, in a summary report in mid-April, 1934, a month after the precious print match].
>
> However, it subsequently was stated by various employees of the Union Railroad Station at Kansas City, including H. House, a redcap, that the man who sat in the chair of Mrs. West was Harry Blanchard, another employee at the Union Station.

Trainor went on to report that "the photograph of Floyd was not identified by any other witness in a manner which would establish a positive identification."

No witness even mentioned Richetti.

But Hoover's men simply had nowhere else to go. And, according to the Bureau's Washington laboratory, the print did appear to place Richetti, and therefore Floyd, in Verne Miller's house within a few hours of the June 17 massacre. Because of circumstances, they reasoned, the print couldn't have been left before midnight or so on the sixteenth when Floyd and Richetti arrived in town with Sheriff Killingsworth as a hostage, nor could it have been left after June 19, when the house was vacated.

Trainor's mid-April report was a watershed. It focused on Richetti, his background as a poor Italian kid in Oklahoma, and his friendship with the Pretty Boy. Richetti family members from Texas to Ohio would have their phones tapped and their mail covered for months.

And none of it led anywhere. In fact, Floyd and Richetti, well aware Floyd had been named in the original list of suspects, were nowhere near the heartland. They were quietly going stir crazy in a small apartment in Buffalo, New York. Their companions, the Baird sisters, only slightly less buggy after months in hiding, were after them constantly to head back home. Wisely, they didn't.

■   ■   ■

Ironically, Hoover's investigation, long stymied by the gangster/police/politician brotherhood in Kansas City, took a great leap forward because of a feud within that corrupt family. In the early morning hours of July 10, 1934, after making his usual rounds, mob strongman Johnny Lazia was gunned down on the streets near his home. Expecting no trouble, he was accompanied only by his wife, Marie, and his trusted driver. When they pulled under the canopy of the Park Central Hotel, a new building at 300 East Armour Boulevard, Lazia got out to help his wife through the front door. He didn't get far.

A stream of machine-gun bullets ripped through his body, leaving him to die slowly the next day. Three transfusions and nine physicians couldn't help. His last words were said to be a plaintive lament that anyone would want to do such a thing to Johnny Lazia. "Why to me . . . the friend of everybody?"

Obviously, not everybody. Among those not fond of Johnny Lazia were Jack Griffin, a St. Louis gangster who had come a year earlier to the greener western pastures, and James "Jimmy Needles"

LaCapra, a former boxer and career thug in Kansas City's Italian community. LaCapra, who always had a big mouth, didn't much like his neighborhood reputation—high on ambition, short on brains and guts—but he was stuck with it. Nearing middle age, he was going nowhere with the criminal organization, and he knew it—because Lazia had told him so just a few weeks before his untimely death.

It happened when Griffin and LaCapra muscled their way into ownership of the Saratoga Horse Room, a booze and gambling joint at Armour and Troost. The former owners complained to Johnny Lazia that it wasn't right, especially after they'd paid their protection money and helped the Democratic Party.

Lazia agreed and ordered Griffin and LaCapra to give the club back. But LaCapra thought he and Griffin had muscled in fair and square, and he didn't want to leave. After all, they'd worked on Election Day too, he argued.

So Johnny offered a compromise. They could open a joint somewhere else, but they had to give up the Saratoga. End of discussion.

Griffin and LaCapra opened in the 1900 block of Main Street, a good spot, and they soon had another place across the street. But they still felt they'd been wronged. It got worse when Griffin and a third friend, Al O'Brien, tried to muscle in on a Teamsters and Milk Drivers Union, and the Italians blocked them again. Griffin, a former bank robber, was having little luck working into Kansas City's closed system, and he didn't keep his complaints to himself.

So the mob's verdict on Griffin, LaCapra, and O'Brien was reached quickly. When Lazia's followers finished a huge wake and respectful funeral, they took to the streets for revenge. Somebody caught up with Griffin on the evening of July 30 as he left Al O'Brien and their wives on the porch of the Buckingham Hotel to walk to the corner drugstore for cigarettes. He made it just as far as the sidewalk before several gunshots pierced the early evening air and left him cringing on the grass. Only a gathering crowd saved him from a final farewell bullet in the neck.

Hoover's agents found Griffin in the hospital, his left leg broken in two places, a deep flesh wound in his right hip, and a wound that started through his cheek and came out the back of his neck. Four Kansas City policemen stood guard outside his room, but Griffin did not feel safe. He wouldn't say much, nothing definitive, but he told the agents to come back the next day. Maybe then he'd have something to tell them.

They never saw him again. The agents would later find out that Lieutenant Jeff Rayen, a KCPD detective known to do bloody side jobs for the mob, had taken Griffin away in an ambulance, destination unknown. Griffin's fate darkened when it turned out the judge who signed his arrest order in fact had been out of town on vacation at the time. Nonetheless, for days KCPD Chief of Detectives Tom Higgins, who earlier had told agents that the "Wops" were trying to get Griffin out of the hospital so they could "put him on the spot," would claim he could lay hands on Griffin anytime he chose. He evidently never chose. Griffin was never heard from.

Meanwhile, O'Brien also vanished, either by his own choosing or with some professional help. So did Nugent "Little Nugie" LaPlumma, a neighborhood friend of LaCapra's and the man some say was the actual triggerman the night Lazia died.

That left Jimmy Needles LaCapra, now on the run and scared out of his wits—for good reason. Two days after Griffin was hit on his doorstep, LaCapra was chased at breakneck speed down Independence Avenue by three serious-looking fellows with guns in their hands and murder on their minds. The two cars slammed to a stop, and three hit men ran after LaCapra, who was dodging and firing over his shoulder as he stumbled into the post office at Independence and Benton. The three in pursuit fired several shots, witnesses told Sheriff Tom Bash, and started to follow LaCapra inside. However, they changed their minds and sped away just as police arrived.

LaCapra got the message. It was time to visit family in rural Kansas.

Argonia, population 500, not far from Wichita, wasn't far enough from Kansas City. Sometime after midnight on August 31, LaCapra's car was overtaken by a Ford V-8 sedan with black wire wheels. When it pulled alongside, a spray of bullets came at LaCapra and his two female companions. Nobody was hit, but LaCapra ducked low, pretending he was injured, and the big Ford sped on down the road.

LaCapra ran for the police immediately, and the would-be assassins ran into a ditch a few hours later. They all joined up at the Kansas State Highway Patrol headquarters in Wellington, Kansas, LaCapra in custody because he wanted to be and the three hit men under arrest because of three Colt .45-caliber automatic pistols found under their coats.

Back in Kansas City, Agents Harold Anderson and W. F. Trainor read an early-morning press report about the assassination attempt and sought permission to go ask a few questions, though the investigation was to be "in absolute secrecy due to the fact that no apparent jurisdiction had as yet occurred for this division." It was a hunch well played.

They found the three shooters, identified as Robert McCoy, John Pace, and Jerome Cretes, in rough shape. "It was obvious from the appearances of the three . . . that they had undergone physical punishment, probably at the hands of the Kansas Highway Patrol, as this was stated by the three parties when they were interviewed," Trainor wrote. But the real treasure trove was waiting in the next room.

Trainor and Anderson found Jimmy Needles LaCapra panicked and ready to babble. The men in the black Ford had stomped out whatever courage he had left. He begged for protection from the mob and the Kansas City police, and he tried to buy sanctuary with his words. The agents' only problem was making sense of it all.

"The statements of LaCapra were, of course, very jumbled and rambling and he appeared to be under a very great nervous strain," the agents reported to Hoover, apparently compelled to offer a telling disclaimer, "although he did not appear to be out of his mind in any manner."

In short, he spilled his guts, and Hoover's men scooped up every morsel. They started listening in the early evening of August 31 and let him talk until 4:30 A.M. September 1, asking everything they could think of. In his terror, LaCapra held nothing back. He named names, gave dates, trashed friends, settled old scores, and tried to buy back his life with the only currency left to him.

By dawn, the agents had a solution to the Union Station Massacre case.

■　　■　　■

LaCapra's midnight ramblings would take over the investigation. From that moment, all new information would be viewed through the prism of his words, measured against his recollections, weighed according to how it fit with his incredible story. Indeed, what he had to say was compelling, once the disjointed parts were assembled.

LaCapra explained that he was already a close friend of Griffin and a St. Louis gangster named Edward Wilhite when the two rolled into Kansas City about the last day of April 1933, driving a black Buick sedan that they wanted to hide somewhere for later use. They said they had stolen it in St. Louis. LaCapra led them to the Trafficway Garage, on Locust Trafficway near Missouri Avenue, and arranged to have the big Buick parked in a dark faraway corner of the garage.

It sat there through May and most of June. Then, about a week after the June 17 massacre at Union Station, according to LaCapra, he and his two St. Louis friends received a visit from LaCapra's brother-in-law, a mobster named Sam Scola. Johnny Lazia, as La-Capra quoted Scola, wanted the big Buick that Griffin had brought to town. And something else, Scola added. Johnny wanted Griffin and Wilhite to escort somebody out of the county.

Scola then told them the true story of what had happened at

Union Station. ("And Scola knew more about what was going on in the mob than anybody in town," LaCapra assured the agents.) Later, LaCapra swore, Johnny Lazia would repeat the whole thing to him personally. Pieced together, it went like this:

> When Pretty Boy Floyd and Adam Richetti left Sheriff Killingsworth and the kidnapped farm manager on the street in the West Bottoms near midnight June 16, Floyd already had hooked up with a gambler named Dominic Benaggio and, through him, the Kansas City mob. Floyd's contact was Steve Oliver, Benaggio's brother-in-law, who owned the nightclub Floyd had walked into as Killingsworth watched from the corner.
>
> For a price or because of previous friendship, Benaggio offered Floyd and Richetti shelter, but only after he had sought and received the permission of Johnny Lazia, who insisted on knowing everything that happened in any part of his organization, any time, night or day. Benaggio took Floyd to a hideout somewhere in the West Bottoms, as unaware as Floyd or Richetti that history was about to be made.
>
> The other links in that chain of circumstances were being forged at virtually that same time when Verne Miller, upset about the arrest of his friend Frank Nash, approached Lazia at his favorite late-night restaurant, Harvey's in Union Station.
>
> "Johnny, I want to use a couple of your boys to take my partner away from the officers," Miller told the crime boss.
>
> "I won't let you have any of my boys, but I have a fellow you might use," Lazia said, thinking of the call he had just received from Benaggio. It seemed a perfect fit. Favors done all around, but his boys not fouling their own nest. "How about Pretty Boy Floyd?"
>
> Miller and Floyd met for the first time in the back room of the drugstore at Missouri and Grand. The plan, Miller told Floyd as he had outlined to Lazia earlier, was to scare the federals spitless

and take Frank Nash away without firing a shot. Scola was with them at that meeting, sent along by Lazia to make introductions. Also, following Lazia's instructions, Scola gave Miller a machine gun to use; Floyd had his own.

The next morning, it just went wrong. They got the drop on the officers, all right, but after Miller said, "Come on, Frank," Nash stumbled getting out of the car. The sheriff he was handcuffed to fired quickly, hitting Floyd in the left shoulder. And that triggered the bloody firefight.

"It was them or us," Miller would tell Lazia later. The shooters laid up all day in Benaggio's hideout, nursing Floyd's shoulder wound. After dark Miller was back out on the streets, looking for Johnny Lazia and shocking those few who knew what he'd done. Miller caught up with Lazia, again at Harvey's, barely a hundred yards from the site of the massacre, where the crime boss sat with some of his boys, Tony Gizzo, Charley Gargotta, Charles Carolla, and Sam Scola.

"I've been looking for you all day," Miller said, in a voice a bit loud for the circumstances. "I don't think I would have to lose as much time waiting on the Pope as I do waiting on you."

That embarrassed Lazia in front of his people, so Miller tried to smooth things over with a joke about Johnny not wanting to stand the heat now that it was turned on. Then Miller apologized for the bloody events of the morning.

"I know it couldn't be helped," Lazia said.

"I'm glad you know that it couldn't be helped," Miller said, inviting Lazia to a brief and private huddle beside the table. Later, Lazia would tell his boys, in every detail, Miller's account of the massacre.

Miller left town as the heat intensified, leaving Lazia with an injured Floyd, a drunken Richetti, and a town full of angry cops. If Floyd's intention was to lay low until he healed, Lazia had other ideas.

"We have to get that fellow out of town," he told Benaggio.

Benaggio wasn't so sure. "He's in pretty bad shape, Johnny," he said.

"Well, try to see if he can make it," Lazia ordered. He sent Sam Scola in search of a safe car and some muscle.

When Griffin heard what Scola wanted that morning, he exploded. Lazia could have the car, but expecting Griffin to step into the massacre mess was crazy.

"You tell John Lazia to go to hell! He has his own boys," Griffin roared. "They been feeding off the fat of the land. Let them escort Floyd out of town. I don't want no heat like that."

Sam Scola left LaCapra, Griffin, and Wilhite at the Trafficway Garage. But he drove away in Griffin's big stolen Buick, heading for the Bottoms. Later, he would pick up his narrative to LaCapra:

Charley Gargotta, Tano Lacoco, Tony Gizzo, Sam Scola, and Dominic Benaggio were all in the car when it arrived at Missouri and Grand. Lazia was waiting on the street. They all walked quickly into the drugstore. Behind the prescription counter, a swinging door led to a large room with a bar on one wall and a big round table in the center. They found Floyd and Richetti inside, standing nervously against a windowless wall.

"Are you going to be able to make it?" Lazia asked Floyd.

For an answer, Floyd picked up a machine gun from the table, hefted it with his injured left arm, and pointed, not too far from the line of mobsters.

"I think so," he said softly.

"Stay close to them," Lazia loudly told his boys as he threw a smile at Floyd and Richetti. "If anything happens, go the limit."

But as the group crossed the street, Lazia called Charley Gargotta back for a private word. "Don't pay no attention to what I said in there," he whispered. "That was for Floyd's benefit. If anything comes up, go the other way."

LaCapra's story was riveting, rich in detail, colorful in characters, and sprinkled with virtually every murder and kidnapping over the previous ten years. And names, lots of names. He even fingered the young intern who secretly treated Floyd, a man who was the first Italian-American doctor in Kansas City and later head of a large local hospital. Within the Bureau, LaCapra's story became a sensation, especially as other evidence seemed to bolster his basic themes.

When agents talked to Edward "Speedy" Wilhite in the Iowa State Prison in Fort Madison, for instance, he confirmed the outlines of what LaCapra said. The agents had, after all, brought a note signed by Jimmy Needles asking for Wilhite's cooperation. Wilhite began by telling the agents that "LaCapra, to my knowledge, has learned as much about the Kansas City massacre as anyone now alive."

Wilhite confirmed LaCapra's version of events surrounding the car and said he also had heard Scola's account of the massacre and its aftermath. He even claimed that Johnny Lazia had told him personally, just as Lazia had told LaCapra, about all the particulars. Yet, unlike LaCapra, Wilhite didn't want to flip completely for the federal agents. He didn't want to be known as a snitch. But he said, according to the report, the government got a lucky break in securing the information from LaCapra "as it is not generally known in the country, even in the underworld, who participated in the shooting."

The agents even showed LaCapra's lengthy written statement to Wilhite and asked him to affirm or deny it. He thought about it a long time, then backed away, saying Floyd had never done anything to him.

"I am not going to say whether that is right or wrong, but if I were in your shoes, and knew what I know, I would say that you have the Kansas City massacre solved," he said. Then he asked the agents to come back when the two men the government was chasing, Floyd and Richetti, were killed. With a friendly smile, he promised to have positive information about the case at that point.

That sounded very close to an endorsement of LaCapra's story, and Agents Trainor and Anderson were quick to tell Washington so. More good news came to the agents from Ohio. Both LaCapra and Wilhite had said that the Buick later turned up near Akron, badly burned and containing a corpse. Agents confirmed that the burned-out car indeed had been found several days after the massacre with the body of New York gangster Nathan Gerstein inside. He'd been shot in the back of the head. And a check of the odometer showed the car had traveled 1,700 miles since it was stolen— very close to their calculation of 1,655 miles from St. Louis to Kansas City to Cleveland to Akron.

Best of all was Floyd's shoulder wound. It fit perfectly with the bloody rags found in the attic of 6612 Edgevale. It looked like Wilhite was right about the agents having a "solution" close at hand. Maybe LaCapra did know more about the massacre than "anyone now alive."

Yet "alive" was an important qualifier. Sam Scola, after all, was now dead, murdered by the very men with whom LaCapra swore Scola had been so intimate—perhaps because, as LaCapra maintained, Scola had known too much; or perhaps because Scola appeared to be getting a bit too close to the upstart Griffin-O'Brien-LaCapra faction. In any case, he had been taken for the classic gangland ride, so he would never personally endorse his own version of the massacre as recalled by LaCapra and Wilhite.

Griffin was dead too. And O'Brien was missing, presumed dead.

Others would verify the removal of the Buick from the garage, but its intended use as a Floyd-Richetti getaway vehicle depended on LaCapra's word, bolstered to a degree by Wilhite.

The Bureau's enthusiasm might have been dimmed by other considerations too, though there's no indication in the file that those mitigating factors, reasons for doubt, were ever thoroughly explored.

For instance, there's the Benaggio connection. There was no love lost between LaCapra and this man he accused of harboring Floyd and facilitating the massacre. In fact, it had been Benaggio who had appealed to Lazia when LaCapra muscled into Benaggio's Saratoga Horse Room. Benaggio got LaCapra's hands smacked and his pocket picked by Lazia. More important, it was Benaggio who focused Lazia's watchful eye on the Griffin-LaCapra operations long before their challenge to Lazia led to the boss's assassination. That's a lot of reason for a LaCapra grudge against Benaggio.

Then there's the question of why Lazia would have turned to an upstart rival like Griffin for help with someone as dangerous as Floyd at such a crucial time when the heat was so high. And if Lazia had asked, would he have allowed Griffin to turn him down so contemptuously?

What about Scola? If he was so much an insider, privy to all the secrets of the temple a year ago, why was he dead now?

And why would Johnny Lazia confirm "all the particulars" of such a sensitive and incriminating matter to distrusted rivals like LaCapra and Wilhite and Griffin?

Last, but probably foremost, is James "Jimmy Needles" LaCapra's state of mind. He was far beyond frightened. He was terrified.

"I am willing to do anything," LaCapra told the agents several times, according to a transcript of one long session. "I am willing to do anything you ask me to do."

Was he also willing, therefore, to *say* almost anything to save his scalp, even for a little while? A reading of the panicked transcript screams "Yes!" If LaCapra told the truth that night, it was only because it worked. If it took lies to hold the agents' attention, he would have told lies as quickly and as easily as truth.

In fact, he was absolutely right to be terrified. Jeff Rayen and two other KCPD detectives were already hanging around that Kansas jail. They arrived not long after the federal agents, demanding possession of LaCapra for return to Kansas City on an old robbery charge. However, Rayen and his friends showed little interest at all in the three men who had tried to assassinate LaCapra. So the local prosecutor, saying he "doubted their sincerity," refused to hand La-

Capra over. Rayen, frustrated and angry, resorted to uncharacteristic frankness.

"He's committed crimes against the Organization," Rayen told the small-town prosecutor.

The prosecutor still refused, but he quickly let LaCapra know what was waiting just outside the interrogation room. And LaCapra understood what that meant.

"If they take me, I'll go into the river," LaCapra pleaded with the agents. "I'll never get to Kansas City alive."

Hoover's men did help him for a while. They lodged a federal car theft charge against him and had him placed in Sheriff Bash's Jackson County jail, out of reach of the KCPD.

Meanwhile, the mob's hatred for LaCapra was bubbling over. Not only did they believe he, along with Griffin and O'Brien, had killed Lazia, they knew his elaborate confessions to federal officers had led to raids all over town. Benaggio's house at 1208 Admiral Boulevard was raided in search of the machine guns LaCapra said would be hidden in a secret subbasement and for traces of Floyd's presence. Agents found neither. A mob arsenal at 4th and Oak streets turned up empty when agents got there. Other mob haunts named by LaCapra were raided with similar negative results.

LaCapra recognized how hopeless his situation had become. Agents began receiving pathetic letters, some sent anonymously, pleading for protection for LaCapra. Some were written by his brother; most were written by Jimmy Needles himself. He wrote J. Edgar Hoover in November:

> The Kansas City Machine will stop at nothing to get me after the embarrassment I have caused them, no where can I get any help. I am helpless as a child, so I am calling on you to see that I can get some justice, in the name of God is their [sic] no more justice? . . . I have went through the torches of the devil.

He had only a little further to go. Not quite a year later, no longer under any protective wing and traveling under any name but his own, he wandered into Kingston, New York. Somebody caught up with him there. He was murdered and left on the street. The local sheriff, thinking LaCapra might be someone important, sent his fingerprints to Washington. No, the Bureau responded with unintended irony, "he is not wanted by us."

The local undertaker boxed him up and sent him home.

.   .   .

In the end, LaCapra's fascinating statements simply are not as definitive as they must have sounded to overworked and increasingly desperate agents in September 1934. Other facts were needed to fill out the picture. For example, Griffin and Wilhite themselves had a very strong previous connection to both Verne Miller and Frank Nash. In the first hours after the massacre, the agent in charge of the Bureau's St. Louis office alerted Kansas City to the possibility that Griffin and Wilhite were the shooters. It was, in fact, his first thought after hearing of the massacre.

The St. Louis office knew Griffin and Wilhite had passed stolen checks from a Nash bank robbery in early 1933 and knew Griffin was strongly suspected of pulling a bank robbery in Fairbury, Nebraska, along with Nash and the Barker Gang, only two months before the massacre. So Agent D. M. Ladd flatly stated that Griffin was close enough to Nash to want to be in on any rescue attempt.

And it turned out Griffin was even closer to Verne Miller, probably as one of the many visitors to 6612 Edgevale. He and Miller definitely pulled bank jobs together over a period of several years. So he had a double motive to participate.

Then there's the matter of the machine gun. When Bureau ballistics technicians eventually matched the impressions of a machine gun bolt on a shell casing from the Union Station Massacre scene to the impressions of a bolt on a shell casing from the Johnny Lazia assassination scene, Hoover's men first said the same machine gun was used in both killings. And they took the gun match as a link of the massacre to the Kansas City mob and, therefore, somehow to Floyd.

But there is serious question that the Bureau's lab was right on this one. After all, that machine gun, which was recovered from a Chicago lagoon, had been in the possession of the Valparaiso, Indiana, police department until it was loaned to the Crown Point, Indiana, police—and John Dillinger stole it—on March 3, 1934. That's a long time after the massacre.

The Bureau's senior field agents promptly marked off the match and, therefore, any links as a mistake. Hoover's headquarters, however, maintained that the match was in the bolt, not the barrels or the overall gun. Therefore, according to their most improbable theory, someone would have had to use the bolt in the Union Station Massacre and the Lazia assassination, then switch it with the one in the Valparaiso arsenal that Dillinger later stole in Indiana. Not terribly likely.

But even if the ballistics match was accurate, the connection between the Lazia assassination and the massacre could just as easily lead from Verne Miller to Jack Griffin. After all, if it's possible that the Kansas City mob somehow provided the machine gun for both jobs, it's just as possible (and more likely) that Griffin provided the machine gun for both jobs.

As to the Buick, it's clear from corroborating statements and many small details that someone drove that car out of the Trafficway Garage and on out of Kansas City a few days after the massacre. It wasn't Verne Miller; he drove the Chevrolet sedan used in the massacre on to Chicago, and it was sold part by part out of a garage in suburban LaGrange. But it could have been almost anybody else.

Or it could well have been Floyd and Richetti. They had to get out of Kansas City somehow. But simply driving that Buick ties them to the massacre only because LaCapra says it does. That

Floyd, with no car of his own, had someone's help leaving town is obvious. The question is, Who and why?

Neither the federal agents nor their leader were cursed with many of those doubts or questions in early September of 1934. They knew who they were after. And they were about to use and abuse a beautiful young woman to convince themselves they were right.

CHAPTER THIRTEEN

VI MATHIAS

VI MATHIAS was unshakable those first few months after the terrifying shootout at the Sherone Apartments. Though Hoover's men sometimes would question her all night and then all day, she would say nothing. When it was clear she was going to prison for harboring Verne, she said nothing. Even when the agents rushed to tell her Miller was dead, to lay out the worst gruesome details, to try to shock her into opening up about the days in Kansas City, she only cried softly and brushed them aside.

She offered exactly two pieces of information. Yes, the man in her Chicago apartment had been Verne Miller. No, he didn't have anything to do with the massacre in Kansas City. Only once did she even give away her frustration with the endless questions.

"I have never been a stool pigeon," she said through clenched teeth. "Not now or ever will I be a stool pigeon. I would not tell you anything I knew, assuming that I did know anything, that would get any of Verne's friends or enemies into trouble."

She and Bobbie Moore went to prison together, each sentenced to a year and a day in the Federal Prison for Women at Alderson, West Virginia, for helping the fugitive Miller. At least, they thought, they would have each other.

But the Bureau wasn't through with Vi Mathias; Hoover's agents never quit working on ways to crack her shell. And in early 1934, Agent Harold Anderson recruited a most unlikely ally in Leavenworth's Federal Penitentiary. Machine Gun Kelly, the tough-talking bank robber now serving a life sentence for the Urschel kidnapping, was trying hard to make new friends.

"Do you guys know it was Verne's habit to confide in Vi and even seek her advice?" he asked Agent Anderson one day, carefully laying the groundwork for his pitch. "I'll bet if somebody could get close to her, she'd tell the whole story. You would find out everything you want to know."

And Kelly had just the right secret operative in mind, the woman who had manipulated his own career and reputation for years. Kathryn Kelly was already a guest of the federal government in Milan, Michigan, serving time for her role in the Urschel case. It would be a simple matter, Kelly explained, for Kathryn to lead Vi to believe that she intended to escape and that she had the unrecovered portion of the Urschel ransom money hidden away.

"Kelly says that he believes that this would appeal to the cupidity [sic] of Vi and would do much to cement her confidence in Kathryn," Anderson reported.

"Once Kathryn and Vi get together on common ground," Kelly promised, "Kathryn will have no trouble in obtaining the story of the massacre."

Hoover bought it. Within a few days several women, including Vi Mathias, were transferred to Milan, apparently for bureaucratic reasons. The agents were careful to ensure that Bobbie Moore was not among them. They wanted Vi alone, with no other confidantes, when Kathryn Kelly made her play.

The plan fell flat. Vi wasn't particularly interested in a new best friend and certainly not a confidante with the reputation for self-promotion that Kathryn Kelly had earned throughout the underworld. She didn't tell Hoover's spy a thing.

Now it was getting personal. Hoover's well-documented inclination to see a devious woman behind every evil man came to focus on the Minnesota farm girl turned gun moll. As she came closer to finishing her prison sentence, Hoover put out the word that he wanted her questioned and cracked. His agents were to figure out how.

They didn't let him down. A few days before Vi's scheduled release, R. E. "Bob" Newby, a trusted headquarters supervisor, sent forward a plan he and field agents had worked out together.

He first passed along Agent S. P. Cowley's brags that the "success obtained at the Chicago office in questioning . . . women has been the result of holding them indefinitely and breaking down their mental resistance and obtaining from them, piece by piece, the story of their activities." That was the game with Vi—only in spades.

The plan called for Vi Mathias to be dumped on the steps of the Milan prison, no warning, no one to meet her, and no money. The idea was to have "Vivian released unexpectedly from the institution where she is held so that there will be no attorneys or any other person present at the time she is released, and that she then can be taken by agents of the Division and held incommunicado in some apartment where she can be thoroughly questioned concerning the massacre case," Newby explained.

She would not be arrested, Newby said, because there was nothing with which to charge her—and she had already served her prison time. She would simply be . . . well . . . taken.

If that sounds remarkably like kidnapping, nobody pointed it out. Not only were there no objections to the plan, Hoover gave his resounding approval. Now they had to get the prison to go along. Agents D. E. Hall and Ray Suran approached John J. Ryan, superintendent of the prison, and Ryan said he would cooperate fully with whatever the Bureau wanted.

At 8:30 P.M. on September 18, 1934, Vi Mathias was escorted out the front door of the prison farm and left standing alone on the front steps. But not for long. Agents D. P. Sullivan, Hall, and Suran grabbed her, put her into a waiting car, and headed toward Detroit. They "proceeded by unfrequented roads," meaning they lost any potential tails, and ended up at 12134 Lincoln Avenue, Detroit. Suran and Sullivan had rented the apartment earlier, stocking it with food and supplies for a long siege.

They would need their supplies. Though alone, with no idea where she was, and surrounded by a stream of federal agents night and day, Vi held out. Sullivan and Suran started the grilling, and when they got nowhere Hoover sent in fresh interrogators. No one will ever know exactly what went on in that dark and secret place, but it could not have been pretty. No reports of the actual interrogation have survived, only reports of the results. What *is* known is the mood in the Bureau at that time, as illustrated by what was happening in different parts of the country to two other massacre figures. In all three simultaneous situations, the pressure to produce was tremendous.

Richard Galatas, the Hot Springs fixer who started the conspiracy that led to massacre, was finally run to ground in New Orleans while Vi was being held incommunicado. Agent Anderson flew down from Kansas City, but he did not immediately get the information Washington wanted from Galatas. Headquarters was in no mood to be patient.

"I informed Mr. Clegg [a D.C. supervisor] that I am very much disappointed in the information that Anderson has obtained," Edward A. Tamm, a senior supervisor, wrote in a memorandum for Hoover; "that we sent Anderson down from Kansas City and he has been there since yesterday afternoon and they haven't got anything yet; that what we want is a good vigorous physical interview."

Lest there be any doubt what "a good vigorous physical interview" meant, Tamm followed up with another memorandum to the director the next day.

> I called Mr. Vetterli at St. Louis and told him that we need a substantially built agent in New Orleans for a few days; that in looking over his list, I was wondering if he could spare Bush for a few days. Mr. Vetterli stated this would be satisfactory and I told him to have Bush report to Dwight Brantley at the St. Charles

Hotel in New Orleans; that he is not to go any place else but to the St. Charles Hotel. I told Mr. Vetterli to wire me as soon as possible the hour of his arrival in New Orleans so that I can relay it to Mr. Brantley. I stated that the agent does not have to identify himself to anyone but Brantley; that he should go there and get in touch with Brantley.

Galatas later complained in court that he had been tortured, but the Bureau emphatically denied it.

A couple of days later, Fritz Mulloy was pulled off the streets by Hoover's agents. Though Mulloy's family protested that he had disappeared, probably kidnapped, the Bureau said it had no idea where Mulloy might be. In fact, he had been spirited to Chicago, where Agent Sam McKee was about to get very busy.

"McKee can work on these people for the persuasive part," Tamm wrote Hoover.

Vi Mathias required a lot of McKee's "persuasion" before "breaking down," as Newby called it, and giving the agents what they wanted. She had disappeared from the steps of the prison on the evening of September 18. Through September 27, she had told them nothing at all. Agent Earl M. Black replaced Suran as chief inquisitor, but he got nowhere. Then, on the morning of September 30, Agents Black, McCallum, and Sullivan loaded Vi Mathias into a car for a fast ride to Chicago. It was time for her to meet McKee.

His "persuasive" skills worked within hours. By that night Vi Mathias finally signed a statement. For twelve days and nights she had been alone, lost, and in the hands of a revolving cadre of Hoover's angry young men—in their hands psychologically, almost certainly physically, and possibly sexually. Yet she had held out.

Neither Vi nor Mulloy ever talked about what McKee did to them. Galatas's allegations may be instructive; they may not. But his complaints read like pages of a torture handbook:

■ Denied sleep and rest for five days, not allowed to lie down during that time

■ Given no food first day and practically none thereafter for five days

■ Curtains always drawn in private apartment, held incommunicado

■ Threatened with death frequently

■ Confronted with guns constantly

■ Sat in stiff chair, manacled, against the wall

■ Mercilessly questioned, grilled, and interrogated for long, continuous hours by armed officers after being verbally assaulted, profaned, struck, cursed, and while suffering agonizing pains of hunger and mental distress

■ Told "You're going to tell us what we want to know," "You haven't any rights . . . till we finish with you," "I ought to kill you now," "We're going to get the story one way or another," "You could be found dead on the street and all we would have to say is you tried to run"

■ Told a "team" was coming to "get" a story if he didn't give it

■ Had statements reworded to suit agents

In any case, whatever Agent McKee brought to the Vi Mathias situation when she arrived in Chicago surpassed all that had gone before. Vi's statement, though loaded with detail, lacked any of her normal vitality. But it touched all the bases Hoover wanted touched, dovetailed beautifully with other evidence and theories, and nailed down the "solution" that Jimmy Needles LaCapra had offered.

She told them everything they wanted to hear. Pretty Boy Floyd and Adam Richetti were the shooters. She had seen them. She had fed them. She had served them coffee and beer after they staged the massacre at Union Station.

But she talked only after Hoover promised to keep her cooperation secret.

And the Bureau has kept that promise for over sixty years.

I Vivian Mathias [her statement began] *make the following voluntary statement to R. C. Suran and S. K. McKee, special agents of the division of investigation, United States Department of Justice, having been told I need not say anything, but that anything I did say would be used against me.*

She told about moving into the house on Edgevale where Verne Miller passed himself off as a salesman for the Educational Finance Corporation of Oklahoma City and went by the name Vincent C. Moore. She told about their friends, among them Frank Nash, known by her to be an escaped convict. And she told them finally about the massacre.

It all began, she said, about 5 P.M. on the afternoon of June 16, when she got a call from Fritz Mulloy. Mulloy was eager for Verne to get in touch with him, so she called the Milburne Golf Club where Verne was playing and asked them to have him call home. When he did, she told him to get in touch with Fritz Mulloy right away. About an hour later Verne came home, talking about Frank Nash being picked up by federal agents in Hot Springs. She assumed he got that information from Fritz Mulloy.

Verne left the house about nine o'clock that Friday evening, while she was putting her daughter, Betty, to bed for the night, but he didn't tell her where he was going. A couple of hours later, the phone rang. It was Esther Farmer calling from Joplin. She wanted Verne, but she was willing to leave a message.

She said that "that party" had left Fort Smith [Vi said in her statement]. *She told me the time the train left and I made a note for Verne on a piece of paper. I cannot now remember the time she furnished. Esther was the only person I talked to at the time of this telephone call.*

Vi went to bed, but she was hardly asleep when Verne returned. He told her to get Betty from her room and move her into their bed because he had brought some friends who needed a place to sleep. She did as she was told. Verne soon came to bed, sleeping with Vi and her daughter.

She didn't hear Verne leave the next morning, but about 9 A.M. he came into the bedroom and awakened her. He seemed agitated, telling her to get dressed, call Fritz Mulloy, and tell him to come over and get her and Betty. She sensed something was wrong, but she asked no questions. And she knew from past experiences that such requests were not unusual. She went to the Mulloys and stayed there until after breakfast, when Miller called and told her to leave Betty there and come back home.

The cab driver talked about some people being killed in a gun battle at Union Station just a few hours earlier, but she paid little attention to him. She made no connection between the shooting and Verne.

> On arriving home [her statement continued], *I found Verne and two men whom I had never seen before. Sometime during the day Verne told me one of them was named Floyd. He did not tell me the name of the second man. I have been shown the photographs of Charles Arthur Floyd alias "Pretty Boy" and Adam Richetti and recognize them as the pictures of the two men who were at our home with Verne. Floyd was in Betty's bed because of a wound he had in his left shoulder. I do not know how serious his wound was, but do know that no one was called to treat him. Verne had a small wound on his right little finger, but he did not tell me how he had acquired it. Verne told me that they had been to the station to get Frank; that there had been some shooting and that Frank had been killed. He also said Floyd had been wounded. I do not remember whether he said anything about any officers having been shot. I knew that he felt badly about the matter from the way he looked and talked.*
>
> *I went to the kitchen and prepared breakfast. Verne and Richetti drank some coffee and I took a cup in to Floyd. None of them cared for anything to eat.*

The four of us remained in the house during the entire day, which was June 17, 1933. Sometime during the day Verne remarked that he, Floyd, and Richetti had used his, Verne's, Chevrolet in making the trip to and from the Union Station. Floyd and Richetti remained in the bedroom all day, with the exception that Richetti came to the dinette a second time for coffee. I believe I took coffee to Floyd a second time. I did not have anything to say to either Floyd or Richetti about what had happened and they did not say anything to me.

Sometime after dark Verne left the house by himself. He was away for about an hour. I do not know where he went. After he returned we were talking in the living room when I heard someone walk onto the porch. Verne asked me to go into our bedroom, which I did. I at no time saw the person who came onto the porch and have never known his identity. I remained in the bedroom about twenty minutes. When I came out into the living room both Floyd and Richetti were gone.

During the day when the daily newspaper was delivered to the house Verne read the account of the shooting at the Union Station and remarked, after reading that five or six men had been involved, "That's what the newspapers can do." He stated at this time that only the three of them had been at the station.

Vi explained that she, Verne, and Betty stayed in the Edgevale house that Saturday night. And they lingered longer than they should have through much of Sunday. But late in the day a friend of Verne's, a local jeweler named Martin Schwartzberg, came by to drive Vi and Betty to Des Moines. Schwartzberg knew nothing of what had happened; he was just doing a favor for a friend.

Vi caught a night train out of Des Moines and met Verne the next afternoon, June 19, outside Madame Therese's dress shop at Harding Avenue and Cermak Road in Chicago. He took her to the home of fellow gangster Volney Davis in suburban Maywood. Two days later, Verne flew to New York City. She waited a day and then flew with Betty to her parents' home in Minnesota. She did not see

Verne again until he showed up at the Sherone Apartments in October just before the shootout.

Vi also told the agents about the premassacre visits to 6612 Edgevale by the Barker brothers, Alvin Karpis, Volney Davis, Frank Nash, and others. They often talked about their bank robberies, she said. As to the bloody bandages found by the agents in the attic, she said there could only be one explanation.

"It was her opinion," the agents wrote in their report to Hoover, "that any bandages or other medical supplies found in the attic after she and Miller departed from the bungalow would have been there as a result of the shoulder wound which Pretty Boy Floyd had suffered."

And one other vital addition: "It should be stated here that Vivian Mathias has advised that Pretty Boy Floyd did not drink any beer on the day of the massacre because of his wounded condition."

With that, about everything was covered. It explained why Richetti but not Floyd would leave a print on a beer bottle. It focused the agents, yet again, on a Floyd wound in the shoulder, going along with previous indications and especially LaCapra's account. And, as Tamm wrote to Hoover while the statement's ink was still drying, "This information, which I consider authentic, in view of Vivian Mathias's former association, definitely places Floyd and Richetti in Kansas City immediately following the massacre."

All in all, a very good week for Hoover's Bureau. Galatas's statement out of New Orleans confirmed the genesis of the Hot Springs end of the conspiracy; Mulloy's interrogation in Chicago pretty much locked up the Kansas City end of the conspiracy. Now Vi's statement, combined with LaCapra's, gave Hoover's men important new reassurance that they were on the right track in chasing Floyd and Richetti.

But this peace of mind had come at a price. Vi Mathias's bargain with Hoover would lock her words away, well out of the courts and off limits to the lawyers. Her information was to be held in strict secrecy; Hoover was very serious about that. Throughout the massive file, every reference to her statement repeated the admonition that in every respect it was to be kept strictly confidential. When federal prosecutors later wanted to renege on the deal, to "introduce the statement as a free and voluntary confession regardless of what might have been said to the woman," Hoover would have none of it.

"As we have given our word to her to keep the statement in strictest confidence," he told Tamm and others, "it was not my desire to break the trust."

When prosecutors came back with the argument that Vi's statement was "the basis of the entire case," Hoover's counter argument was that the point was bigger than Vi or even the Union Station Massacre case.

"If those statements were made under certain conditions and promises made by Division agents we should adhere to these statements, providing the defendants made good their promises," Hoover told Vetterli, "owing to the fact that if such were not the case, word would no doubt be scattered from coast to coast . . . making it exceedingly difficult for the division to work with the underworld in the future."

But Hoover's principled argument also had a very practical side. Mulloy and Vi Mathias had promised to plead guilty if Hoover kept their statements secret. So Hoover also was getting automatic victories in the courtroom. And he desperately needed victories—and the positive publicity they would generate—after so many setbacks in the Union Station Massacre case.

So agents made sure that even the mob didn't find out about Vi's statement and her cooperation with Hoover's men. If the mobsters had known, they almost certainly would not have provided the lawyer to represent Vi in the conspiracy trial. She actually consulted, much later, with agents to make sure her plea protected her cover.

In point of fact, however, Vi's statement and LaCapra's statements were not the hand-in-glove fit that agents wanted to believe.

LaCapra, for instance, had said with certainty that Floyd and Richetti were sheltered by Dominic Benaggio in the Bottoms, not by Miller in a house on the upper-middle-class South Side both before and after the massacre. And, though the agents tended to skip over it, LaCapra's first statements were that Scola came for the Buick almost a week after the massacre, not the next day when Vi said Floyd and Richetti left her home. Of course, both Vi and La-Capra could be somewhat accurate if Floyd and Richetti were first at Miller's Edgevale house and then moved to Benaggio's Bottoms hideout, but LaCapra, who claimed to know everything about the massacre, had said nothing about anything like that.

And then there is the whole manner in which Vi's "voluntary statement" was obtained. Matters of propriety, legality, and morality aside, there's the practical question of how much she was told, as well as asked, over those long days and nights in confinement. How much was she led by agents desperate for a "useful" statement? Could she have well understood, after twelve days, what they wanted and needed her to say—and simply said it?

In any case, the foundation was in place: the fingerprint, the wound, the car, and now the crucial eyewitness. If they could never put her on the stand to confirm, she would certainly never dare deny.

The solution, therefore, appeared to be in hand.

CHAPTER FOURTEEN

THE SOLUTION

J. EDGAR HOOVER had hoped to resolve the Union Station Massacre case the clean and final way, with the arrest and perhaps the consequent death of his two remaining nemeses, Pretty Boy Floyd and Adam Richetti. He had, after all, promised his wounded agent Joe Lackey that the killers would be "exterminated, and exterminated by us."

But that wasn't so easily done. For one thing, Floyd and Richetti were not cooperating. Despite rumors of sightings from Florida to Texas to Maine, agents could pick up no fresh trail. By early October 1934, the exasperated director was preparing to send a team of undercover agents into Oklahoma's Cookson Hills, where he believed Floyd to be. The agents would pretend to be rug salesmen, moving all over the region, from house to house, making friends and looking for clues. Just why Hoover thought rug salesmen would be any more welcome there than any other strangers in that most strange territory he did not say.

Hoover's men had a couple of other tools, too. Fritz Mulloy's kidnapping and interrogation by agents in Chicago had left him a changed man. Though agents would allow him to come back to Kansas City, load up with liquor, and protect his gangland reputation by telling friends and family he had been on a big drunk, they expected him to come through on his secret promise to pump friends in Kansas City for information and to put Floyd on the spot if at all possible. Mulloy, agents told Hoover, was now "willing to do anything he can, and he is in a better position to do some good than anybody else."

Finally, in the depths of the Depression, there was another tool—money. Though it was never made public, Hoover ordered his agents to circulate the word: "We will pay $2,500 to $3,000 for information furnished to us resulting in Floyd's apprehension." The figure reflected Hoover's frustration; only $500 had been paid for Underhill's scalp. And the method reflected the Bureau's tactics. "I don't believe we should tell it direct to police departments, but people we contact should know about it," Tamm wrote to Hoover.

Agents in the field got the message clearly, but the finality of it worried some of them. There had been concerns early on, voiced in Kansas City by Agent E. E. Conroy, that, since Floyd was not at that point indicted, "agents who effected [Floyd's] arrest would not be sufficiently protected, especially in the event that it should become necessary to kill Floyd in order to take him in custody."

Now the same sort of questions arose about Richetti. Hoover's mania for secrecy about the beer bottle fingerprint "match" meant that the Bureau had never even issued an identification order on Richetti. So as far as the public was concerned, the Bureau didn't even want him. And as far as the various states' laws were concerned, federal agents had no legal claim on him.

All that put the director in a quandary. If the Bureau didn't ballyhoo the search for Richetti, "it will be difficult," as Agent Tamm phrased it, "to later convince anybody of the facts" if Floyd and Richetti were "knocked off" by somebody else. On the other hand, "If the public knows about it and these people are knocked off, this will be a solution of the case."

In other words, if the Bureau wanted public credit for solving the Union Station Massacre case, it better grab that credit *before* some local sheriff or even Hoover's own agents killed Floyd and Richetti.

That argument, for the publicity-hungry director, was persuasive, but what he heard next was absolutely compelling. Agent

S. P. Cowley called Hoover from Kansas City, warning that the Kansas City Police Department had heard rumors of the Bureau's progress.

"He mentioned the fact that if the Kansas City Police Department should break the case it would spoil it for us," Hoover wrote in a memorandum to Tamm, "and Mr. Milligan [the U.S. attorney] is of the opinion that this might be done at any time."

That did it. No one was going to steal his Bureau's thunder. Two days later, at noon on October 10, 1934, J. Edgar Hoover, to all the capital fanfare he could muster, announced the "complete solution" of the Union Station Massacre.

"Verne Miller was identified as the leader of the gunmen," read the six-page, single-spaced publicity release, "and through exhaustive investigation it has been conclusively established that the other assassins were Charles Arthur 'Pretty Boy' Floyd and the latter's lieutenant, Adam Richetti. . . . Floyd," the announcement concluded, "was wounded in the skirmish and since that time has successfully remained under cover."

For the first time Hoover ordered preparation of an identification order on Richetti.

The public relations triumph was short-lived. Hoover's grand display of satisfaction turned into acute embarrassment before the week was out. In Kansas City and then around the country, newspapers picked up and repeated the stark, flat, biting message of Merle Gill, the ballistics expert who had been at the heart of the Union Station investigation from the first day:

"Pretty Boy Floyd had absolutely nothing to do with the massacre."

Gill blasted the Bureau's case from several directions at once, ripping viciously at the evidence Hoover thought he had laced together so well. Right off the top, Gill said, the Bureau had misled everybody, including him, about the most essential facts. And, the ballistician implied, those facts only emerged after Hoover's "announcement" triggered leaks from disgruntled local police officers.

"Until yesterday I was unaware that Chief [Otto] Reed had a 16-gauge shotgun with him when he was killed," Gill wrote the Bureau, with a timely copy to the *Kansas City Journal-Post*.

Knowledge of the existence of that gun, especially in a lawman's hands, would have been crucial information for the man who was putting together the ballistics case and doing all the ballistics matches. Yet the Bureau had maintained even to Gill that the lawmen carried only two 12-gauge shotguns that morning. Therefore, when exploded 16-gauge shotgun shells had been found on the massacre scene, their presence had demanded an assassin armed with a 16-gauge shotgun. In fact, the exploded shells were much of the reason the number of shooters was generally assumed to be four, not three.

But that was just the first link in Gill's devastating chain of logic. If Chief Otto Reed, sitting in the rear seat, was armed with and fired a 16-gauge shotgun, Gill reasoned, that would explain one exploded 16-gauge shell casing found inside the agents' car, on the floorboard by the rear seat, and a second that rolled out onto the running board when the door was opened. And those two shots might explain Frank Nash's fatal wound to the back of his head.

And Hermanson's wound through his head.

And Caffrey's ball bearing in the brain.

But Gill offered more than speculation and circumstance. "The next day after the shooting we opened up an unexploded 16-gauge case in the Justice [Bureau] office and found three ball bearings in place of the regular buckshot," he wrote to the Bureau.

The unexploded 16-gauge shells, he said, had been taken from the pockets of Chief Otto Reed. And the ball bearings, a special load created personally by Reed, matched the ball bearing from the brain of Agent Caffrey.

Gill laid out his alternative scenario succinctly:

Chief Reed, sitting in the left rear seat, fired the shot that took off the back of Nash's head, one of the ball bearings from that same shot also killing Caffrey. Then Chief Reed fired a second shot to his right, hitting detective Hermanson as he stood or crouched between the cars.

Hoover was outraged but also knocked off balance. He concealed the balance problem, but he let the world know of his outrage. He had never liked using Gill, as he was quick to remind his subordinates. "Well it serves us right for ever having dealt with Gill," Hoover wrote on the bottom of the first memorandum about Gill's disloyal theories. "I always opposed it and never approved the turning over of the evidence to Gill."

He was right about that. As early as March 20, 1934, Hoover scrawled on a "personal and confidential" letter about the ballistics evidence, "I deplore the use of private detectives or of experts upon government work. Our K.C. office should never have gone along on this set-up without getting our approval."

But there Hoover's memory was a bit selective. In fact, his Bureau had leaned on Gill from the start and paid Gill for his services, and a letter requesting one of those payments the previous October bore Hoover's personal stamp of approval and his signature.

On June 17, 1933, the date of the commission of the above Federal offense, the services of a ballistic expert became immediately necessary. The urgency of the investigation, which was started on that day, required the immediate expert examination of bullets and firearms. As the investigation continued, the comparison of other suspected firearms with those originally analyzed became necessary, and it was essential that the investigation be conducted by the same person, who was familiar with the investigation from its inception.

At the time this investigation was begun, there was no other qualified person available to perform these services. So far as could be ascertained there was no person regularly employed under the Civil Service rules and regulations of the United

States whose services could be immediately procured for the necessary examination, and the exigencies of this case would not permit of any delay incident to ascertaining the availability of such a person.

As the spitting match between Gill and the Bureau degenerated, Hoover would chastise his Kansas City office for not depending from the beginning on the Bureau's own technical laboratory. But Hoover forgot that the Bureau's laboratory was only created a few months before the massacre and was hardly in full swing when the Kansas City office needed it. In point of fact, the legendary Charles Appel had started Hoover's laboratory in 1932 with only a single microscope and a lot of ambition.

Nor was the Hoover-Gill clash rooted only in technicalities and evidence. Both men craved publicity. Actually, both depended on it, in one way or another, for their success. In Gill's case the link was more direct. As a private practitioner, receiving public credit for his findings led to more jobs, more money, greater fame, and more success. A few years later, when the Bureau lab was thriving and performing work for police departments all over the country, Gill would complain that "examinations free of charge by the Bureau tend to put private ballisticians such as himself out of business," and he would threaten to appeal to Congress about the unfairness of it all.

Ultimately, of course, Gill was right. Hoover and the Bureau did want private ballisticians out of the game, just as they wanted the Bureau to be the dominant force in laboratory analysis of all things criminal. That technical and laboratory supremacy, once achieved, remained in place, unthreatened for half a century, at least in the eyes of the public. Today virtually all ballistics and forensics experts in America are tied to the Bureau by methodology, by standards, and, most important of all, by training. The FBI course is a must for such specialists.

So the Hoover-Gill animosity festered long before Gill's outburst.

When Gill went public, however, people were far more interested in what Gill was saying than in why he might be saying it. And what they heard, especially in Kansas City, was that Hoover's "complete solution" was dead wrong.

If Hoover was thrown off balance, it was because none of this shotgun talk had been part of the Bureau's ongoing investigation of the massacre, at least as far as the official file reveals. There is no record of agents in Kansas City opening the unexploded 16-gauge shell, though Gill said that Agents George Harvey, Gus Jones, Reed Vetterli, and others were present. In fact, the only previous references to the lawmen's shotguns indicate that they were both 12-gauge and that neither was fired at all.

Agent Joe Lackey, in his report to Hoover immediately after the massacre, said he never fired his shotgun. "Agent had his shotgun pointed toward the floor, and the muzzle of the gun was between the driver's seat and the door, the butt of the gun being between agent and the [left] side panel," Lackey wrote. "In endeavoring to cock this gun to fire, it jammed, and to the best of agent's recollection, he was unable to get it unjammed during the proceedings."

Agent Frank Smith was just as precise about the dead Chief Reed, the only other lawman with a shotgun: "Chief Reed was instantly killed."

Lackey soon would take it a step further. In a memorandum to the director, the field agent would say Gill's conclusions simply were impossible. "The writer is thoroughly familiar with shotguns and is positive that the gun carried by Chief of Police Reed was 12-gauge," Lackey wrote. "The writer was sitting within two feet of Chief of Police Reed in the rear seat at the time that this shooting took place and has always been firmly of the opinion that no shots whatever were fired by Chief of Police Reed and certainly that no shots were fired from a shotgun by Chief of Police Reed."

These are very strong denials. Unfortunately none of them are true.

Lackey lied. Knowingly and with intent, he lied to Hoover about the shotguns, just as he would lie again and again in the months ahead.

The Reed gun was indeed 16-gauge. In fact, Reed's descendants in Oklahoma still have his shotgun, a treasured family heirloom since its return after the massacre. It is a 16-gauge pump with a sawed-off barrel. The author has seen it. The shotgun recently has been inspected and test-fired by the Kansas City Regional Crime Laboratory. The chain of ownership and possession is irrefutable. There simply is no doubt that 16-gauge shotgun is the one Chief Reed took to the massacre.

Nor is there any possibility that Lackey made an honest mistake. He would one day testify in court that the reason he knew Reed's gun was a 12-gauge was because Lackey gave Reed the ammunition with which Reed loaded the gun. That is a physical impossibility. Because of the size of the barrel, a 12-gauge shell cannot fit into a 16-gauge gun. The shell is too big.

But Lackey wasn't alone in the lies. Vetterli personally handed the shotgun over to Reed's family shortly after the massacre, and Gus Jones, an old hunter and firearms expert, had inspected the gun closely. Both were present when Gill opened the 16-gauge shell in the Bureau office and found the telltale ball bearings that morning. Yet neither said anything; neither acknowledged any connection between the recovered shell and Reed's gun. Neither filed a report on the shell, the gun, or the gauge to Washington, at least not a report that has survived.

Nor did any of the other agents in the Kansas City office.

Nor, for that matter, did Gill make an issue of the recovered 16-gauge shotgun shells until he got miffed when Hoover gave him no credit in the grand solution of the case. Yet Gill admitted he knew all along that the ball bearing–laden 16-gauge unexploded shells came from Reed's pockets. And he knew a ball bearing had been retrieved from Caffrey's head. Even if he did not learn until after Hoover's announcement that Reed actually carried a 16-gauge shotgun, he must have wondered early on about the remarkable coincidence of ball bearings in Reed's pocket and an identical ball bearing in Caffrey's head. And he had said nothing about any of it.

The file shows that Hoover launched a mini-investigation around the shotgun controversy. Agents were sent to Reed's family, and the 16-gauge shotgun eventually was inspected and test-fired for the very private record. Those agents confirmed from family members that Reed packed his own load for police use, three large ball bearings. In short, the agents could find no way to discredit Gill's theory of the massacre. The 16-gauge shotgun had been there, and it could have done all the things Gill claimed it had done.

Nor did the other technical evidence help the Bureau much. Consider Frank Nash's wound, for instance. In the early days after the massacre, Vetterli had reported that the jacket of a .45 slug fired from a machine gun was found stuck in the blood of Nash's scalp, thus bolstering the theory that the huge hole in his head had been caused by a machine-gun bullet. That story had been repeated often. In fact, however, the file reveals that the shell jacket actually was found lying in the front seat beside Nash. So there is nothing to indicate the massive hole in Nash's head was inflicted by anything other than the most logical source of such wounds—a shotgun blast from the rear at very close range.

Regarding Frank Hermanson, the file throughout the case is consistent. Though the autopsy does not say precisely what weapon caused the wound, ballistic and Bureau reports repeatedly assume he died from a shotgun blast that entered above his left ear and exited the back of his head. Certainly the wound was most consistent with a shotgun blast.

And Caffrey's case leaves no room for doubt, since the ball bearing fell out of his brain.

There were other troubling indications. The roof post on the Plymouth parked to the right of the agents' car clearly showed evidence that a projectile had ripped into it from the direction of the agents' rear seat. There was the second ball bearing, matching Caffrey's, found on the floorboard of the Plymouth, about where the driver's heel would be.

And there was the front windshield of the agent's car, the glass blown outward, away from where Nash sat in the front seat, scattered fragments of glass all over the hood. Like a blast from the backseat, perhaps.

Finally, there was the troubling business of Chief Reed's wounds. One was a machine-gun bullet in the head, easily enough explained by the firefight. But the other was a .38-caliber slug. Nobody but lawmen were even suspected of carrying .38s that morning. If the Bureau's "solution scenario" was correct, Miller and Floyd were armed with machine guns, and Richetti had two .45-caliber automatic pistols.

So who shot Chief Reed in the right temple with a .38?

Gill's theory was that Mike Fanning, the KCPD officer who ran out of the station and fired blindly into the massacre scene, in fact hit Otto Reed. But that's unlikely, since Reed sat in the backseat facing south, away from the station and Fanning. More likely a bullet that would hit Reed in the right temple would come from the west or southwest, where detectives Grooms and Hermanson had stood talking with Agent Vetterli.

Gill's very public theories rattled the Bureau. After fourteen months of massacre talk, after a highly successful campaign to stir public outrage toward gangsters and empower Hoover's Bureau, after a carefully orchestrated effort to paint the agents as outgunned underdogs, they now heard Merle Gill saying that four of the five dead had lawmen's bullets in their brains. Worse, he was saying that he could find nothing that in any way linked Pretty Boy Floyd to the shooting, and that he believed Floyd had absolutely nothing to do with the Union Station Massacre.

If correct, Gill's conclusions ground Hoover's "solution" into dust. So the Bureau might have been expected to suffer convulsions, not just mild shivers. Yet for all the subsequent Bureau correspondence about shotguns and gauges and ball bearings, and for all the agents rushing around to find technical answers and file reports, the scope of the Bureau's response was remarkably limited. The inquiry focused on guns and shell casings and test firings— things.

Crucial evidence apparently had been overlooked or misinterpreted or falsified or mishandled by Hoover's own agents, yet there was no discernible Bureau effort to figure out who had done what.

No fixing of blame; no retribution.

And there was no effort at all to correct the official record. When Lackey testified months later at the Richetti trial that the lawmen's shotguns were both 12-gauge, no one contradicted him, though they all by then knew the truth. The lie stood.

Yet as sensational as they were, Gill's revelations would soon be forgotten. That technical/ballistics/evidence debate was about to be overtaken by events.

Pretty Boy was on the move.

CHAPTER FIFTEEN

THE KILL

Though Charles Arthur Floyd kept a wife and son tucked among his extended family in the Oklahoma hill country, he really had but one true love in his life, the dark and pretty Juanita (who sometimes went by the name of Beulah), one of the classy Baird sisters of Kansas City. And why not? She had stayed with him through the five dangerous years since he left the Missouri State Penitentiary at Jefferson City in 1929, had shared hideouts and tourist camps with him all over the country, and even had taken a bullet meant for him one particularly bad morning in Ohio.

And she brought along an equally dark and even prettier sister, Rose, who shared her taste for the exotic and adventurous. So when Floyd and Richetti retreated into the shadows after the massacre at Union Station, they quite naturally took the Baird sisters with them.

But it was hardly the adventure the girls had anticipated when they hurriedly left their Toledo, Ohio, apartment. Rather, they found themselves with two ultra-cautious men who stayed indoors, spent little money, and brought them only crushing boredom laced, too often, with high anxiety.

For over a year, from September of 1933 until October of 1934, the four nearly hibernated in Apartment 821, at 8 Eighteenth Street, in Buffalo, New York. Almost from the first day, the five rooms and single bath began to close in on them. When the girls finally talked about it to agents, after promises of confidentiality, there was more than a hint of bitterness.

"Charlie and Eddie [Richetti] remained in the apartment constantly," Rose would complain later, "with the exception of a few trips. They would leave at night and be gone one or two days, sometimes two or three weeks."

The jaunts brought money, for all the good that did. They'd spend it only on food and rent. No nights out on the town. No entertainment. Richetti, often drunk, grew increasingly morose. "He always walked around with his head down, saying nothing, which aggravated us," Rose recalled. "During the time we were in Buffalo we barely got along and did not have any extra money, staying in the apartment practically all of the time."

The only visitors were poor kids from the neighborhood asking for food or money, but neither Floyd nor Richetti ever answered a knock at the door. Instead, they would walk quietly into another room. They didn't pick up guns or act afraid, Rose said, but they always left the room. Conversation often lagged, mostly because there was so much the boys would never discuss. Past jobs, for instance, were off limits, even though Juanita still bore a long, ugly bullet scar beneath her hair from one of those escapades. Rose said she knew Floyd and Richetti were wanted for the Union Station shooting, but she also knew better than to ask. So the massacre was never mentioned at all.

The caged atmosphere in Buffalo fit not at all with the Floyd myth seeping out of the Cookson Hills. Though Floyd was far away, in and around upper New York State almost all the time, rumors of his desire to surrender floated daily among the hill people, most of the rumors probably started by worried family members. Ex-cons, small-town lawmen, even a Fort Worth radio preacher wanted to talk to the agents about Floyd's plans to surrender. Everybody wanted promises that the Pretty Boy would not be gunned down the first time he showed his face.

Hoover's men talked to one and all, even tried to cultivate some of the would-be negotiators. But the director was wearing out with it all. On June 23, 1934, he told Pop Nathan, his deputy director, to drop everything else and get Pretty Boy Floyd.

"I would, therefore, like to have you take this case as a personal special assignment and proceed with it until Floyd is apprehended or surrenders," Hoover wrote in a memo for Nathan. At that point, even before LaCapra or Vi Mathias had talked to agents, Hoover clearly was convinced Floyd was their man, saying that "from the information received Floyd was an active participant in the Kansas City Massacre."

Two months later, Hoover was completely fed up with the surrender talk. He wanted action, and he wanted it quickly.

"I do not desire . . . to waste any more time in these suggested or attempted [surrender] negotiations," Hoover wrote to Nathan, now working out of the Oklahoma City office. "It is my desire that Floyd be apprehended at the earliest possible date and accordingly I desire that vigorous and intelligent steps be taken in all field offices to assure his apprehension without further delay."

Just in case Nathan still didn't get the point, Hoover made his feelings perfectly clear.

> I am disgusted at the attitude of lethargy which is being assumed in this case, it appearing to be the idea of the various special agents in charge that all that it is necessary for them to do is to wait for something to happen in some other district which will develop leads in their district. As I have indicated heretofore, I desire that appropriate contacts be made to assure the Division's receiving reliable information concerning Floyd's whereabouts; that appropriate inquiries be made wherever desirable; that mail covers, telegraphic covers, and telephone taps, if necessary, be utilized to bring about Floyd's apprehension. In short, I desire that the Division's representatives locate and cause the apprehension of Floyd rather than remaining in a semi-waiting attitude.

Floyd could not have been so isolated in Buffalo that he did not know how much the heat had been turned up in his old Oklahoma stomping grounds. In fact, his staying so deeply underground indicates that he knew precisely how badly Hoover wanted his hide. Hoover's announcement of the "complete solution" to the Union Station Massacre was big news from coast to coast.

Yet something was afoot. For months, when the Baird girls talked wistfully about the Middle West, they drew no response at all from Floyd and Richetti. "We were all more or less homesick, but Juanita and I were the only ones that mentioned that we would like to go home," Rose said.

Then one day that attitude abruptly changed. Maybe Floyd's homesickness got to him; maybe he believed when his relatives said it was possible for him to surrender. In any case, he and Richetti suddenly asked the girls if they were ready to go home and gave them $350 to shop for a new car. The sisters bought a Ford V-8 at the Niagara Motor Company, signing the papers as Byrl West of the 400 block of Rhode Island Avenue. The next day, October 19, 1934, happy for the first time in months, the four were on their way, a machine gun riding comfortably between the two front seats.

Floyd was driving when their luck turned bad. About three o'clock in the morning in the rain and fog just inside the eastern edge of Ohio, the powerful Ford slipped out of his control and slammed into a telephone pole. No one was hurt, and the damage to the car wasn't extensive, just enough to make it inoperable. Floyd told Juanita to hike into the next town, East Liverpool, and bring back a wrecker; Rose would wait with the car. Floyd and Richetti, not willing to sit like a couple of ducks alongside the road, wrapped a blanket around their machine gun and disappeared into the nearby woods.

Juanita found a wrecker, all right, and she got the car towed into town. But the garage wasn't a Ford dealership, and the mechanic had trouble getting parts. The sisters could do nothing but cool their heels in the waiting room. It was almost noon when they heard that the local sheriff had scared up a couple of guys in the woods outside of town.

"I figured it was Charlie and Eddie," said Juanita, who had to wait several more hours, until almost dark, for the car to be fixed. When it was ready, the sisters did the prudent thing.

"We told the garage man we were going to Chicago," Juanita said, "and we headed straight for Kansas City."

■   ■   ■

It should have been a good plan. All Floyd and Richetti had to do was keep out of sight, catch a little sleep, and wait for the girls to get back with the car. But they managed none of it. When Joe Fryman walked from his house down to Silver's Switch about ten o'clock that Saturday morning to talk to his son about hauling a load of coal, there they were, two guys sitting on a blanket, out in the open. They didn't belong, and they didn't look right.

Well, Fryman thought to himself, as he veered off the path, I can always say I'm looking for pears.

That would have been a lot better line than what Floyd came up with when Fryman stopped to talk. "Just out taking pictures," the Pretty Boy said. "We had a couple of girls, but we got lost."

With blankets, overcoats, cushions, and no sign of a camera, they didn't much look like they were taking pictures, Fryman thought, and they didn't seem at all worried about the girls they'd "lost." Something wasn't right. He walked up the hill to Lon Israel's farm and told his friend about the strangers down below. Israel didn't much like it either. So they hurried over to Frail's Store and called J. H. Fultz, the police chief in Wellsville.

William Irwin and a man named Potts were in the police station at the time, so Chief Fultz casually asked them to come along. On the way he told them two suspicious characters were hanging around Lon Israel's place. They left their car at the fork of the road and walked up the hill till they met Israel on the path. They'd just started toward the strangers when someone came around a tree.

"Maybe this is one of the fellows," Chief Fultz said. Then he saw the gun pointing at his midsection.

"Hands up, all of you. Get 'em up," Floyd ordered.

"I won't put 'em up," Fultz said, his bluff apparently throwing Floyd off stride. "I am going down to the brickyard to work, and I don't see why I should put my hands up."

Fultz walked on toward Floyd despite repeated orders to stop. He finally did, when the muzzle of Floyd's .45 automatic touched his stomach. "You wouldn't shoot a working man, now would you?" Fultz taunted Floyd.

The theatrical exchange continued as Floyd fell in behind the single file, led by Fultz, then Potts, Israel, and Irwin. Twice Fultz started to reach for his pistol, and twice Floyd threatened to kill him on the spot. Floyd told them repeatedly not to run; Fultz's response was a sarcastic, "Nobody's going to run, nobody's done anything to run for."

Richetti was lying on the blanket when the little troop arrived. Fultz again applied the bluster. "Hello, buddy, how are you?" he said to Richetti. "You seem to be taking it pretty easy."

But Pretty Boy had had enough. "Don't let him kid you. Shoot him. He's an officer," Floyd snarled.

Richetti tried to do just that. Pulling his own .45 automatic, he, Fultz, and Floyd fell into a blistering close-order gunfight, with the others caught in the triangle. Yet for all the bad intentions, nobody hit anybody. Fultz even reloaded, at least getting two shells into the cylinder, and chased Richetti down the hill.

"I ran him I believe one hundred feet and he jumped down over something, I guess a fence, and ran down into a house about one hundred feet ahead of me, and just as he went to go in the door, I cut loose at him again," Fultz later told a coroner's inquest. "The bullet hit about two feet from him, even with his shoulders. When that shot was fired he threw up his hands and said, 'I give up,' and come running back towards me, pleading not to kill him. He said, 'For God's sake don't shoot me, don't kill me, I am done.'"

But Pretty Boy wasn't. As Richetti and Fultz disappeared over the hill, Floyd went the other way, up the slope toward Israel's house. But the others—Israel, Irwin, and Potts—got there first and armed themselves with Israel's generous supply of shotguns and ammunition. When Floyd showed his face over the ridge of the path, he was met with a torrent of buckshot, some of it lodging in his back as he dived into a ditch. He let off one burst with the machine gun and another with a handgun, wounding Potts in the arm; then he literally headed for the hills.

Within the hour, Adam Richetti was locked up tight in the Wellsville jail, and Chief Fultz took time to look through the W. J. Burns Company catalog of Wanted posters. Picture number nine jumped out at him. "He is a fellow anybody can recognize by his picture," the chief said later.

The word went out. Charles Arthur "Pretty Boy" Floyd was on the ground and vulnerable. When similar word had passed, incorrectly, a few days earlier, Tamm had made the Bureau field agents' worries clear to Hoover. "Mr. Cowley [in Chicago] stated that he has an idea that these people up there will have Floyd bumped off and Richetti too," Tamm wrote; "that he hopes we can beat them to it as he would rather get them first than have them bumped off before we get to them."

But J. Edgar Hoover, so close to a dramatic rescue of his "complete solution" to the Union Station Massacre, wasn't about to let locals get in his way.

■   ■   ■

Hoover's men descended on Wellsville by rail, road, and air. By midnight, twenty-four agents from offices as far away as Kansas City were stomping all over the town—and all over the sensibilities of the local establishment. The agents swept into the hill country like royalty, some by charter airplane, demanding not just to question Richetti but to take custody of him. And they were told, not so politely, to go straight to hell.

"Mr. Purvis telephoned in from Wellsville and advised that the situation there was rotten, that the Chief of Police has refused to turn Richetti over to us, that they are going to prosecute him there,"

Hoover wrote in a memo to Tamm. "Mr. Purvis says they are all a bunch of hardheaded men."

If Hoover was furious when his name and reputation didn't sway the small-towners, he was livid when his threats of Bureau retaliation brought little more than laughs. Purvis and his men started finding themselves locked out of rooms, excluded from strategy meetings, and generally the butt of jokes. First Purvis used the phony name of Marshall so as not to overwhelm the locals; then he was insulted when he produced his real name and impressed absolutely no one.

"Mr. Purvis suggested I call the Attorney General . . . the governor. . . . I told him I had in mind calling the mayor myself," Hoover wrote. That didn't work either.

The problem was that everybody wanted the limelight, and the locals had it for the moment. Worse, without local help, the federal agents had little chance of regaining center stage by finding the slippery Floyd in the hills and hollows around Wellsville. Agent reports are full of references to Bethel Chapel, Sheep Skin Hollow, Echo Dell, Bell School House, and a dozen other places unlikely to turn up on any map. More than once, local posses came upon bands of Hoover's men wandering the back roads without a clue as to where they were heading. And in the middle of it all, Hoover had Clyde Tolson diving into Bureau records.

He was already planning retribution.

"Will you please inquire and ascertain whether the Chief of Police of Wellsville, Ohio, is on the list to receive releases from the Division and what participation that police department takes in the work of our Identification Unit," Hoover instructed Tolson. "In view of the attitude of the authorities at Wellsville last night and today in connection with the Pretty Boy Floyd and Richetti matter, I want to make certain exactly what cooperation we are extending to them."

And, he might as well have added, what we can withhold from them in the future.

. . .

Floyd's flight from Israel's farm took him deep into the woods. He was traveling light now; he had dumped the machine gun in the backyard of a nearby house. It was too heavy to carry, he would tell someone later. In fact, the stock had broken, and it was almost useless.

No one knows where he slept that Saturday night, probably in an untended barn. And he stayed out of sight all day Sunday while local lawmen and citizens and the growing army of federal agents combed the area. No one turned up anything.

By noon on Monday, he was on the move again. He had not shaved and had eaten little. And he didn't know where he was going. His wandering took him to the Peterson Brothers Garage, where Ted and Bill Peterson were about to leave for an appointment across the river. They had to be there at one o'clock, and that was only twenty minutes away. They were surprised when a man in a dark suit and no hat drifted in from the woods.

"He wanted to know if we would be interested in taking him to Youngstown, said he would give us five dollars," Bill remembered. "We asked him why and he said he went up past the brick works in a car hunting duck and had went over the hill and broke the machine. We said we didn't think so, and he raised the price from five dollars to ten dollars and pulled the money out of his pocket, and I judge he had six or seven ten-dollar bills."

In the midst of the Great Depression in an exceptionally depressed region, that was enough to make anybody wonder. The Petersons were about to take Floyd up on his offer when their mother stuck her head out the door of the nearby house.

"You can't take this man to Youngstown and get across the river by one o'clock," she said, flashing them a look they well understood.

"We knew she didn't want us to go," they admitted later.

What they did not know at that moment was that their bright-eyed younger sister had spotted a rust-colored stain on Floyd's pants just below the belt. Blood, she suspected, and she told her mother. That's when the maternal glare passed their way.

George MacMillen, sitting nearby, had too much time and no mother to look after him. He took Floyd's offer. They were only a few miles down the road when he regretted it.

"I suppose you know who I am," the stranger said. "I'm Floyd, Pretty Boy. The radios are flashing it all over the country."

MacMillen, who had no radio and read only the funnies, didn't know any of that, but he knew he had made a bad deal. When they came to a hill, he slyly pulled out the choke and waited for his old Ford to die.

"We're out of gas," he told Floyd. "You push."

Floyd tried, but with a little discreet coaxing from MacMillen, the car ended up in a nice deep ditch. MacMillen thought he was safe until Pretty Boy spotted a nearby farmhouse. The farmer, whose name was Baum, was not much help.

"I ain't got no gas."

"How about draining some out of your car?" Floyd asked.

"Can't," he said. He'd tried that before.

Then could he take them to get gas? That he could do. The three loaded into Baum's 1929 Nash sedan. They had only gone a mile or so when Floyd, sitting in the rear, leaned forward.

"Old man, I have a little surprise for you," he said, resting his gun on the front seat. "I want you to keep on driving. . . ."

Frightened beyond good sense, Baum took him at his word, driving so fast that the accelerator stuck and the Nash almost crashed into the side of a hill. Then, a few miles farther, Floyd exchanged shots with a Wellsville policeman, shooting out the other car's windshield and rear window and leaving MacMillen and Baum even more terrified. Baum slammed on the brakes, swerving the Nash into a ditch.

Floyd ran into the woods. Baum ran directly toward the protection of the policemen. They promptly shot him, though his wound was not serious. Word passed along the roads, and lawmen flocked to the area. The net was closing quickly.

Floyd was about exhausted, but he still managed to be polite when he stumbled up to the Conkle farmhouse, where Ellen Conkle was alone while the men worked the fields. He knocked gently on the back door about three o'clock that afternoon.

"He asked me if I would give him something to eat, said he was hungry and lost, that he and his brother had been out hunting and he had got lost from his brother," Ellen Conkle said later. "I asked him what he was hunting and he said squirrels or just anything he could find."

She told him he surely wouldn't be hunting squirrels at night, and he tried again. To be honest, he said, he had been drinking, and had too much.

"I got him a lunch and he asked me if I would get him some meat; he said he was hungry for meat," she recalled.

Floyd told her it was a meal "fit for a king" and gave her a dollar. She said she didn't want to take anything, but he insisted. He had been there over an hour by then, and she was getting scared. She doubted his story, mostly because she could tell he had not really been drinking. She didn't know the law was looking for him, but she knew she was afraid of him. And she didn't want him in the neighborhood overnight.

"I look like a wild man," he said, as if reading her mind, when he had finished his meal. She didn't respond. "Well, I feel just that way," he said. "I'll go down to the car and wait."

He had asked her to take him to Youngstown, but she had said she couldn't. Then he asked if anyone else in her family might. Knowing her brother was nearby husking corn, she said he might take Floyd.

A while later Steward Dyke, Ellen's brother, walked up to the house, with his wife, Florence. Floyd was fiddling with the keys in Dyke's car's ignition. "Hello, there," Floyd said, startled. "Your sister said you would take me to the bus line."

Dyke said he didn't think he could do anything like that, mostly because he had other plans for the evening. But the truth was he just didn't like the look of things. So he walked away. Florence, unaware she faced a killer, reached in front of Floyd, pulled out the car keys, and dropped them in her pocket.

When Dyke and his wife came back out of the house a few minutes later, Floyd was still there. As they walked toward their car, he approached them again.

"My wife, she didn't like it very good because he was going to ride, and I said for her to get in the backseat," Dyke recalled. "I walked around to the front of the car to talk to him."

Dyke could see over Pretty Boy's shoulder that something was terribly wrong. Two cars slipped partway up the long lane, then parked as though to block the path. A passing policeman had spotted Floyd pacing; now he was leading a posse to investigate.

"I knew something was going to happen, I didn't know what," Dyke said. "I had a stranger, and I knew their business, so I figured the worst was yet to come."

He told Floyd, who had not seen the police, to get in the car. Then Dyke backed up and wheeled the nose down the lane. "As soon as I run back of the building and they all stood across the lane there, he saw them at the same time. He juked [sic] down beside me, and said, 'Drive behind that building, they are looking for me.'"

When Floyd pulled out his gun, the grizzled farmer leaned over and unlatched the door.

"Get out, you son of a bitch," he said. Floyd obeyed.

The line of lawmen, four East Liverpool policemen and four federal agents, moved toward the house as Floyd ran behind a corn crib. Some of the lawmen could see his feet as he raced from one side to the other, as if trying to decide which way to run. Finally he chose, sprinting across a clover field toward the crest of a small hill.

The officers fired in unison, shotguns, machine guns, and pistols spewing lead at the Pretty Boy.

"As he ran, he ran with a swinging kind of half-turning motion as though he was trying to dodge or sideslip any shots [that] were fired at him," recalled Glenn G. Montgomery, a local policeman.

"As he came to this high raise, he kind of cut sideways like he had been hit in the arm. His arm kind of flew like one of the shots had hit in his arm. He ran on and fell on his left side."

Chester Smith, another East Liverpool policeman, reached him first, grabbing his right wrist and twisting the .45-caliber automatic out of his hand. Montgomery was right behind, pinning his other arm down. Herman Roth, also a policeman, reached in and grabbed a second .45-caliber automatic from Floyd's belt.

Floyd was down but not out. At first he wouldn't admit who he was. But soon he said, "Yes, I am Floyd."

Hoover's men ordered the police officers to step back while they questioned Floyd about the Union Station Massacre. According to both policemen and agents, they got only a string of profanities for their efforts.

A few minutes later, Pretty Boy Floyd was dead.

CHAPTER SIXTEEN

THE DOUBTS

Hoover basked in the warm media glow, fielding reporters' calls personally and making a quick record of what he told each. To Pat Frank, *Washington Herald*: "Come by, we'll give you a picture." To the *Pittsburgh Sun Telegraph*: "A squad of our agents had engaged in a gunfight with Floyd . . . and mortally wounded him." To Conner of the *Chicago Daily News*: "We will have nothing to say about who fired the fatal shot."

In fact, the generalities were far more comforting to both the director and the public than the whole truth would have been. And Hoover always tried to puff up his Bureau, like the bit about the "squad of agents" that ignored an equal number of local policemen who were also on the scene. He did not point out that Purvis and his boys had been lost when the East Liverpool policemen took them in charge and led them toward the Conkle farm. Nor that it was an alert local policeman who spotted Floyd pacing in the Conkle yard.

There were some other interesting aspects that never got much play either. For instance, Ellen Conkle, her brother Steward Dyke, and his wife, Florence, never heard anybody shout for Floyd to halt before the blaze of gunfire. Nor did any of the three, all caught between Floyd and the officers but off to the side, ever see Floyd pull out a gun or wave one around. They said he simply ran from behind the corn crib and started across the clover field.

"I suppose he got five hundred feet away before he dropped," Ellen Conkle said.

Hoover made no secret of his glee at Floyd's death, especially considering the circumstances. Just minutes after the killing, he reported the details to Acting Attorney General William Stanley, as they were passed along from Purvis by telephone from the field. Hoover's memo for Tamm outlined the crux of that conversation.

"I remarked that we were glad to be able to shoot Floyd ourselves because he killed one of our men," Hoover wrote.

Many years later, serious question arose about just how literally Hoover meant that statement. In 1979, Chester Smith, one of the East Liverpool policemen on the Conkle farm that day, told the world he wanted to unburden himself of an ugly secret he had carried since 1934. In short, Smith, then an eighty-four-year-old retired police captain, stated that Hoover's men executed the helpless, wounded Floyd while the local policemen stood by and watched.

Smith agreed with other accounts about Purvis and the agents telling the police officers to back away while they questioned Floyd, who was wounded but sitting up in the clover field. Purvis's first question, according to Smith, went to the Bureau's obsession: "Were you in on the Kansas City Massacre?"

Floyd, according to Smith, spat back, "I wouldn't tell you son of a bitch anything."

Smith said Purvis then told Agent Herman Hollis, "Fire into him!" Hollis, according to Smith, raised his revolver and shot Floyd in the lower chest at point-blank range.

Smith said he later asked Purvis why they had murdered Floyd, and he got only a terse response: "Mr. Hoover, my boss, told me to bring him in dead."

Even after all those years, Smith's allegation brought rage from the Bureau. Besides the official denials, W. E. "Bud" Hopton, the only living member of the Bureau's squad that day, called the story "absolutely false." Herman Hollis wasn't even there, Hopton said.

That was true. Agent Hollis, who would be killed a few weeks later in a gunfight with Baby Face Nelson, was down the road with other agents at the moment of Floyd's death. The agent closest to Purvis, physically and otherwise, that afternoon was Sam McKee, the "persuasive" inquisitor from the Chicago office. Though Hoover never wanted any single agent to take credit for Floyd's fatal bullet, agents would whisper years later that McKee had fired it, though they always claimed it was from a machine gun at several yards.

Yet it is interesting to note that of the four East Liverpool policemen present that day in the clover field, Chester Smith was the only one *not* questioned under oath at the coroner's inquest and *not* represented by some sort of post-killing statement in the Bureau files. Then there's the fact that the remaining three policemen couldn't agree on the most historic moment they would ever experience, exactly when Pretty Boy Floyd breathed his last.

> Chief H. J. McDermott: "I told the police officers that was guarding him to carry him from the field to the road for the purpose of putting him in the ambulance, and he died on the way out to the road."
>
> Officer Herman Roth, when asked if anyone was sent for help after Floyd was shot: "Yes, Mr.—the head man—Purvis, and so by that time he had died. I would say maybe about twenty minutes, and Smith and I, and I believe Curly [Montgomery] carried him from where he fell and laid him under a tree in this lady's yard until Mr. Purvis came back."
>
> Officer Montgomery, when asked if Floyd died right there on the ground: "Right there where he went down. After he died and was dead we carried him from there over to the main highway and laid him down on a grassy spot there under a tree until we got the car straightened up to bring him."

But the most intriguing question of all is just why Chester Smith would want, nearly on his deathbed, to take himself out of the category of folk hero and into that of murder conspirator. If not a guilty conscience, what compelled him at the end of his life to sully his own reputation with family, friends, and the rest of the world?

In truth, Smith's revelation was not the surprise in East Liverpool that it was everywhere else. Though the national news media finally picked up the story in 1979 and *Time* magazine ran a detailed account, the Bureau-bullet-in-the-chest version of Floyd's death had been circulating around eastern Ohio for years. Smith's mea culpa only added an official public stamp after the other three local policemen were dead and gone.

■   ■   ■

Not all the Bureau's disappointments were forty-five years in coming. Hoover's moment of triumph was tainted immediately by the continuing disinclination of the Wellsville police to give up Richetti. Hoover, who knew something about sour grapes, thought he saw it at work here.

"The thing is, they were the heroes yesterday and we are today," he wrote to Tamm. "I instructed Mr. Cowley . . . to let the press know that this Wellsville crowd is blocking one of the most important investigations of the country."

Beyond that, there was Hoover's personal problem with Melvin "Little Mel" Purvis. By the time Floyd was shot, Purvis, nicknamed because he never reached five feet in height, had fallen out of favor with the director. In no small part, that was because he had come *into* favor with the American people. Purvis had become a mini-hero when he led the squad that killed John Dillinger that summer outside the Biograph Theater in Chicago; he became a figure to rival Hoover himself when the Dillinger episode was highlighted on the *G-men* radio show. But J. Edgar Hoover liked anonymity, not competition, from his agent underlings.

So when a few weeks later it turned out that Purvis had played a major role in the Floyd killing, Hoover took no chances. First, he ordered Purvis to leave East Liverpool that very night, have "the curtain pulled down on the publicity," allow no photographs of himself to be taken, and "go to Chicago and lay low" in his apartment for several days. Under no circumstances, according to Hoover's orders, should Purvis talk to the press.

For good measure, Hoover later made Tolson call Purvis in Chicago and ask if Purvis had fired any shots in either the Floyd or Dillinger episodes. Purvis responded that he had not fired at all in the Dillinger capture, but he had fired six times with his .38 revolver at Floyd. Hoover apparently expected Purvis eventually to try to take credit for Floyd's demise, which Purvis in fact did a few years later.

The director was downright livid when the nation's newspapers quoted Purvis at length the morning after Floyd's death. Worse yet, several reporters wrote that Purvis had said Floyd lived long enough to deny any role at all in the Union Station Massacre. That brought a Hoover explosion, and Purvis tried to cover his tracks with a story that both contradicted the reporters and disagreed with all the later testimony from policemen and civilians who were at the Conkle farm.

Headquarters supervisor Bob Newby expressed the director's displeasure to Little Mel two days after the shooting:

> I called Mr. Purvis's attention to the fact that he is extensively quoted here in the East, from East Liverpool, as to the conversation which he had with Floyd, in which he, Mr. Purvis, stated to the papers that Floyd made a statement that he was not in the Kansas City Massacre. Mr. Purvis emphatically stated that he did not even talk to Floyd and he made no statement to the newspapers to this effect. I asked if any of our men talked to Floyd and made such a statement. Mr. Purvis replied that Agent McKee talked to Floyd, but he [McKee] did not make a statement to anybody. Floyd stated to Mr. McKee: "I won't tell you nothing," using some very obscene oaths.

Finally, the local folks knew a good souvenir when they saw one, so nobody in Wellsville wanted to give up the .45-caliber automatic pistol Richetti carried when he was caught or the machine gun

Floyd had thrown away. Hoover's protests that the guns were crucial evidence in "the most important investigation" in America had little effect. So the director significantly increased the stakes. He was prepared to invade.

"I told Mr. Cowley that I felt he should gain possession of the guns, even if he might have to use force, that they are needed in our case," Hoover wrote in a memo to Tamm.

The Wellsville authorities soon relented, turning the two guns over to the Bureau. A short time later, Hoover showed that he too knew a good souvenir when he saw one. After a few test firings for ballistics purposes, one of the two pistols taken from Floyd, part of what Hoover had called crucial evidence, was permanently altered, rendered inoperable, and its ballistic characteristics forever destroyed by a welder's torch.

Hoover then had it mounted in his personal trophy case.

■   ■   ■

The director's vanity would only complicate what was about to become a very confused ballistics situation. Hoover had been correct to assume Floyd's .45s were potentially crucial to the Union Station Massacre investigation. After all, Merle Gill in Kansas City and the Bureau's own ballistics experts in Washington had been examining bullets and shell casings for months, hoping to make a match to those found at the massacre scene. And, though the Bureau lab people maintained they had a match in the bolts of the machine guns used in the Lazia assassination and the massacre, there was no ballistics evidence to tie a Floyd, a Richetti, or even a Verne Miller gun to the massacre scene.

At that point, immediately after Floyd's death, relations between Merle Gill and the Bureau were far beyond strained. Hoover had ordered agents to have "nothing to do with Gill" and to avoid him absolutely after Gill's public assault on the director's "complete solution" to the massacre case. That was not easy, since Gill was handling the massacre evidence for both the state and federal prosecutors in Kansas City. When Assistant Attorney General Joseph B. Keenan said the U.S. Attorney in Kansas City wanted to use Gill's expertise and asked the director's opinion on that, Hoover wrote in a bold hand across the bottom of the letter: "Certainly I would never recommend this man Gill for anything. Tell the Criminal Division that in view of our experience with him we could not conscientiously concur in any recommendation where his [Gill's] veracity or integrity is involved."

It wasn't just a personal grudge fight between Hoover and Gill either. Charles Appel, the renowned founder of the Bureau's technical laboratory, had given Hoover a scathing analysis of Gill and his methods on August 11, 1934, well before Gill's October broadside against the Bureau. Appel wrote the report shortly after Gill had brought his massacre ballistics evidence to Washington for Appel's inspection and then taken it back home. The report deserves quotation at length.

> In the examination of the above cartridge cases the examiner [Appel] observed that each and every one has been sprayed with a white solution which is sometimes used by photographers to assist in the photographing of metals in order to cut down the highlights and smooth out the surface. In their present condition the examiner considers that these specimens are not suitable for introduction in evidence because of this disturbance of their normal condition. A photograph of the base of one of these shells no doubt may be made to look more natural by this means as many of the small abrasions and irregularities in the surface will not appear. When it is considered, however, that these photographs are enlarged a great many times so as to show microscopic marks made by the gun, and the identification is to be based on this, it can readily be seen that such a method renders any photographs taken for any examinations made after the deposit of this material on the shells absolutely without value. *Unquestionably, such evidence would be ruled out of Court if it should be discovered* [emphasis added]. This method of spraying metallic objects is one

regularly employed by photographers and is not, therefore, in itself questionable. It is only when it is applied to microscopic work that it becomes improper.

The writer has on several occasions observed photographs made by Mr. Gill, has been unable to reconcile these with specimens which he has seen, and *now that the method by which they were made has been found could not approve any identification in any part based upon photography* [emphasis added].

In short, Appel trashed Gill's methods and conclusions and their admissibility in court.

That knowledge must have thrown Hoover into something of a quandary a few months later when, in the aftermath of Gill's attacks and Floyd's death, Gill suddenly announced that he had matched a test casing from one of the Floyd pistols to a casing recovered at the massacre scene.

Gill obtained the test casing secondhand, through the Missouri State Highway Patrol, since Hoover forbade any direct Bureau–Gill contact. What really mattered, however, was that Gill now said he had what Hoover's men had wanted from Day One—a ballistics link between a specific gun, in this case Floyd's, and the massacre.

But this breakthrough came from the very man whose scientific methods had been judged by the Bureau in August to be unfit for any court. Quietly, Hoover had his own ballistics people take a look at Gill's alleged match, and the results were not encouraging. Since Gill would not part with the original shell casing, Hoover's men had to work from photographs, and the same old problem arose. In their view, the photographic evidence was inconclusive and Gill's methods rendered the alleged match meaningless.

That left R. B. Nathan, the agent in charge in Kansas City, impaled on the horns of a dilemma. On the one hand, he was trying to build a case against Richetti; on the other hand, he knew his own Bureau's top scientists wouldn't accept the ballistics match. He laid out his problem on January 15, 1935, in a letter to Hoover.

State and federal prosecutors, Nathan said, wanted to use Gill's testimony, especially the critical part about the ballistics match. But they wanted the Bureau's stamp of approval.

"I will appreciate further advice as to whether I should advise [U.S. Attorney] Milligan of the fact that the Division's experts do not consider Mr. Gill's identification in this matter accurate," Nathan wrote.

Hoover's response was political, not professional. He wrote Nathan on January 18:

> With regard to the identification of shells from this [Floyd] gun with a shell found at the scene of the [Union Station] Plaza murder reported by Merle A. Gill, you are advised that the Division Laboratory has been unable to concur with the findings of Mr. Gill on the basis of the photographs submitted. It is suggested the U.S. Attorney may care to request that the original shell, found at the scene of the Plaza murder and reported by Gill to have been identified, be submitted to the Division to determine if the Division Laboratory can, from the original evidence, confirm the findings of the expert Gill. In this request the Division Laboratory would have the further advantage of having available the bolt on the gun itself for comparison with the alleged markings on the shell. Should the findings of the Laboratory be in accord with those of Gill, the services of a Laboratory expert might be desired by the U.S. Attorney to collaborate the testimony of Gill regarding the identification. Should the experts of the Laboratory be unable to confirm the findings of Gill, the information would undoubtedly be of value to the U.S. Attorney in planning his prosecution.

In other words, Hoover had the gun and wouldn't give it to Gill, and Gill had the shell casing and wouldn't give it to Hoover. And Hoover's experts were unwilling to accept Gill's highly suspect match without a look at the original specimen, the shell casing.

On one level it was a petty turf battle. Clearly, Hoover wanted his technical laboratory to be *the* authority, and he wanted *his* experts testifying in any upcoming court case. Local police forces all over the country would become very familiar with this haughty, superior attitude over the years ahead.

On another level, if you were Adam Richetti, for instance, or an impartial judge sitting behind a high bench, the Bureau's negative conclusions as to the accuracy, legal admissibility, and worthiness of Gill's findings would be a crucial piece of evidence in a capital murder case.

But it all died right there. Prosecutors were told little and defense lawyers nothing at all about the Bureau's disdain for Gill's competence in general and his match specifically. The Gill ballistics match has stood, unquestioned, to this day.

For those who study J. Edgar Hoover, however, that is no particular surprise; withholding crucial evidence at the expense of those he believed to be criminal was not unusual for the director. Anthony Summers, in *Official and Confidential: The Secret Life of J. Edgar Hoover*, pointed out that on the strength of handwriting evidence Kathryn Kelly went to prison for twenty-six years in the Urschel kidnapping case.

"Only in 1970 did it emerge that the Bureau had suppressed its own handwriting expert's report, which flatly exonerated Mrs. Kelly," Summers wrote.

■　　■　　■

The Bureau's keen anticipation of Floyd's death or capture had been deeply rooted in what the agents were convinced they would find when they finally brought the killer down. Both Jimmy Needles LaCapra and Vi Mathias had described in great detail the wound to Floyd's left shoulder, and Vi's house on Edgevale even had provided the bloody dressings for that wound. Now the wound's still-fresh scar would justify their faith in their two witnesses and provide ironclad proof that Floyd had been involved in the massacre.

But the scar wasn't there. The wound had never been there.

The two doctors who performed the autopsy were precise about Floyd's wounds, thorough in every detail, including the facts that "the ends of the fingers have been made smooth, apparently by some abrasive substance" and "there is a tattoo mark on the palmar surface of the left forearm composed of the face of a nurse within a rose." But they did not mention any shoulder wound.

When Hoover caught that omission, he demanded an explanation from his subordinates. Tamm tried to put the best possible face on the autopsy report.

"The body of 'Pretty Boy' Floyd was not examined by medical experts with a view to determining whether he had been wounded in the left shoulder, as reported by Vivian Mathias, for the reason that it was overlooked at the time," Tamm wrote Hoover on January 18, 1935, nearly three months after Floyd's body was buried.

That simply would not do. Bob Newby, writing for Hoover's signature, fired off a letter on February 9, 1935, to the Detroit office, which was responsible for the Ohio area, demanding clarification and further investigation.

> From a review of the findings of Doctors Roy C. Costello and Edward W. Miskall it has not been possible to determine whether the examination of the body of Floyd reflected a gunshot wound in the left shoulder which may have been inflicted approximately fifteen months prior to his death.
>
> With this end in view you are instructed to have an agent interview Doctors Costello and Miskall to determine whether they recall having observed such a wound on the body of Floyd. This matter should receive the immediate attention of your office.

Dr. Costello was unequivocal in his response. Agent William Larson wrote back to Hoover nine days later that "Dr. Costello advised agent that there was absolutely no indication of a gunshot wound in the left shoulder of subject Floyd at the time he examined him."

There was no doubt in the doctor's mind. The fact that the autopsy report did not state that there was no wound, he said, was totally understandable. They recorded what was there, not what wasn't there.

"With regard to the fact that a review of the findings made by himself and Dr. Miskall failed to indicate whether a gunshot wound appeared in the subject's left shoulder, Dr. Costello advised that these findings represented only the positive facts brought out by the examination," Larson wrote. "He stated further that he had since talked with Dr. Miskall concerning this matter and it was also that doctor's opinion that there were no scars at all appearing on subject's left shoulder indicating a possible gunshot wound."

When Larson reported that Dr. Miskall was doing post-graduate work at Tulane University in New Orleans, an agent was dispatched to question him about the wound. But the second doctor was just as adamant.

"Dr. Miskall advised Agent Olson that he did not observe any indication of a gunshot wound in the left shoulder of subject Floyd at the time he examined him and that he would answer that question a positive way, *that there was no sign of a gunshot wound on the left shoulder of subject Floyd* [emphasis added]," Agent D. W. Magee wrote Hoover from New Orleans. "Dr. Miskall recalled having discussed this case with Dr. Costello sometime after the examination, and that it was their opinion that there was no mark indicating a gunshot wound in the left shoulder of subject Floyd."

But if there was no wound, what did that do to the believability of Vi Mathias's statement, which a U.S. attorney had called "the basis of the entire case"? Agent Sam McKee, the inquisitor in the Chicago office, was dispatched immediately to again interview Vi Mathias. Suddenly, her story changed dramatically.

The bloody rags found in the attic at 6612 Edgevale really had nothing to do with Floyd at all, she now admitted. Rather, they had been used to treat Earl Christman, member of the Barker Gang and a participant in the Fairbury, Nebraska, National Bank robbery not long before the massacre. Christman had been shot in the chest during the robbery, she said, and brought to the Miller house a few days later by other members of the gang.

She described how he had been delirious, calling for his mother and saying he was going to die. "The odor from the wound was obnoxious," she told the agents.

When Christman finally died after three excruciating days, Fred Barker and Alvin Karpis carried him out while Vi left the house to avoid the stench. She wasn't sure what they did with the body, but she thought Fritz Mulloy had something to do with it, maybe burying it in his garden.

One other thing, she added: "That was the only part I wasn't telling the truth about in the first statement."

Considering the emphasis Hoover and his men had placed on the left shoulder wound and its prominence in Vi's original version of what happened, it was a crucial lie, whether she told it to avoid "harboring a fugitive" charges, as she claimed, or because she had picked up what the agents wanted to hear and fed it right back to them during the Chicago interrogation. In either case, it must have caused Hoover to wonder about the veracity of his star, if supersecret, witness.

But it didn't even end there. Over the next few weeks Hoover's dedication to a Floyd shoulder wound was jolted twice more when first Juanita Baird and then her sister Rose swore that Floyd had had no shoulder wound or any other wound during those long months of hiding in Buffalo. And both professed intimate knowledge of Floyd's body in all its particulars.

Yet, in a greater sense, none of it much mattered anymore. Miller was long dead. Now Floyd was dead. The people on the Joplin and Hot Springs ends of the conspiracy really didn't know anything about the identities of the shooters Miller had recruited anyway. And Vi Mathias and Fritz Mulloy were locked into Bureau-designed sweetheart arrangements that would keep them from ever saying anything publicly about the massacre if they wanted to avoid long jail terms.

That left only Richetti. And Hoover knew Richetti eventually would have to come back to Missouri to face what prosecutors were calling a "gilt-edged" case for killing the highway patrolman and county sheriff near Columbia two days before the Union Station Massacre.

Then, quite unexpectedly, somebody else confessed to those two killings. Richetti was off the hook.

With their case privately falling apart, Hoover's agents would have to do it the hard way. They would have to convict Adam Richetti in a very public court.

CHAPTER SEVENTEEN

THE TRIAL

NOBODY REALLY wanted to take Hoover's case against Adam Richetti public, including J. Edgar Hoover himself. Though pride made him fight like a demon to get Richetti into federal custody after the Ohio capture, the director had no illusions about the strength of the murder case his agents had built.

"I also called attention to the fact that we could not prove our charge [against Richetti] without using some witnesses whom we do not want to use," Hoover wrote to Tamm, recounting a phone conversation with Agent S. P. Cowley. "I also pointed out that the evidence we have is evidence from a confidential source [Vi Mathias] that we would not want to use publicly."

But Hoover wasn't the case's only skeptic. After Richetti's capture, federal prosecutors in Kansas City could see court coming down the road at them. So they renewed their pleas to renege on the Bureau's promise to keep Vi Mathias's statement confidential. Let's introduce it as "a free and voluntary confession regardless of what might have been said to the woman," the lawyers proposed at a December 1934 planning session in St. Louis.

Hoover still wouldn't go along with breaking the promise, but he authorized agents to take another run at Vi Mathias. Hoover wrote in a memo to Tamm:

> I told Vetterli [by then agent in charge in St. Louis] that, in view of the above facts, it would be desirable to have a re-interview

with Vivian Mathews [sic]; further, that I had no objection to the presence of the United States Attorney at this interview; that the interviewing agents should endeavor to get her permission to let the statement be introduced at the trial. I told him that, in view of the fact that the statement which she gave us was of utmost importance in the case.

Vi Mathias, however, had no intention of going public. She held Hoover to his deal. And that soured Maurice Milligan, the U.S. attorney in Kansas City, who then refused to bring Richetti to trial on any federal charges at all.

That left only the Missouri state courts, dominated like everything else in Kansas City by the Pendergast political machine and political maneuvering of every sort. Hoover warned his agents to be careful with whom they had dealings in those courts.

"It should also be ascertained immediately whether the Prosecuting Attorney is a man of honor or whether he is a crooked politician."

In fact, Michael O'Hern, the local assistant prosecutor who would have to carry most of the load in taking the case to court, was a successful and very savvy lawyer not thrilled with his assignment. Less than a month before the trial, he told Hoover's agents flatly that he was "inclined to doubt the fact that there is sufficient evidence to convict Richetti."

However, his boss, the extremely political W. W. Graves, knew his own political bosses wanted the whole ugly matter closed and forgotten. So they would go to trial.

If the evidence wasn't there, they would make up for it in razzle-dazzle. Graves named Russell Boyle, a seasoned prosecutor, to work with O'Hern and himself, in no small part because Boyle knew his razzle-dazzle. The first thing Boyle did was ask Hoover if Agent Harold Anderson, slick, smooth, and thoroughly familiar with all aspects of the case, could sit at the prosecution's table during the trial. Boyle should have known better; Hoover never let his men shine individually. Better, the director said, if Anderson sat with the other agents.

But that was almost as good. Throughout the four-day trial, the first row behind the prosecutors was filled with Hoover's men, even then looking neat, clean, and as identical as Bureau haircut and dress code regulations could make them.

That was just the beginning of the show. Boyle tried to pile every gun related to the case in front of him, directly in the jurors' line of sight. Anytime anyone mentioned a machine gun, Boyle would pick up Floyd's Thompson and parade it around the courtroom, until the defense's objections finally got to the judge. Only then was Boyle's arsenal set aside.

Boyle and O'Hern would also take full advantage of the Bureau's well-rehearsed fingerprint presentation, complete with huge charts, pointers, coordinated markings, and lots of big words. In those early days of fingerprint testimony, the Bureau men already knew that this bit of showmanship went over well. E. P. Coffey, one of Hoover's scientists, had written an enthusiastic report about his men taking the presentation before a Kansas City grand jury.

"In response to numerous questions from [the prosecutor] and various members of the jury, [lab expert] Mr. [Jerry] Murphy described at some length the work of the technical experts of the Division's Single Fingerprint Section and Identification Unit," Coffey wrote with obvious pride. "The jurors appeared to be quite interested in the identification work and quite convinced of the soundness of fingerprint evidence."

Fingerprint evidence, after all, was not then the common thing it is today. Richetti's jurors would be made to feel, correctly, that they were in on something exciting and novel in law enforcement.

Then there was the other side of the courtroom. Richetti, thoroughly sober for the first time in years, sat forlorn and disconnected much of the time, talking only infrequently to his two court-appointed lawyers. Ralph Latshaw, none too articulate and prone to bluster, led the defense team. He was supported by James Daleo, a young lawyer with deep roots in the Italian community. Both men objected frequently to the prosecution's antics, but for the most part they were overruled and overlooked by the judge.

Ray G. Cowan, as revealed by the transcript, was not a judge troubled by nuance or inclined to break new legal ground. It didn't take him long to throw out the defense's motion to quash Richetti's indictment on the grounds that no "Negroes, Italians, Japanese, or Chinese" were included in the pool from which Richetti's grand jury indictors were selected. Besides, those kinds of discriminatory omissions really wouldn't have been news to any Kansas City judges or to many citizens. Judge Cowan was more inclined to get to the meat of things and let the prosecutors present whatever they liked however they liked. More than once he told young Daleo to sit down and shut up.

The trial opened June 13, 1935, just four days short of two years after the bloody massacre. Officially, though five men died that morning at Union Station, Adam Richetti was charged only with the first-degree murder of Frank Hermanson, one of the Kansas City detectives. So from the beginning it was the trial of a support player for the murder of another support player. Not surprisingly, both often would be crowded offstage by the real stars of the drama. Boyle seemed never to get it straight that there weren't defendants, plural, meaning Richetti *and* Floyd, despite objections from the defense and admonitions from the bench. And Latshaw wanted to blame all Richetti's transgressions on the Pretty Boy.

For most of the first day the jurors were entertained by tales of guns and gangsters, much of it having nothing at all to do with Richetti's guilt or innocence. Nash's colorful background was explored in detail. So was Pretty Boy's capture and death, recounted with dubious accuracy by Agents Purvis and McKee.

But Sheriff Jack Killingsworth, the man Floyd and Richetti had kidnapped in Polk County, very clearly placed Richetti in Kansas City only hours before the shooting, and J. H. Fultz, the Wellsville,

Ohio, police chief, tied Richetti to Floyd and a shared machine gun sixteen months later. At the end of the first day, the circumstances were in place for the jury. They still needed hard proof, and that came when Hoover's men trooped to the witness stand the following morning. Tom Baughman, one of the Bureau's most senior administrators, testified that he had taken delivery of the two .45-caliber automatic pistols that Purvis and field agents had taken off Floyd's body. Lab specialists testified to test-firing them and sending the test shell casings and bullets to Kansas City.

That set the scene for Merle Gill's big day. After testifying that he had examined 11,000 guns and 20,000 bullets over the eight years since becoming a professional ballistician, Gill got down to business. Yes, he had examined the test shell casings sent from Washington, and, yes, he had compared them to a shell casing Detective Tom Higgins had given him from the scene of the Union Station Massacre.

Yes, he said, it was his opinion that the two were fired from the same pistol.

Ironically, he brought along an enlarged photograph, reflecting precisely the sort of technique that made Hoover's scientists reject his match entirely. Yet Hoover's ballistics experts sat right there in the courtroom and listened quietly; none raised a hint of objection. As far as the jury was concerned, there was nothing but unanimity among the experts.

In truth, Gill was closer to Floyd's automatic at that moment than he ever had been or would be again. Hoover had let the prosecutors have the guns only so they could be part of Boyle's showboat arsenal to impress the jury. But the guns were to be used only for display. Gill was to keep his hands off.

Agent E. E. Conroy, in charge of the Kansas City office, had known full well the director's hatred for Gill when he broached the subject of bringing the crucial weapon out for the trial.

"In connection with the above I had in mind particularly the possibility that there might be an attempt on the part of the office of the Prosecuting Attorney to secure possession of weapons for the purpose of having same turned over to Merle A. Gill, local ballistician," Conroy wrote Hoover only a month before Richetti's trial. He continued, a few paragraphs later, "That, in other words, the gun would not be forwarded merely for examination by Merle A. Gill, but would be forwarded if the United States Attorney was of the opinion that it was necessary evidence."

Gill never touched either gun. And the day after the trial ended, the guns were back in Bureau hands and locked up.

Latshaw and Daleo knew nothing of all the conflict and doubt surrounding the ballistics match. So they were left only to argue that none of the extensive gun evidence meant anything anyway. Even if Floyd's gun was at Union Station, they argued, Floyd was not on trial. Richetti was.

But that didn't really wash. The chain of logic was obvious enough for the jury, especially with the prosecution's not-so-subtle guidance: If Floyd's gun was there, then Floyd was there, and if Floyd was there, Richetti was there.

A single spark of hope for Richetti did come during Gill's testimony, however. It happened during cross-examination, when Latshaw tried to establish a link between the ball bearing that killed Agent Caffrey and whatever ball bearing–loaded shotgun shells Gill might know about. After the prosecution objected repeatedly, Latshaw confided his defense strategy to Judge Cowan during a bench conversation out of the jury's hearing.

"We offer to prove by this witness that he made a request for a test bullet from Otto Reed's gun to determine whether or not any of those bullets compared with the bullets in evidence in this case, *it being our theory that Otto Reed shot and killed Frank Hermanson* [emphasis added]," Latshaw said.

In fact, that "theory" turned out to be one of the best-kept secrets of the trial. Neither Latshaw nor Daleo ever clearly articulated it within hearing of the jury. It wasn't mentioned in opening or closing arguments. It wasn't even pursued when they had before them on the witness stand the very man who had publicly pushed that theory into the newspapers of Kansas City nine months earlier—Merle A. Gill.

Somewhere along the line, Latshaw and Daleo decided, perhaps with some encouragement, to keep their theory of the case to themselves.

Nor did Gill volunteer to resurrect it, certainly not the part about Floyd having "nothing at all to do with the massacre." The atmosphere around Gill was getting a bit strange by then anyway, and he may have had good reason for reticence. After all, two days before the trial he had mysteriously disappeared. No one had any idea where he might be. His wife, according to reports in Hoover's files, was "frantic because of the disappearance." But he turned up just in time to testify—exactly as the prosecution and Hoover wanted him to testify.

Oddly, Gill later would ask the Bureau for some public recognition of his services in the Union Station Massacre case, maybe even a letter of appreciation from the director who hated him. That letter was not forthcoming. But despite blistering private criticism of Gill and secret memos to the effect that "for a few dollars [Gill] will testify either way," the Bureau did nothing to block his ongoing private practice as a ballistician.

For the record, Gill was known to have on hand in his private collection several spent Floyd shell casings from various shootings around the region. So his personal integrity would have been the only barrier to a quick switch—and a perfectly accurate ballistics match between Floyd's gun and the Union Station Massacre.

■　■　■

The prosecutors tried hard to keep the jurors from too much deep thought about the guns. Instead, they wanted the jury to feel the menace of the guns and to soak up the deadliness that surrounded Pretty Boy Floyd and, by extension, Adam Richetti. Boyle's arsenal certainly did that. Sheriff Killingsworth, testifying with the machine gun on his lap, went into great detail about the rubbed-out serial number and how he remembered it clearly from all those hours when he had expected a spray of bullets to kill him at any moment.

And the whole courtroom was fascinated by the .45-caliber automatic pistol that yielded the ballistics match. That gun had a special attachment at the rear that made it look a little funny, but the fascination came from Purvis's explanation that the conversion made it a "full automatic."

"What do you mean by that," Boyle asked, "'full automatic'?"

"I mean by that that as long as you hold your finger on the trigger and press, as you would ordinarily, shooting a forty-five-caliber automatic pistol, it will continue to fire until the magazine is empty."

Floyd, in short, had created the sort of weapon not available to his successor gunmen for a good many years, a pistol that spat like a machine gun.

Thus primed for bloody violence, the jury watched Agent Frank Smith, a physically unscathed survivor of the massacre, take the witness stand. He was a good leadoff choice for the prosecutors. One of the pre-Hoover old guard, already in the Bureau well over twenty years, Smith was a little overweight and highly sympathetic as the victim of unprovoked assault. Besides, his "nerves were shot" after the shootout, according to Bureau reports, and the jurors undoubtedly could see and sense that.

Smith described the arrest of Nash in Hot Springs, the escape to Fort Smith, the train ride to Kansas City. He took the jury into the parking lot and carefully began loading the car for them, himself in the middle of the rear seat. Only then did he veer away from the reports he had sent to Hoover right after the massacre.

"Now, where was Mr. Lackey located with reference to the back seat there as to reference to the left or right side?" Prosecutor Graves asked.

"Mr. Lackey was on the west side of me and Mr. Reed was on the east side of me," Smith answered.

That was a reversal of the positions of Lackey and Reed and a contradiction of all the Bureau reports over the months. It was a crucial alteration, but the defense team didn't know that. Denied access to the Bureau's massive file, Latshaw and Daleo did not recognize perjury when they heard it.

There would be much more.

Well, after the shooting started I raised up and I saw Nash's head go back and some blood fly out of it, and a man raised up over the front hood of the—over the fender of the car that was parked just west of us. He raised up over there with a gun in his hand, I couldn't tell what it was, but he just raised up and begin to shoot right at my head, like that [indicating].

A little later he added, "I fell over and I felt the heat of the bullets go by my face, burned my face as they went by."

Graves then handed him a picture of Vernon C. Miller.

"That was the man that shot at my head," Smith said.

This from the agent who told Hoover he saw absolutely nothing that morning. In fact, his report to the director a few hours after the shooting hardly could have been more precise:

At the first volley . . . the writer [Smith] dropped his head down below the front end as if shot and remained in that position until the firing ceased. While the writer observed by a glance a man behind the machine gun pointed and shooting in his direction, he was unable to obtain any kind of a description of him and was unable to see anyone else who did the shooting.

Nonetheless, the jurors heard Verne Miller identified as a shooter.

A couple of hours later, Agent Reed Vetterli came to the stand. Despite his thinly disguised offers over the months to identify almost anyone (Bob Brady, Machine Gun Kelly, Floyd) as a shooter, he still was not back in Hoover's favor. But he came through for the

Bureau that day. Graves handed him pictures of Verne Miller and Pretty Boy Floyd and asked "whether or not you saw either one of those two men there firing upon this car of Agent Caffrey and you gentlemen there that morning."

Vetterli answered without hesitation. "I identify the picture of State's Exhibit Number Three of Pretty Boy Floyd as the individual I saw."

That didn't square at all with his report to Hoover soon after the massacre. "I saw but one man, who was operating the machine gun from my right," Vetterli had reported back then. And after looking through photographs a few hours later, he had been able to offer a little more. "I am convinced that the man who first opened fire from our right, with a machine gun, is Bob Brady."

Nonetheless, the jurors that morning heard Pretty Boy Floyd identified as a shooter.

But Adam Richetti, the man on trial for his life, still hadn't been placed at the massacre scene. That would be left, in part, to Mrs. Lottie West, the fifty-one-year-old woman who ran the Travelers Aid Society desk at Union Station. She had told Hoover's agents an elaborate and daring story of her exploits that morning, beginning when she found a man sitting at her desk when she arrived at 7 A.M. Though agents later learned from other station employees that man was Harry Blanchard, who also worked at the station, neither they nor she flinched in court when she told the jury the man was Pretty Boy Floyd.

"How far was he from you?" O'Hern asked.

"About two feet," she responded.

"Two feet?"

"Two or three feet, I would say."

"You mean as close as I am to you now?"

"Yes, sir."

A solid identification. No room for doubt.

But Lottie West wasn't finished. She then told the jurors how she had watched the lawmen cross the lobby and very soon thereafter she followed in order to help six Benedictine Sisters, in full habit, who were in search of a taxicab.

"When the shooting started, I was standing on the edge of the sidewalk, under the east canopy of the station," she said.

She described two men with machine guns, one of them the man who had sat at her desk. And she described a third shooter who was armed with twin pistols, one "a blue gun" and the other "nickel plated." She remembered it glinting in the sunshine. That man, she said, went around the back of the agents' car and continued firing into the men.

"Do you, Mrs. West, see that man in the courtroom, that third man that was doing that firing with those two revolvers?" O'Hern asked.

"Yes, I do," she said.

"Will you point him out to these gentlemen and to the court, please?"

"He is right back of Mr. Daleo."

"You are pointing to this defendant, Adam Richetti?"

"Correct."

Now Adam Richetti was placed at the scene as one of the shooters.

■   ■   ■

With all three shooters now fixed at the scene by eyewitness testimony, the prosecutors might have quit right there. But they had one more eyewitness, and he would do far more than strengthen the prosecution's case. He would destroy any possibility of a Richetti defense.

There simply is no question that the oath administered to Agent Joseph Lackey that morning meant nothing at all. To begin with, his eyewitness identification of Richetti as one of the shooters was as perjured as the identifications made by the other two agents. In response to Boyle's questions, Lackey precisely tracked a shooter from the right front of Caffrey's car, alongside the Plymouth parked to the right, and behind the agents' car.

"Officer Lackey, do you see that man in the courtroom?" Boyle asked at last.

"I do," Lackey answered.

"Will you point him out to these gentlemen?"

"Right there" (indicating).

"You are pointing to this defendant, Adam Richetti, is that right?"

"Yes, sir," Lackey said.

Compare that to Lackey's report to his feared Bureau director immediately after the massacre, the same report that had guided the Bureau's investigation for almost two years:

> Agent [Lackey] saw these men through the window glass on
> the windshield of the Plymouth, which was none too clean, and
> therefore a clear view could not be obtained by agent. . . . Agent
> got such a hurried glance at these two men and this glance was
> through a none too clean window and windshield of the
> Plymouth, that he is not sure that he could identify either
> of these men.

Latshaw tried to attack Lackey's identification of Richetti. Though Latshaw had never seen and would never see the Bureau reports, he did have newspaper accounts in which Lackey was quoted as saying much the same thing, that he had seen no one. Lackey brushed those accounts aside by swearing to Latshaw that he had intentionally misled the reporters. Years later, he would repeat that to a *Kansas City Star* reporter.

"I was in enough danger already," he said in 1971, adding that he had received death threats. In fact, he said, he had got a good look at two of the killers' faces.

At Richetti's trial, the hawk-faced agent with the pinched nose was smug in his replies to Latshaw.

"I did not testify in [federal] court that I could not see who those men were," Lackey said. "I told them that I told the newspapers that."

Lackey blamed this on Bureau policy.

"We are confined in our interviews with newspaper men," he said. "We will not make a definite identification or give the name of any person sought without previous authority."

It sounded good enough, but it was nonsense. The explanation ignored the fact that Lackey had told his boss precisely what he told the newspapers—that he could identify no one.

Still, that little manipulation of the truth was child's play for Agent Joe Lackey. He would do much better in the minutes ahead. And when he finished, Latshaw's "theory of the case" would have absolutely nowhere to go.

It began subtly when Boyle asked who sat where in the backseat of the agents' car, which faced south that morning. Lackey simply switched sides with the dead Otto Reed.

"I was on the backseat on the right or west side," Lackey responded. "Next to me in the center of the car was Frank Smith, and Otto Reed was on the east side."

Although that agreed with Agent Smith's strange testimony from the day before, both testimonies flatly contradicted the version of the facts that had stood for two years and had been repeated in dozens of formats. "Agent [Lackey] got in the backseat on the left-hand side, Smith got in the backseat in the center, and Reed got in the backseat on the right-hand side," Lackey had written at the time.

It was not a simple error. That initial report was replete with similar references that put Lackey behind the driver's seat, including one reference to Lackey seeing blood drip down in front of his own eyes from the head of Nash, who was positioned behind the steering wheel. At another point Lackey wrote precisely that "the agent [Lackey] was crouched down back of the driver's seat."

When Lackey switched sides with Reed, Smith's perjured testimony suddenly made sense: Smith knew Lackey was going to make the switch. The lie had been choreographed.

But why was it so important that the jury and history record Lackey as being on the right side, not the left side, of that backseat?

The answer lay in the defense's hinted but thus far unexplored theory of the case that might have blamed Chief Otto Reed for much of the killing. When Merle Gill had first advanced that theory through the newspapers, he clearly identified the left rear seat, behind the driver, as the firing position based on his ballistics evidence. Not privy to the Bureau's reports, Gill thought that's where Otto Reed had been seated. If the left rear seat was to become the hot seat during this public trial, Lackey clearly did not want to be in it.

That left the gun, the 16-gauge killer, to be dealt with. Lackey chose simply to lie it right out of existence. The door was opened as he testified about the specifics of the shotgun he carried that morning and how he had it "stuck down beside of me, I had it muzzle down."

The opening didn't just happen. The question was designed for it.

"Was that your gun?" Graves asked, throwing open the door and stepping aside as Lackey hustled the jury through.

"To the best of my recollection, when I got off the train to meet the officers the gun that I had belonged to the Oklahoma City Police Department and was borrowed, just prior to leaving Oklahoma City, and was not my personal gun; it was a gun I had been using. And then when I got off to meet the officers that morning I just picked up a shotgun.

"At that time I noticed it was Otto Reed's gun instead of the gun belonging to the Oklahoma City Police Department that I had previously had, and to the best of my recollection I still had that gun at the time."

Lackey had taken Reed's seat and now his gun as well. In short, Joe Lackey had taken himself out of the shooter's seat, yet placed himself in an authoritative position to deal with any possible questions about gauges of shotguns or ball-bearing loads in shotgun shells or shots fired. He could deny it all.

And he did.

He set up the scene as he had for Hoover, only in mirror image. He had told Hoover that his shotgun was "pointed toward the floor, and the muzzle of the gun was between the driver's seat and the door, the butt of the gun being between agent and the side panel."

Now he told the court, "My gun, the muzzle was toward the floor and the butt was between the seat and the side of the car resting up here [toward the roof]. . . . The last I saw of [Otto Reed's] gun it was in the same position as mine was, on the opposite side. . . . It was on the left."

With all that firmly in the juror's minds, Lackey simply began to deny, to undercut any foundation Latshaw might try to build. Lackey said that he had never fired a shot himself and that he didn't believe Reed had. Six months earlier he had told Hoover categorically that Reed had not fired.

No, he didn't know what had become of Reed's gun, but he was sure it was not a 16-gauge.

"Are you positive of that?" Latshaw asked.

"I gave Reed ammunition for it at McAlester," Lackey stated flatly.

Latshaw must have thought he had him. The defense attorney walked to the prosecution table and demanded the two spent 16-gauge shells found in the backseat with Lackey and Reed.

"Did you ever see these before, Mr. Lackey?" he asked.

"I never saw those before yesterday—before this week in the prosecutor's office; that is the first time I ever saw those shells," Lackey answered.

"Will you say that neither one of those shotguns there were loaded with these?"

"Yes, sir, I will."

"What shotguns did you see there, Mr. Lackey?" Latshaw pressed.

"The only shotguns I saw were the one that I had and the one that Otto Reed had."

Latshaw gave up.

It must have been a tense moment for the row of Bureau firearms experts and agents behind the prosecution table. All of them knew that the Bureau had long since recovered Reed's shotgun from the family, verified that it indeed was a 16-gauge, and extensively test-fired it. Of course, they had given none of the test cartridges to Gill or anyone else for examination, and they had not shared their research on the shotgun controversy.

So they could be reasonably confident that they were the only ones with the certain knowledge that Agent Joe Lackey was lying through his teeth. But then, Smith's perjured testimony and Graves's leading question "Was that your gun?" amplify the lie into conspiracy. And the Bureau's silence expands it all into cover-up.

They knew in advance that Lackey would lie. They listened to him lie. And they said nothing.

■　　■　　■

Richetti's coup de grace came with the Hoover traveling fingerprint show. It was performed smoothly and flawlessly, again as though there were no seams in the perfect weave.

Agent John E. Brennan testified efficiently about finding the print on the beer bottle at 6612 Edgevale. He explained carefully how he had a local photographer take pictures of the latent prints. He did not, however, explain to the jury how he failed to match Richetti's scarred print to the scarred print from the bottle. The agents chose to keep all that to themselves.

Brennan was followed by Jerry Murphy, the Bureau fingerprint specialist from Washington, D.C., who skipped the interval from June 1933, when the print was found, to March 1934, when the match was made, without so much as clearing his throat. He preferred to talk about the four million sets of prints then on file at Bureau headquarters. Latshaw never even asked about the interval between the finding of the latent and the identification of the print.

When Latshaw asked how a print, which depends on the moisture of body oils, could survive twelve hot days in June under dust in a cellar, Murphy brushed him aside.

Of course it could, the expert said.

But few modern experts could be so offhand about that. Even with today's tools and techniques, twelve days of dust is a formidable foe.

No one posed the most obvious question: Is it logical that a consummate alcoholic, a man known to drink a case of beer a day, would leave only one print on one bottle over the course of sixteen or so very tense hours before and after committing a massacre?

Ironically, Murphy only hesitated on one question, when Latshaw pressed him about published reports of Bureau efforts to see if fingerprints could be transferred, say, from a card to a bottle.

"In other words, then, you would say that you couldn't transfer a fingerprint and make it appear as a latent fingerprint?" Latshaw asked.

"I would say that I have never seen it, nor heard of it being successfully done," Murphy hedged.

Again, modern experts know better. Transferring a fingerprint to a hard surface such as a bottle is not difficult. All you need is cellophane tape and a print, such as those on millions of fingerprint cards made this century. The real trick, almost impossible, is to leave no microscopic traces of tape or other telltale materials for the defense team's experts to find. But in 1935, all the scientists and fingerprint experts worked for the prosecution. Richetti had no such expertise to rely on.

So, without a hint of challenge, Murphy summarized his devastating expert testimony: The print on the bottle was Richetti's.

The Bureau was delighted at how well it all went down with the jury. Coffey fired off a memo to headquarters immediately, bragging that "the members of the jury appeared interested and apparently comprehended the purpose and method of the testimony." But beyond that, both he and Hoover knew important precedents had been set. "Defense attorneys objected to the introduction of the fingerprint evidence on the ground that the latent fingerprints were discovered at too distant a time from the date of the massacre, and to the introduction of the charts on the ground that the witness had not personally made the photographs," Coffey reported. "The court overruled both objections."

Hoover was quick to grasp the significance. "A very good ruling and one we should keep in mind for future use," he wrote in the margin.

That left only the coroner's testimony about the cause of Hermanson's death, though by that point it seemed almost perfunctory. Yet from the beginning the most curious aspect of Adam Richetti's trial was the charge itself, the murder of Frank Hermanson.

After all, the state's case demanded that the jury believe Richetti was armed that morning with two .45-caliber pistols. Yet throughout the two-year investigation, Bureau and ballistics reports had said Hermanson was killed by a shotgun blast. That conclusion was repeated at least a dozen times in the file and about as often in public. In fact, it had provided impetus for the long search for a shotgun-armed shooter.

So how would the prosecution finesse all that in court?

Easy. They simply didn't tell the jury about any of it. Instead, prosecutors waited until the end of their case to call Dr. C. G. Leitch, chief deputy coroner of Jackson County, who promptly stood that aspect of the investigation squarely on its head.

It was a gunshot wound, Leitch testified. The bullet entered above Hermanson's left ear and exited at the lower back of his head.

But, Latshaw asked, couldn't that wound have been "caused by a small ball bearing shot out of a shotgun?"

"I don't think that it could have. It had the appearance of having been inflicted by a bullet," Leitch testified. "I don't think that it is possible."

And with that, the State of Missouri rested.

■   ■   ■

Latshaw's defense immediately went after Lottie West, and in that single area he was a raging success. The quiet, matronly giver of aid and directions soon was shown to be a veteran member of the law enforcement community. She had worked for the Welfare Board in Kansas City, attached for over two years to the Kansas City Police Department. Almost every day during that period, according to her own testimony, she was called to assist in arrests, sometimes using force.

She called herself, during that time, "an acting policewoman." Latshaw showed her to be clearly enamored with police work and policemen, in modern terms a groupie or wanna-be.

But the real damage to her veracity came from her friends, people who knew her at Union Station and who had been there with her that morning. First of all, nobody could remember the six Benedictine Sisters in full habit she claimed to be helping when the shooting started. And none of those pinned to the sidewalk by fear of bullets remembered seeing her there with them.

Dan Lynn had just pulled up to the east doors in his cab when all hell broke loose. It was all he could do to get out of the line of fire.

"When the shooting started, I opened this right front door to take the passenger's bag, and when I opened this door the shooting started, and I went right on out the door, got down on the north running board of my cab, and laid there till the shooting was over. Then I got up," he said.

During all that time he had no choice but to face directly into the east doors. He was too afraid to look anywhere else. Robert Earl Fritts, the cab starter who ran the taxi stand, was behind the same car's front wheel.

And neither of them ever saw Lottie West standing invincibly on the sidewalk under the canopy. In fact, they didn't see her even step outside until well after the shooting was over. A half dozen others trapped behind cars or in doorways told very similar stories about her. All were hiding for fear of their lives, as sensible people do under such circumstances. And none saw the valiant Mrs. West standing on the sidewalk watching it all happen, as she claimed to have done.

Fritts seemed to speak for all of them: "When it was over with, I seen her coming out of the station."

But if Lottie West's testimony dissolved into more wishful thinking than fact, the three agents remained, each swearing to the identity of a different one of three shooters. And that left the defense trying to prove a negative. Several of the witnesses they produced said the man they saw was *not* Richetti, but none got such a good look at all the gunmen as to be able to say that *none* of the shooters was Richetti.

The phrase "I will say that the man I saw was not Adam Richetti" became a defense anthem, but even taken together the disclaimers proved nothing.

In desperation, the defense lawyers called their own client. At least they could give Adam Richetti a chance to proclaim his innocence. His testimony was brief. He stated his name, said "Yes, sir" when asked if he was the defendant, said "No, sir" when asked if he was in Kansas City on the morning of the massacre, and said "No, sir" again when asked if he was at Union Station that morning. That's all.

Normally, in a murder trial prosecution lawyers pounce on such an opportunity to rip the defendant apart. This time, they didn't ask a single question.

The agents knew at that point that they'd pulled it off, and for all the bluster they showed the world, they were secretly shocked at their success. "Mr. Tolson was advised by Mr. Conroy that the Richetti case will go to the jury tonight and that it looks very good. Much better than expected," read an urgent memo circulated around headquarters.

The jury took little time to find Richetti guilty, and the judge took even less to pronounce sentence. Adam Richetti was to be hanged by the neck until dead.

■   ■   ■

The eighty-nine-volume Union Station Massacre file and its long-kept secrets now cast the Richetti trial and Hoover's case against Floyd and Richetti in a considerably different light. It focuses around Latshaw's closing argument that this was a "save your face" case on the part of the Bureau.

The first question, after all, was never whether Richetti deserved execution for his various crimes but whether he was guilty of that crime at that time. And the second question: Did Hoover just need somebody, anybody, to take the fall—and close the file?

Now that Hoover's entire case can be compared to his own file, that case can itself be seen as a carefully staged crime, whether or not it stumbled across any truth:

■ Agent Reed Vetterli lied about his identification of Pretty Boy Floyd as one of the shooters. In fact, he could identify no one.

■ Agent Frank Smith lied about his identification of Verne Miller as one of the shooters. In fact, he could identify no one.

■ Agent Joe Lackey lied about many things, several times, including his identification of Adam Richetti as one of the shooters. He could identify no one—and he had his own secrets to protect.

■ Lottie West's testimony was so contrived and contradictory as to be useless. She was a well-intentioned police wanna-be trying hard to please.

■ The Richetti fingerprint on the beer bottle was at best highly suspicious and at worst a Bureau fake. Hoover's version of the truth surrounding the print is, in a word, unbelievable.

■ The Merle Gill ballistics "match" of Floyd's gun to a massacre shell casing was probably inaccurate, maybe faked, and most certainly unacceptable as evidence in court.

- Floyd's shoulder wound did not exist.

- Vi Mathias's statement was recognized by Hoover himself as the linchpin of the case. Yet when her crucial lie about Floyd's wound in the left shoulder is considered, her entire statement becomes at best highly suspect. As noted earlier, she was a survivor.

- Jimmy Needles LaCapra's extensive statement, given his desperation and panic at the time and his probable involvement in the Lazia assassination, was most likely a self-serving and unsuccessful attempt to stay alive. He would have said anything.

At this late date, none of that means much to Adam Richetti. His conviction was appealed to the Missouri Supreme Court, but the justices had little trouble tossing the appeal aside. By the time all the formalities were done, Missouri had finished construction of its new gas chamber at the state prison in Jefferson City, and his sentence was changed. At 12:10 A.M. on October 7, 1938, Adam Richetti was the first to try it out.

It worked.

CHAPTER EIGHTEEN

THE TRUTH

Based on a thorough analysis of the FBI's own file, this is what really happened on June 17, 1933, at Kansas City's Union Station.

A GENT JOE LACKEY hung from the door of the slowing train, his eyes scanning the faces on the platform, searching for the men who would help relieve the gnawing anxiety he'd now felt for a good many hours. The weakest link of their plan, after all, was just ahead, the transfer of Frank Nash to a waiting car and on to the federal prison in Leavenworth.

Kansas City had been a problem from the beginning. When R. H. Colvin, his boss in Oklahoma City, had told him the night before to board the Missouri Pacific out of Fort Smith, Arkansas, they'd talked at length about the one-hour layover at Kansas City's Union Station. Even with a lot of firepower, that was a very bad idea.

Colvin solved the problem with a call to his friend Reed Vetterli, who said he would arrange for some local muscle to help them with Nash's transfer. No problem.

But there were problems. Though Kansas City police detectives Frank Hermanson and Bill Grooms got the message to take their armored car to the station the next morning, someone else in the KCPD got a second crucial message. So during the night the machine gun that was standard equipment on the Hot Shot car was quietly removed. The detectives didn't have time to look around for it the next morning before going on to the rendezvous at Union Station. The machine gun would turn up a few hours later. Just a bureaucratic foul-up, senior officers would claim.

Vetterli had a little trouble with his own men, too. When he tried to phone Agent Kenneth McIntire, who was just beginning what would become an illustrious Bureau career, he got nowhere. Vetterli would not know until later (and would never report to Hoover) that McIntire had flaunted Bureau regulations for the sake of a few cents.

"I had given the office my downstairs neighbor's number," McIntire told the author in 1983. "Those were hard times. You tried to save a nickel here, a dime there. So that night I had to come downstairs to answer the phone. By the time I got there, Vetterli had hung up."

Vetterli had then called Agent Ray Caffrey, the new guy in the office. Yes, Caffrey would pick him up well before 7 A.M.

It was Vetterli's face that Lackey sought and found that morning as he hung from the train's doorway. Lackey quickly recognized Caffrey, too, and assumed the other two men were local police. After quick introductions and a few words of planning, Lackey reboarded the train.

McAlester, Oklahoma, Police Chief Otto Reed and Agent Frank Smith listened to Lackey's hurried briefing, and the three lawmen left the train compartment quickly with their handcuffed prisoner sandwiched between them. Outside, the others fell in around the edges, forming the V-shaped wedge that so many in Union Station that morning would remember for the rest of their lives.

They were an imposing lot. Hermanson and Grooms, deprived of their machine gun, carried only .38-caliber handguns, but they let their guns be seen by those they passed. Most of the time, the guns were out of their holsters and in the detectives' hands.

Agent Frank Smith carried two handguns, a .45 automatic and a .38, one of them in his hand most of the time. Agent Caffrey carried a .38-caliber pistol, at times jabbed into Nash's ribs. Only Vet-terli was unarmed.

Lackey and Reed provided the lawmen's real firepower. Lackey had borrowed a 12-gauge pump shotgun from the Oklahoma City Police Department before the trip into Arkansas. Reed had brought along an old family favorite, a 16-gauge pump shotgun that he used for both fun and work. He owned two interchangeable barrels for the gun, one long for buckshot and wild game and the other sawed off short to spread the special load of ball bearings he packed for human quarry. This was a short-barrel job.

Reed knew the gun very well, and like all hunters he was aware of his gun's eccentricities. On this gun, for instance, there was no separate safety switch. The only safety was placing the hammer at the half-cocked position. If you didn't thumb the hammer back the rest of the way, it would never fire.

That morning, walking through the station, Reed may have re-alized he was carrying the wrong shotgun. Since he knew the feel of his 16-gauge gun so well, he probably did know something was amiss. But that was no time to play kid games, no time to be pass-ing guns around. Lackey, nowhere near as familiar as Reed with guns in general or that shotgun in particular, mistakenly had picked up Reed's 16-gauge. But the switch wasn't crucial at the mo-ment, as long as they both had loaded shotguns held at the ready.

The formation walked briskly across the lobby, past Lottie West's untended Travelers Aid desk (she was across the lobby gossiping with the restaurant manager), and out the doors that exited south from the eastern end of the station. With only the slightest hesita-tion, they walked in a tight bunch to Caffrey's Chevrolet, parked in the first row of cars and facing south away from the station.

Caffrey opened the passenger side door on the right or west side of the car, and the party began to board. Lackey got in first, slid-ing all the way to the left rear side directly behind the driver's seat. Then Reed climbed in, settling in the right rear. Nash, no stranger to being arrested, immediately climbed into the rear seat between the two lawmen.

But Lackey objected. "Get up front," he ordered. "We'll ride like we did out of Hot Springs. That way we can all watch you."

So Nash, handcuffed and clumsy, climbed back out the passenger door and onto the front seat, sliding all the way over behind the steering wheel so that the passenger-side backrest could be pushed forward, allowing Agent Frank Smith to get into the middle of the rear seat.

Lackey and Reed fiddled with their shotguns, trying to make room for six men and a small arsenal inside the little car. Lackey wedged his shotgun's barrel between the left edge of the front seat and the driver's door, the stock between his own left hip and the side of the car. The bulkier Reed pointed his barrel down toward the floor to the right of the front seat but raised the stock up toward the roof.

Outside, Vetterli stood beside the passenger door, facing into the car. Hermanson and Grooms stood just a pace or two beyond that door, almost beside the right front tire. Grooms faced away from the car and toward the southwest; Hermanson stood directly in front of Grooms, his back to the southwest. Caffrey closed the passenger door and squeezed past the two detectives, heading around the front of the car to take up his position as driver.

The stage was set for massacre.

■　■　■

Fewer than fifty yards away, Verne Miller watched the phalanx of lawmen come out of the station. Frank Nash's rescue was about to begin. Slowly, the driver edged Miller's Chevrolet forward until it was about a hundred feet south and west of Caffrey's car. Miller, sporting the machine gun a friend had loaned him during the wee small hours of the morning, walked briskly toward the agents, using parked cars as shields.

Miller and a second machine gunner peeked over the hood of a car just a few spaces west and south of Caffrey's. Both men knew the plan: Get Nash and go. Surprise and overwhelming firepower were their strongest weapons. In fact, neither expected to fire a shot.

What happened next took only seconds, from the first shot to final dying gasp. It was, by all accounts, a blur of smoke and fire. But, thanks to the extensive file, everyone's movements can be reconstructed and reviewed like a film in slow motion.

"Put 'em up! Up! Up!" Miller shouted, leveling his machine gun at the agents over the hood of a car. A few feet away, the other machine gunner moved closer, a bit more in the open.

In the backseat Joe Lackey was already reacting, whether alerted by the words or by seeing the gunmen.

"In endeavoring to cock this gun to fire, it jammed," Lackey would report to Hoover, "and to the best of agent's recollection he was unable to get it unjammed during the proceedings."

In fact, that was only a very small piece of the truth, though everything that was about to happen did indeed hinge on Lackey's utter incompetence to handle the shotgun he held. That gun, Reed's gun, was nothing like the more conventional pump shotgun Lackey had borrowed in Oklahoma City and carried through Arkansas. It didn't work the same way; it didn't respond the same way. And those differences were about to change the course of history.

The gun in Lackey's hands was a Winchester Model 1897, a fierce weapon that helped tame the last of the American West, cut down opium-crazed natives in the Philippines, and even triggered a sharp protest from Germany when its Trench Gun Model hit the Western Front with the doughboys in World War I. The Model 97 had several tricky but lethal features, especially as compared to other shotguns.

First of all, the Model 97 had no separate safety switch or button. Its hammer, when pulled back only halfway, was the only safety mechanism.

Second, the Model 97 was constructed so the recoil from a fired shot naturally slid the pump's forearm grip forward a little, thus releasing an action slide lock and allowing the next backward pump of the forearm grip to begin the process of ejecting a spent shell and seating another in the chamber. However, in order to eject an *unexploded* shell without the benefit of that firing recoil, it was necessary (1) to lower the hammer manually by simultaneously squeezing the trigger and easing down the hammer with the thumb and (2) to push the forearm grip *forward* to release the slide lock so that the grip could then be pumped backward to begin the ejection and chambering process.

The third special feature of the Model 97 allowed it to fire virtually like a machine gun. With no trigger disconnector, if the trigger was held back during operation, the gun would immediately fire each new round as it was chambered and seated. In other words, with the trigger held back, the gun was loaded, cocked, and fired with each pumping motion of the forearm grip.

In the right (skilled) hands, the Model 97 could spray lead balls at an astonishing rate that, for a few seconds, outperformed any machine gun; its short-term firepower could be devastating. But in the wrong (untrained) hands, its idiosyncrasies made it clumsy or, worse, chaotic. And Joe Lackey's were the wrong hands indeed.

That morning, in the grip of blind panic, Lackey yanked at the shotgun wedged between his left hip and the car's side panel, trying to get it up into firing position as the gunmen advanced. The hammer may have become jammed, by a coat sleeve or jacket or the car fabric. Or, knowing little or nothing about the Model 97, Lackey simply may have failed to pull the hammer fully back, out of the half-cocked safety position and into firing position. Or the chamber may have been empty. In any case, Lackey could not make the gun fire.

Instinctively, he tried to pump a new shell into the chamber by pulling back the forearm grip. But Lackey didn't know he first had to lower the hammer manually. Nor did he know that, in the absence of any recoil, the Model 97's slide lock would hold firm, waiting for the slight forward movement of the forearm grip that would enable the ejection and chambering sequence.

Joe Lackey knew only that the damned gun wouldn't work.

With adrenaline surging throughout his body and terror gripping his mind, Lackey fumbled frantically, desperately, at the pump, trigger, and hammer mechanisms. Finally, perhaps only five or six seconds after he first recognized the danger, he hit on the right combination. Somehow, with his thumb or his other hand, he jammed the hammer all the way back, out of the safety position and into fully cocked firing position—or, if the chamber was empty, he blundered into the proper changing sequence. And with Lackey's panicked finger gripping the trigger, the Model 97 did just what it was designed to do: It automatically and immediately released that hammer and discharged, firing an unaimed and unintended load of Reed's homemade ball-bearing shot into the back of Frank Nash's head.

The blast killed Nash instantly, blew a hole through the front windshield, spread glass straight out across the hood of the Chevrolet, and finally slammed a ball bearing into Caffrey's head as he walked or stood near the front of the car.

Now Lackey's panic was total. Not only had he blown much of his prisoner's head off, he had triggered a raging firefight. And he had no idea how he had fired the shotgun and little notion of how to fire it again. Frantically swinging the shotgun generally toward the gunmen at his right front, he pointed and pumped. And with Lackey's finger still locked over the trigger, the Winchester again responded, firing instantly.

That blast caught Frank Hermanson in the side of the head, blowing his brains out. From the wound's position, it's as though Hermanson was dropping toward a crouch. Or he may already have crouched between the cars and was hit when he rose slightly to see what was happening.

That same blast also smashed through the left side window and windshield of the Plymouth in the adjoining space. One ball bearing ripped the metal of the roof post forward, and another ricocheted around inside the car before coming to rest on the floorboard near where the driver's foot would be.

Lackey started to fire yet again, kicking the second exploded 16-gauge shell casing onto the floorboard, but he was done. Bullets ripped into him, and he collapsed forward over his knees. One slug knocked his revolver out of its holster.

Detective William Grooms reacted quickly to the first blast from Lackey's shotgun. Well over six feet tall and built like a truck, he was used to carrying a machine gun that earned any respect that his badge did not. And he wasn't inclined to be intimidated. Grooms's .38 barked almost immediately, but it was no contest. He took two machine-gun bullets in the chest and was dead before he hit the ground.

Reed Vetterli, on his belly and crawling toward the rear of the car, suddenly sprang to his feet and sprinted toward the station's doors. The staccato of machine-gun fire followed him. Bullets danced off the polished granite facade, spraying dust and fear on those who huddled near the doorway.

The gunmen, though shocked at meeting any resistance, quickly focused with amazing accuracy on Lackey's position in the car, hitting him three times. Smith, sprawled forward across the folded-down backrest and literally touching Lackey, played dead and never was hit at all. Chief Reed, hit from both the front and the rear, died instantly.

When the firing stopped, one of the gunmen stepped to the driver's side of the car, looked in at Nash, and said, "He is dead." Some witnesses swore they saw that gunman, who was standing within arm's reach of Lackey, grab the barrel of a shotgun, pull it out of the car, and throw the gun to the ground.

It was all over in fewer than a hundred seconds.

Though Lackey later would lie about almost everything, there's no real doubt about his actions that morning. For one thing, Harry Orr, a Yellow Cab driver, watched Lackey struggle with the "jammed" gun, describing it much like Lackey himself had described his efforts to fire.

"As they got across and some of them got in the car, I saw one man with what looked like a shotgun, and he was trying to fire it," Orr told a grand jury.

And Orr, from his position in the line of cabs to the east, could only have seen Lackey struggling with the "jammed" gun if Lackey sat on the car's left side behind the driver's seat. For it to be otherwise, Orr would have had to look into the car, across the backseat, and past two people to the far side of the car.

Orr's testimony adds another significant bit of information. Orr saw Lackey frantically working on his shotgun from the earliest moments of the ambush, before the firing started. And that matches recollections of the late federal judge William Becker of a most private conversation he had decades ago with a federal agent intimately aware of what happened that morning. Together, their words confirm that Lackey fired the shot that started the war.

Judge Becker was preparing to leave the federal bench in the late eighties when he whispered the story to a friend, who still wishes that his name not be used.

"Our agent sitting in the backseat pulled the trigger on Nash, and that started it," the old judge quoted the senior agent as saying, with deep embarrassment that bordered on despair. "The machine gunners didn't shoot first. Our guy panicked."

■   ■   ■

The gunmen sped off into history and obscurity. Despite the legend, despite Hoover's "complete solution," despite the massive file, despite all the evidence of excess and deficiency, we probably will never know the single fact toward which the entire case was focused: just who Miller brought with him to the Union Station Plaza that day.

In truth, it could have been Floyd and/or Richetti, though

Hoover's best and worst efforts never proved it was. It could have been anybody else who happened to be in Kansas City that day.

It could have been elements of the Barker Gang.

It could have been William Weissman, a local killer with close and long-standing ties to Verne Miller. The Kansas City Police named Weissman as Miller's accomplice early on, but Hoover ordered his men not to follow the Weissman trail, so they didn't.

Or it could have been both Weissman and Maurice Denning, another local thug. His name has been kicked around as a possibility for decades, never with any trace of proof.

Or, if Hoover's ballistics "match" that linked the bolt of the machine gun used in the Lazia shootings to the bolt of the machine gun used in the massacre was indeed accurate, it could have been Jimmy Needles LaCapra or his friends Jack Griffin and Al O'Brien. The mob, with pretty good sources of its own, was convinced a year later that LaCapra, Griffin, and O'Brien assassinated Johnny Lazia. If so, maybe one or more of them loaned the same machine gun to their friend Verne Miller to use that morning at Union Station. Or used it themselves.

Or maybe it was someone else entirely.

In the end, the Union Station Massacre investigation sheds far more light on the investigators than it ever did on those investigated. It was a series of dead ends, leads not followed, ignored truths, and buried secrets. When field agents weren't crippled by the director's many obsessions, they were consumed by their own fears of failure and the director's retribution. There's little doubt, for instance, that everybody in the Bureau's Kansas City office knew the true story of the massacre and the consequences of Joe Lackey's wild panic long before they dared tell Hoover. And when they did tell him, Hoover dared not tell the people.

Instead, the Bureau, by then renamed the Federal Bureau of Investigation, chose half-truths, lies, perjury, cover-up, and worse.

Now, more than six decades too late, the file tells the truth that Hoover feared so much:

Lackey killed Nash.

Lackey killed Caffrey.

Lackey killed Hermanson.

Even Chief Reed may have been killed by friendly fire. (There's no doubt that a .38-caliber bullet slammed into Reed's brain, which almost certainly was fired from a lawman's pistol. But a machine-gun bullet also ripped through his head. Either would have killed him. We will never know which got there first.)

That, however, is not the stuff of greatness. Empires aren't built on failed missions and panicked agents and bungled investigations.

Young John Edgar Hoover and his FBI needed a cause, a crusade. He needed good and evil. And he needed victory. The truth would offer none of that.

But the legend provided it all.

CHAPTER NINETEEN

THE LEGACY

IN THE CONTEXT of history, the truth of what happened that day at Union Station matters least of all. Far more important is what came after, what sprang from the guilt, anger, revenge, and fear.

J. Edgar Hoover called the massacre a "turning point in the nation's fight against crime," but that was a major understatement. The savagery of the Kansas City killings suddenly stripped gangsters of their romantic aura. The audacity of daylight slaughter in a city center could not be excused as the work of oppressed country boys in depressed times. Suddenly killers and thieves were judged as killers and thieves. And the public verdict was harsh.

Demands for reform were heard in cities and towns all over the country, but the focus quickly settled on Hoover and his small band of federal agents, in no small part because Hoover reveled in his Bureau's righteous indignation. When Hoover screamed for the umpteen thousandth time that his agents needed more power, he suddenly found sympathetic ears among the public and in the capital. When he bemoaned the Bureau's jurisdictional limitations, as he had for years, he suddenly found people listening—and nodding agreement.

At the time of the massacre, Hoover's men were restricted, with few exceptions, to investigating white slavery (prostitution), interstate auto theft, and federal bankruptcy violations. Agents became involved with Frank Nash only because he was an escaped federal prisoner, and even then the legality of the whole Hot Springs operation was never tested in any court. But the carnage in Kansas City embedded a Hoover versus Gangland image in the public mind. And if the country wanted a gangbuster, J. Edgar Hoover desperately wanted the job.

But he wanted the muscle to do the job, too. When he demanded new, strong laws to fight the gangster element, the nation's lawmakers responded with a vengeance. In May and June of 1934, not quite a year after the Union Station Massacre, nine major anticrime bills were signed into law by President Franklin D. Roosevelt. Those new laws were, as Sanford Ungar noted in *FBI*, his biography of the Bureau, "one of the most important, if least recognized, New Deal reforms." Together, they constituted a federal criminal code, which America had never had before.

Each new law strengthened Hoover and his agents. They not only gave Hoover a broad new mandate but also extensive authority to enforce it. In effect, they gave birth to the modern FBI.

By any appraisal, these powers and jurisdictions remain today at the very core of the FBI's reason for being:

- Robbery of a federal bank or a member of the Federal Reserve System became a violation of federal law and therefore within the jurisdiction of the FBI.
- Transporting stolen property over a state line became a federal offense.
- So did the use of interstate communications in extortion attempts.
- And interstate flight to avoid prosecution.
- And assaulting or killing a federal officer.
- And taking kidnap victims across state lines.
- The Lindbergh (kidnapping) Law was amended to include a presumption of transportation across a state line after seven days, thus allowing the FBI to enter the case.
- FBI agents were given the right to make arrests anywhere in the country, any time.

- And to execute warrants.
- And to carry and use firearms.

But Hoover knew that laws alone would never take him where he wanted to go. So even as he crafted an impersonal aura of efficiency and professionalism around his Bureau, he carefully shaped a cult of the personality around the Bureau's most important asset—J. Edgar Hoover himself. Any agent who let himself shine even briefly in the public eye would quickly be relegated to obscurity, as Melvin Purvis found out the hard way. Yet no praise or gift or honor was too great for the director, as Hoover set about proving over the next four decades.

Still, to cement his role as public superhero he needed more than the standard sit-behind-the-desk and hold-the-machine-gun photographs. He needed to display the same bravery his men showed in the streets. Hoover managed that in 1936 with his widely publicized "capture" of Alvin "Creepy" Karpis in New Orleans. The Bureau story was that Hoover walked up to Karpis's car, put him under arrest, and grabbed the killer's arm before he could reach in the backseat for a rifle. Karpis always remembered it a little differently, beginning with the fact that his 1936 Plymouth didn't have a backseat.

"The most obvious flaw in the FBI story, though," Karpis wrote in his 1971 memoirs, "lies in Hoover's own character. He didn't lead the attack on me. He hid until I was safely covered by many guns. He waited until he was told the coast was clear. Then he came out to reap the glory."

No matter. The charade worked. It played so well, in fact, that Hoover repeated the little caper a few years later with his longtime friend and companion Clyde Tolson as the hero of the day.

But then Hoover always knew what would sell, and he sold it shamelessly. In the wake of Floyd's killing, for instance, the director quickly latched on to the gold watch the Pretty Boy had kept in his pocket.

"Before the watch is turned over [to Floyd's family], it should be photographed in order to have a picture of the ten notches which appear on the face of the watch and on the inside thereof, which probably indicate the number of men Floyd has killed, using the watch for this purpose rather than his gun, which would have attracted more attention," Hoover wrote to Tamm on October 29, 1934.

Maybe, maybe not. At that moment Hoover had absolutely no idea what, if anything, the scratches meant. But that didn't stop him from talking up the trophy to the public, further villainizing Floyd and enhancing the reputation of the Bureau.

None of that would have worked without the legal and psychological base provided by the Union Station Massacre. From that first platform, the director went on to build a series of others, always increasing his and his Bureau's fame and fortune.

First came the gangsters, knocked off one by one by the street-smart crimefighter. Dillinger, Floyd, Karpis, the Barkers: none was a match for the director.

Then came the war years, with the Bureau's expansion to take over all American government operations in South America and heroic Nazi spy-catching operations at home.

Peace brought Red Scare Two, an extension of the old fight against organized communism that had established Hoover's early career. With the Cold War suddenly at the front of everybody's mind, Hoover found a menace truly worthy of the enormous budgets he demanded for his mushrooming Bureau.

That same anti-Communist zeal carried him into the Civil Rights Movement of the early sixties and the anti–Vietnam War protests a few years later, where he seemed to find subversives everywhere. From the students in Chicago's Grant Park at the 1968 Democratic National Convention to Dr. Martin Luther King Jr., Hoover said they were all out to destroy his America, and many Americans agreed.

J. Edgar Hoover died on May 2, 1972. He was seventy-seven years old and still the director of the Federal Bureau of Investigation, revered by thousands of former agents and admired by millions of American citizens. By then, his FBI was a model for the world, an efficient and effective crime-fighting machine.

Such has been the legacy of the Union Station Massacre. But now we can also see the legacy's dark side. History has taught us about FBI excesses, about break-ins and wiretaps and intimidation and deceit and cover-up. Yet the most ardent of the Bureau's supporters cling to the belief that the bad came at the end, in Hoover's dotage, after he lost the shine of youthful honesty and devotion: "Chiefly in the twilight of Mr. Hoover's administration," as former FBI director Clarence Kelley has phrased it.

Hoover's own file screams otherwise. The FBI didn't go bad; it was born bad, right there in the blood of Union Station. The file doesn't speak of a proud birth.

It describes original sin.

EPILOGUE

Agent Joe Lackey, who resigned from the Bureau soon after the Richetti trial, spent the rest of his life promoting himself as a hero —and drifting ever deeper into lies and cover-ups. By 1971 he would tell a *Kansas City Star* reporter that he had been able to identify not one but two of the shooters and that he had recognized Floyd immediately. If he ever regretted anything, he never said so.

Agent Frank Smith, his nerves shot after the massacre according to his supervisors, worked out the rest of his career in the Oklahoma hill country.

Agent Reed Vetterli never regained the director's favor and left the Bureau within five years of the massacre. He returned to Utah, where he ran unsuccessfully for Congress and later for governor, before settling in as Salt Lake City's police chief from 1940 to 1945. He was distributing radio appliances when he died in 1949 at age forty-five.

Agent Melvin Purvis also fell completely from Hoover's favor. Removed from his radio show and retired from the Bureau by the late 1930s, he worked awhile for a small radio station in North Carolina. In 1960, aware that he had terminal cancer, he shot himself with the gun his fellow agents had given him on his retirement.

Agent Gus T. Jones went back to San Antonio, stuck it out in the Bureau a few more years, and then saw the handwriting on the wall.

As one of the old-fashioned hired guns, his era was past, and he left to make way for the lawyers and accountants Hoover valued so highly.

Agent John E. Brennan, despite or because of the Richetti fingerprint blunder, enjoyed a long Bureau career. Though many young agents reluctantly quit or were driven out because of Hoover's frequent and capricious reassignments, Brennan lived virtually his entire career in St. Louis, his family's hometown. Such consideration was seen within the Bureau as a sure mark of the director's favor.

J. Edgar Hoover achieved the ultimate American status: His name became a verb. Today it is used by street cops to describe succinctly the creation, falsification, or manipulation of truth, as in the phrase, "They Hoovered up the evidence."

Sheriff Tom Bash kept his reputation as one of the few honest law officers in Kansas City. He retired to his farm outside of town to raise Missouri foxhounds and long-eared mules.

Merle A. Gill, ballistics expert, was overtaken by events. Though he was a pioneer in ballistics, he could not make a living at it once the FBI and local agencies learned to do the work for themselves. He left the business bitter and broke, cursing his old nemesis, J. Edgar Hoover.

Richard Galatas and **Louis "Doc" Stacci** were sentenced to two years in Alcatraz and a $10,000 fine for their parts in the conspiracy to free Frank Nash. Both later went back to business as usual.

Frank "Fritz" Mulloy also was sentenced to two years and a $10,000 fine. Mulloy served his time and returned to Kansas City, where he kept up his gangland contacts and tried to forget his complete flip for Hoover. He and his family prospered, and today several Mulloy descendants serve as officers in the Kansas City Police Department.

Herb Farmer did his time in Alcatraz and came home to his wife,

Esther, in Joplin, Missouri. They sold the farm hideout and moved into town on Joplin Street. He died there on January 24, 1948.

Harvey Bailey was sentenced to fifty years on Alcatraz for the Urschel kidnapping, but he served only a little over thirty. He was paroled in 1965 and settled in Joplin, where he took a job as janitor in a cabinet shop. On October 14, 1966, he married Esther Farmer, Herb's widow, and they lived quietly as John and Mary, their middle names, until his death in 1979.

Esther Farmer Bailey, who never went to jail for the conspiracy, lived until 1981, always keeping her zest for the old days. Before she died, she made sure her obituary would identify her as a former vaudeville singer.

Frances Nash, because of her cooperation with the agents, did not go to jail. When last heard from she was back in Chicago, where she dropped out of sight forever.

Vi Mathias kept in contact with federal agents until the smoke cleared, asking their advice about steering clear of underworld suspicion and making sure the director kept her secret. With Richetti dead and the Union Station Massacre case closed, she broke off contact with the Bureau and, as she had before, found her own way to survive.

Agent W. F. Trainor was in on the investigation from the first hour, wrote all the important summary reports, and directly supervised the case file during the dark months of dead ends and discouragement. Nonetheless, he was out of the Bureau by 1937. He was mentioned twice in later reports. The first time was when he was obliquely criticized by headquarters for creating, without permission, a card indexing system for the massive massacre file. The second was on July 13, 1937, when an alert field agent reported seeing former agent Trainor in Tulsa, Oklahoma, where he was writing "the true and complete story of the Kansas City Massacre." However, that account was never published. And neither Trainor nor his index was ever heard from again.

Adam Richetti was buried in Greenwood Cemetery in Bolivar, Missouri, after a funeral attended by over three thousand people, most of them just curious. His small, nondescript tombstone, said by legend to misspell his name, in fact reflects the family spelling, Ricchetti, which neither he nor lawmen could ever get quite right. Whether by design or chance, he rests alone, the adjoining plots empty. Though any trace of family has long since moved away, several times each year flowers mysteriously appear on the grave. Always fresh for the summer sun. And silk for the cold dark winter.

AFTERWORD: THE FILE

The eighty-nine-volume FBI file that produced this story, number 62-28915 in the Bureau's elaborate records system, is officially entitled the Kansas City Massacre, the name by which much of the nation knew the events of June 17, 1933, and their aftermath. However, to generations in the heartland the case has always been referred to as the Union Station Massacre, probably because pride in the magnificent building and the shame of the bloody event somehow played off each other in those troubled, depressed, and depressing times. Hence the title of this book.

The file itself started its journey out of obscurity early in 1983 when I was national correspondent for the *Kansas City Times* (which later merged with the *Kansas City Star*). With the fiftieth anniversary of the massacre approaching, we needed some sort of new information in order to produce the obligatory anniversary story. However, a routine request for Bureau records under the Freedom of Information Act (FOIA) did not yield the fat but manageable file we expected. Instead, the Bureau's censors informed us they could produce "only" the first five volumes in the four months then available before the June anniversary.

I wrote a twelve-part series, based on those first five volumes and other sources. Though it was well received by readers, in retrospect it was woefully incomplete. Those initial volumes barely carried the investigation as far as Edgevale Road, left the story with Harvey

Bailey still the major suspect, and provided no hint at all of the Bureau lies, deceit, and perjury that would follow. But, as an early editor at the *Chicago Tribune* once told me, "We don't pay you to write the best possible story; we pay you to write the best story possible under the circumstances." So we went with what we had.

I continued the FOIA request after the series ran, so every six months or so a heavy box of documents arrived until, four years and a couple of thousand dollars later, the file was complete.

Unfortunately, politics, election campaigns, two wars, an uprising, the fall of the Berlin Wall, and a few other things left the file a much-loved but chaotic mess in my study for well over a decade. Eventually, I tamed it with a thirty-two-page computerized index, several thousand hours of reading, and a four-drawer filing cabinet. This book is the result.

The reproduced documents reflect all the quirks of the Bureau and the Freedom of Information Act. For instance, there are passages, long and short, that are carefully inked out. Sometimes an entire page will be blank, except for the "67c" or "67d" notation in the margin, referring to the Bureau's right under FOIA to protect the identities of confidential informants. It is a policy meticulously followed—except when it is ignored altogether. Vi Mathias, the mother of all confidential informants in this file, was never seen as such by the censors, and not a single word of her statements or any reports about her were withheld. On the other hand, the name of the person in Joplin who told the FBI about the Farmers' habits was carefully obscured, although even today everyone in that neighborhood knows who it was.

Much of that relates to timing. Few in the Bureau, especially among the lower-paid clerks and specialists who handle the files, know much about this particular case, no matter how important it was at the time. So they might not fully appreciate that the reason something is missing is because someone wanted it to be missing. Adam Richetti's telling fingerprint record is an example. I found Richetti's print record purged from government records at diverse local, state, and federal agencies all over the country, sometimes after telltale FBI droppings were left behind. Even the Bureau's own Richetti file, despite the historic significance of fingerprint evidence, had been purged. Yet when I stumbled over a very poor duplicate of the critical Richetti fingerprint record deep in the massacre file (where it had no reason to be) and made a routine request for a far clearer photographic copy, the request was granted without fuss or fanfare. No one realized anymore that the record was officially nonexistent.

Likewise, the records reflect the Bureau's history and personality. Memo routing slips chronicle Hoover intimate Clyde Tolson's rapid rise to power. Listed at the bottom in the opening pages, within two years he is near the top, a senior Hoover aide. In the same vein, Hoover's name went on almost everything that came out of the Seat of Government, as he called FBI headquarters in Washington, but a simple code revealed who really wrote the letter or memo for the director's signature. Once broken, that code offered real insight into the power struggles around the great man.

Hoover himself comes alive on the pages, often scribbling an additional note on a letter that already bears his name. When he is angry, the neat, precise writing seems to darken under the pressure of his pen; when he is pleased, the reader can almost feel the flourish.

Yet for all their charm, the twenty thousand pages are also a researcher's nightmare. Some of the papers, perhaps from the fifth carbon on a worn typewriter, are illegible. Others come out only under the urging of a highlighter or a thick magnifying glass. Many pages are badly wrinkled; it is not hard to imagine the food smudges and coffee stains. And some sheets, for instance the page that carries Melvin Purvis's report on the death of Pretty Boy Floyd, are partially torn away, probably from the wear of repeated thumbing. The copy clearly shows the frayed and tattered edges.

Nor is the filing system a tribute to Bureau efficiency. Though the volumes are roughly chronological, any faith in that elementary idea is quickly destroyed. Huge sections are out of order, and there is simply no order at all within shorter periods of time. It is as though the paperwork was allowed to pile up for a week or two before someone decided to put it in the file. And the volumes themselves clearly were created only for size and at the convenience of the file clerk, not in any rational manner. Two crucially important documents generated the same day might be found pages apart and in separate volumes.

But they can be found.

Ultimately, the stones and diamonds lie in a great pile, waiting to be sorted. Detailed evidence of perjury by federal agents might rest next to a well-intended but thoroughly useless letter from a man in Nashville who thought he saw Pretty Boy Floyd. But it's there.

And that, perhaps, is the most amazing part of the Union Station Massacre story.

NOTES

Chapter One: The Legend

Pg. 7. "the Shakespeare collection was missing": Merle Clayton, *The Union Station Massacre* (Indianapolis: Bobbs-Merrill Co., 1975), p. 47.

Pg. 8. "The little formation quickly moved": This passage draws on traditional accounts of the Union Station Massacre found in: Clayton, *The Union Station Massacre*; Don Whitehead, *The FBI Story* (New York: Random House, 1963); L. L. Edge, *Kansas City Star Magazine*, June 17, 1979; *Kansas City Massacre* (teleplay), ABC Circle Films Production, 1975; *Kansas City Times*, 12-part series, June 13–25, 1983; *The Squire's Other Paper*, 60th anniversary series, June 1993; Maurice M. Milligan, *Missouri Waltz: The Inside Story of the Pendergast Machine by the Man Who Smashed It* (New York: Charles Scribner's Sons, 1948); William M. Reddig, *Tom's Town: Kansas City and the Pendergast Legend* (Philadelphia: J. B. Lippincott Co., 1947).

Chapter Two: The Greenhorns

Pg. 13. "The only gun in the office was kept in a safe": Interview by the author with former FBI agent Kenneth McIntire, May 1983.

Pg. 13. "the wrong caliber": Interview by the author with former FBI agent Ray C. Suran, May 1983.

Pg. 14. "unofficial housemother": Curt Gentry, *J. Edgar Hoover: The Man and the Secrets* (New York: W. W. Norton & Co., 1991), p. 67.

Pg. 14. "An avowed patriot": Ibid., p. 68.

Pg. 15. "As the fear and hysteria built": William Preston Jr., *Aliens and Dissenters: Federal Suppression of Radicals, 1903–1933* (Cambridge, Mass.: Harvard University Press, 1963), p. 210.

Pg. 16. "the Bureau of Investigation . . . was in exceedingly bad odor":

NOTES

Alpheus Thomas Mason, *Harlan Fiske Stone: Pillar of the Law* (New York: Viking Press, 1956), pp. 147–49.

Pg. 17. "There is always the possibility that a secret police may become a menace to free governments": *New York Times*, May 10, 1924.

Pg. 18. "hired guns": Gentry, *J. Edgar Hoover*, p. 169.

Pg. 18. "We've got to get Durkin": Ralph de Toledano, *J. Edgar Hoover: The Man in His Time* (New Rochelle, N.Y.: Arlington House, 1973), p. 94.

Pg. 19. "Baby boy" and "ordinary pigeon": Leon G. Turrou, *Where My Shadow Falls: Two Decades of Crime Detection* (Garden City, N.Y.: Doubleday & Co., 1949), p. 109.

Pg. 22. "compromising pictures": Anthony Summers, *Official and Confidential: The Secret Life of J. Edgar Hoover* (New York: G. P. Putnam's Sons, 1993), pp. 241–43.

Pg. 23. "long history of break-ins": Gentry, *J. Edgar Hoover*, p. 284.

Chapter Three: The Pretty Boy

Pg. 26. "We used to stand": Interview by the author with Paul Butler, funeral home director in Bolivar, Missouri, March 1996.

Pg. 27. "My dad was a deputy sheriff": Interview by the author with source near Joplin, Missouri, who asked not to be identified by name, March 1996.

Pg. 28. "Bitzer Chevrolet Garage": Events in Bitzer's garage are recounted by Robert Pearman, *Kansas City Star*, June 17, 1962, and Harry Jones, *Kansas City Star*, June 13, 1971.

Pg. 29. "I still remember that car": Interview, Butler.

Pg. 30. "Decades later, Killingsworth's recollection": Killingsworth's 1962 quotes and recollections of the kidnapping are from *Kansas City Star*, June 17, 1962.

Pg. 34. "At one time a strip of Ninth Street claimed": Reddig, *Tom's Town*, p. 27.

Chapter Five: The City

Pg. 44. "There are lots of ways to define the Goat and Rabbit factions": Reddig, *Tom's Town*, pp. 33–37.

Pg. 45. "In Kansas City": Ibid., p. 183.

Pg. 46. "By contrast": Ibid., p. 215.

Pg. 47. "That same basic philosophy": Milligan, *Missouri Waltz*, pp. 104–107.

Pg. 49. "Upstart outsiders": Reddig, *Tom's Town*, pp. 148–51.

Pg. 49. "My four kidnappers": Ibid., p. 353.

Chapter Six: The Massacre

Pg. 57. "Yet the myth dies hard": Interview, Suran.

Chapter Seven: The Conspiracy

Pg. 61. "He should have called": Interview by the author with former FBI agent Hal Bray, May 1983.
Pg. 67. "We sat there": Interview, Bray.

Chapter Eight: The Manhunt

Pg. 72. "Still the agents took it": *The Grapevine*, official publication of the Society of Former Special Agents of the Federal Bureau of Investigation, January 1992; March, April, and July 1981.
Pg. 76. "The escape": L. L. Edge, *Run the Cat Roads: A True Story of Bank Robbers in the Thirties* (New York: Dembner Books, 1981), pp. 81–101.

Chapter Ten: The Net

Pg. 106. "Though the story made famous the G-man name": Carl Sifakis, *The Encyclopedia of American Crime* (New York: Facts on File, 1982), p. 390.
Pg. 116. "In the end": Interview by the author with former FBI agent Mont Clair Spear, May 1983.

Chapter Eleven: The Print

Pg. 126. "In 1933 the senior Brennan": *The Grapevine*, January 1992; March, April, and July 1981.
Pg. 129. "And the Brennan glory": *The Grapevine*, January 1992; March, April, and July 1981.
Pg. 130. "Interviewed shortly before his death": Gentry, *J. Edgar Hoover*, p. 283.

Chapter Twelve: The Assassination

Pg. 134. "A stream of machine-gun bullets": Reddig, *Tom's Town*, p. 262.

Chapter Fourteen: The Solution

Pg. 164. "Chief Reed": *Kansas City Journal-Post*, November 19, 1934.

Chapter Sixteen: The Doubts

Pg. 186. "Many years later": *Time*, September 24, 1979, p. 25.

NOTES

Pg. 186. "Smith said": Michael Wallis, *Pretty Boy* (New York: St. Martin's Press, 1992), p. 344.

Pg. 194. "Only in 1970": Summers, *Official and Confidential,* p. 69.

Chapter Seventeen: The Trial

Pg. 210. "I was in enough danger": *Kansas City Star,* June 13, 1971.

Chapter Eighteen: The Truth

Pg. 222. "I had given": Interview, McIntire.

Pg. 229. "Our agent sitting": Interview by the author with confidential source, May 1996.

Chapter Nineteen: The Legacy

Pg. 233. "But he wanted the muscle": Sanford J. Ungar, *FBI* (Boston: Little, Brown & Co. 1975), p. 77.

Pg. 234. "Still, to cement his role": Alvin Karpis, *On the Rock: Twenty-five Years in Alcatraz* (New York: Beaufort Books, 1980), p. 7; Sifakis, *Encyclopedia of American Crime,* p. 386.

Epilogue

Pg. 237. "Agent Reed Vetterli": *Salt Lake City Tribune,* June 16, 1949.

Pg. 237. "Agent Melvin Purvis": Gentry, *J. Edgar Hoover,* p. 176.

Pg. 238. "Sheriff Tom Bash": Reddig, *Tom's Town,* p. 321.

Pg. 238. "Herb Farmer": *Joplin Globe,* January 25, 1948.

Pg. 239. "Harvey Bailey": *Joplin Globe,* March 2, 1979.

Pg. 239. "Esther Farmer Bailey": funeral records, Thornhill-Dillon Mortuary, Joplin, Missouri, March 3, 1981.

Pg. 240. "Adam Richetti": Interview, Butler.

INDEX

INDEX

INDEX

INDEX

INDEX